D0021896

MIND-SET MANAGEMENT

658.0019
C897

MIND-SET MANAGEMENT

The Heart of Leadership

Samuel A. Culbert

WITHDRAWN
ST. MARYS COLLEGE LIBRARY

New York   Oxford
OXFORD UNIVERSITY PRESS
1996

LIBRARY ST. MARY'S COLLEGE

Oxford University Press

Oxford   New York
Athens   Auckland   Bangkok   Bombay
Calcutta   Cape Town   Dar es Salaam   Delhi
Florence   Hong Kong   Istanbul   Karachi
Kuala Lumpur   Madras   Madrid   Melbourne
Mexico City   Nairobi   Paris   Singapore
Taipei   Tokyo   Toronto

and associated companies in
Berlin   Ibadan

Copyright © 1996 by Samuel Culbert

Published by Oxford University Press, Inc.,
198 Madison Avenue New York, New York 10016

Oxford is a registered trademark of Oxford University Press

All rights reserved. No part of this publication
may be reproduced, stored in a retrieval system, or transmitted,
in any form or by any means, electronic, mechanical,
photocopying, recording, or otherwise, without the prior
permission of Oxford University Press.

Library of Congress Cataloging-in-Publication Data
Culbert, Samuel A.
Mind-set management : the heart of leadership
/ Samuel A. Culbert.
p. cm.   Includes bibliographical references and index.
ISBN 0-19-509746-7
1. Industrial management—Psychological aspects.   2. Industrial
psychology.   3. Organizational behavior.   I. Title.
HF5548.8.C83   1995
658'.001'9—dc20   94-49133

WITHDRAWN
ST. MARYS COLLEGE LIBRARY

1 3 5 7 9 8 6 4 2

Printed in the United States of America
on acid-free paper

To three fabulous father figures who,
at critical points of my life,
helped with their *great* advice:

Allen Koplin

Bob Tannenbaum

Mort Lachman

FOREWORD

In the interest of full disclosure, I have to reveal that I'm not an impartial person when it comes to Sam Culbert. I have known Sam for over twenty-five years, known him well in a variety of situations, carefully read his previous works, and have admired him and them a lot. But to get to the point quickly, this is by far Sam's best work. I would wager that it will be one of the lasting contributions to our understanding of organizations, the psychology of people who work in them, and—perhaps most of all—a contribution to understanding ourselves.

In large part, this book is about alchemy—not the alchemy of chemical properties, but the alchemy of human relationships. Just as alchemy purported to transform lead into gold, this book is about transforming organizations and people into proactive, creative, productive beings. No easy task, as Culbert makes clear. His starting point is to review with empathy the most current and popular models or organizational life. He rounded up the usual suspects: empowerment, reengineering, TQM, learning organizations, values, and vision. He began to wonder why they weren't working as expected. For example, a recent study cited in the *New York Times* stated that nine out of ten senior executives told the researchers that people are a company's most important resource and 98 percent said improved employee performance would enhance the bottom line. But when asked to rank order what leads to success, *people came last,* if they were mentioned at all.

So what's going on? What is it that seems to mysteriously intervene and disarm the best of our intentions? The best and most enlightened theories? That's what this book is all about: "advice-giving," as the preface suggests. At still another level, and the one that Culbert emphasizes, is *influence*. He says it well: "We're talking about influencing the actions of others when you lack the authority to direct them and have to content yourself with influencing the perspectives, thought, processes, logic, and strategies that give rise to their subsequent actions. . . . We're talking about your eliciting receptiveness and open-minded thinking in people who may not even see themselves needing the advice you want to give."

This may not sound radical, but it is, because Culbert highlights and illuminates the darkness that surrounds this delicate and subtly nuanced operation of leading through influence. In so doing, he provides invaluable help for those of us who work and live in human organizations. He shows how to provide advice that can improve the performance of "the other" without lowering self-esteem, how to be helpful without controlling, and how advice-giving (through Culbert's insights) can not only improve the performance but also *raise* the self-esteem of the advisee.

Sam writes with unusual lucidity. He draws on a rich stock of case studies, not the stilted, predictable kabukilike dramas we usually read about. His descriptions of real situations, real people, and real dilemmas are thoroughly enlightening.

But this book is radical in another way—and perhaps subversive—for it clarifies not only organizational relationships but *all* human relationships. I mean friends, lovers, parents and children—you name it.

So if the reader wants to understand why organizations simply seem unable to walk their walk or why good and deep interpersonal relationships are hard to maintain—read this book, slowly and carefully. You'll be grateful.

Warren Bennis

PREFACE

The essence of management is giving **great** advice—not just any advice, but advice that improves an individual's performance and advances corporate interests. And, most important, it's advice the recipient believes in enough to actually want to follow. Given to work associates, **great** advice is the essence of teamwork; given to organizational units, **great** advice is the essence of leadership. In every instance we're talking about the type of advice that reflects more than the advice-giver's self-interested view of what the other person needs to do to function more effectively. We're talking about the type of advice that enhances a recipient's sense of what's needed to advance the interests of the company in ways which that individual finds personally useful and valid. We're talking about advice that is **great** because the **recipient** finds it empowering.

So what's the "big deal"? Actually there are two. The first big deal is that all executives and managers have a stockpile of improvement advice that they don't offer because they know it won't be followed and fear that the recipients will receive it as criticism and a provocation for hostility. The second big deal is that in lieu of a direct statement of ideas, management turns into a manipulative art where deception, spin, sound bites, maneuvering, guided ambiguity, and other small deceits and sleights of tongue replace straightforward communication.

Whether or not anyone wants to admit it, management needs to become less a manipulative art and more a psychological science. Why would there be any reluctance? It's because most executives, managers, and "team players" don't know enough psychology to get along without engaging in wholesale deception. It's not that they don't try. It's just that conventional wisdom and pop-culture "psychologizing" seldom take them to a place that their advice-recipients find valid. Lacking a psychologically sound model to guide their reasoning, they give advice that usually turns out to be far more relevant to their own agendas than to the interests of the people they seek to influence and "help."

When it comes to giving advice, all psychologists know that they must relate to the context in which their advice-recipient is reasoning—they must "tune in" to where the other person is coming from. They know that, above all else, tuning in entails open-minded listening. Without first listening, there is no rapport and trust and there is no accuracy in understanding what the other person perceives as essential to his or her interests and well-being.

Psychologists know they must refrain from assuming that any individual's situation is a mirror reflection of their own. And they know that their response and advice must be framed in the context of what the other person faces and wants. While most managers generally formulate their advice thinking that they have tuned in to the other person, usually they have listened most intently to themselves.

Mind-Set Management explains what you need to know prior to influencing people and giving them advice. It plays off your desire to get people to open-mindedly consider your ideas by teaching concepts that are essential to the practice of intelligent and effective advice-giving. Thus, while it addresses important topics such as influencing people, empowerment tactics, and giving feedback and advice, this book is far more ambitious. It provides a model for thinking about other people—about their self-interested motives and about their biased and result-focused views of work events—especially when their actions are at odds with what you believe is the most productive track for them to take.

Mind-Set Management asserts that before you can lead, manage, or team up effectively you must comprehend the mind-sets of the people with whom you deal. When you don't, your success is limited. In fact, you may even fail. You won't be able to influence how people perform their jobs. You won't know how they reason or what they think and why, and the advice you give will be anything but **great.** Only after mind-sets are comprehended can management become a psychological science where candor and straightforward talk begin replacing wholesale deception.

The book is ecumenical. It begins by explaining that it doesn't care what managerial "religion" you follow, or which of the new management models you embrace. What matters is that you practice your managerial "religion" with a new mentality—one that recognizes that no matter how much control you exert, you will never succeed in circumventing the distinctive mind-set another individual uses in actually seeing events and responding to them. That's where the need to improve the quality of your psychologizing comes in.

You'll find this book laced with case illustrations and stories that we hope will be easy to identify with. It makes the stories part and parcel to the concepts it teaches. In most books you can skip the stories and go directly to the concepts. In this book concepts and stories are woven together in an effort to present evidence that makes the lessons compelling and personal. Why? Because its task is to do more than show you how to influence other people's mindsets. It includes equipping you to change your own.

In my mind, this book was written with another UCLA professor, Jack McDonough, for his ideas and counsel were with me every step of the way. Our collaboration began over twenty years ago when Jack was on the committee that reviewed my promotion to tenure. Reading my then unpublished manuscript titled *The Organization Trap,* Jack discovered our intellectual symmetry and overlap. He had just finished writing a brilliant analysis of Solzhenitsyn's story *One Day in the Life of Ivan Denisovich,* focusing on the mental structures that determine an individual's experience of "organization," and was in the process of submitting it for publication. My manuscript explored comparable themes.

Subsequently our dialogue and friendship blossomed, and we began working together very closely. There was a formative period in which we met daily to discuss just about every administrative and consultative step either of us took in an effort to apply and extend our theories. Together we wrote two books *(The Invisible War* and *Radical Management)* and many papers, and we helped each other with field research and consultations.

To this day Jack and I meet periodically to discuss theory and the methods and approaches we individually take in our teaching and consulting. There is little I do professionally that, in my mind, doesn't relate to discussions we have had, although I can't necessarily conclude that Jack would endorse all my applications. Accordingly, this book and the experiences, reflections, and insights leading up to it are clearly joint efforts. For this reason, throughout the book I use the pronoun *we* in referring to what I have seen and done individually and often discussed with Jack and *our* in referring to all theoretical perspectives advanced.

Our theory is scientifically derived and grounded in clinical empiricism. It is presented in a format that allows you to participate in its validation, for as confirming evidence we present situations that you may have experienced or observed firsthand. In many instances, preliminary descriptions were submitted to the people featured in our accounts for their reactions, critique, and authentication.

In instances where your experience conflicts with what we are asserting as "fact," you may believe us but not change your actions, no matter how theoretically sound our explanations. However, when the theories we use in explaining events and stating what's desirable match your experience, then you can use what you have personally observed as additional data for validating what we assert and for considering how to modify or extend your present mode of reasoning. Moreover, while the context for our theorizing is placed squarely in the world of work, you're likely to find lessons that apply in other domains as well.

We have taken pains to present what we have seen as accurately as we can describe it. Cases and vignettes have been "doctored" only to conceal the identities of actual participants. If you have seen us lurking in the corridors of your company and think you can guess the names of individuals in our stories, we want to categorically assure you that you are wrong. In fact, just the other day we encountered a humorous situation with a manager to whom we had given a draft of a chapter to read. We gave it to him to illustrate a team-building procedure that we thought could be adapted to fit a problem that he considered urgent. A week later, when we hadn't heard from him, we called to inquire "What's up?" He responded that he found the story we had written *about him* and that reading it had helped him "turn a corner." It took us a while to figure out that he was talking literally, not figuratively, about the first story in the chapter and had never gotten to the team approach story that we thought was going to prove useful to his work unit. It took another five minutes to convince him that he wasn't the person in the story and that it was excerpted from a case we had written a full year prior to meeting him.

As you read this book you'll see how strongly we believe that the distinctive mind-set that an individual brings to his or her experiences at work and uses in making sense out of organizational events is the root determinant of "the organization life" that person lives. It is the mind-sets of the people with whom you work that you need to engage if you are to understand how the organization actually functions, no matter how the powerful people in your company "objectively" depict it for you. In this book our aim is to appreciably increase your capacity to engage people "on sight" *(sic)* in the mind-set organizations where they actually work.

Along these lines we'd like briefly to tell you about two of the most instructive management training films ever made: *Rashomon* and *Nashville.* Actually they weren't made for training; they were produced as entertainment films.

Rashomon is a classic Japanese-made film produced in 1950. It takes a single event and portrays it five divergent ways. Each portrayal corresponds to one participant's report of that event when asked to justify his or her actions in it, and none resembles any of the others.

Nashville depicts an American institution, country and western music, in the early 1970s: People with diverse talents, distinct and blatant limitations, and highly competitive motives, living dramatically different personal realities, interact within an organizational structure that produces the illusion of teamwork and integrated action. *Nashville* shows how self-serving and organizationally erratic expressions inside a system that attributes relatedness, order, and meaning to that behavior can cause everyone's actions to appear far more constructive and coherent than they actually are.

Together these films form a training module that vividly illustrates the basis of "organization." They show that what an individual sees, reports seeing, concludes, and decides to advocate based on those conclusions *cannot* be separated from that individual's personal psychology, life situation, and self-interested agendas at work. They show how subjectivity and political forces are omnipresent and important factors in everything that someone self-conveniently calls "objective," "truthful," and "real." In an organization, personal politics and subjective interests determine how each event, problem, and opportunity gets portrayed; they influence and determine every action that someone advocates as essential.

The implication is simple. If you want to understand what is going on at work, you'd better ask how the people involved see the "organizational" situation and precisely how what they are doing relates to what's important to them and to what they see. When you fail to do this, your chances of misunderstanding them, and, in turn, of their misunderstanding you and the constructive actions you take, are significantly increased. And you well know what happens when people who work together, whom the organization counts on for teamwork, misunderstand one another's actions and intent. Quickly life at work resembles two other films, the *nonclassic Wacky Wednesday* and *Friday the Thirteenth*.

Santa Monica, California   S. A. C.
May 1995

ACKNOWLEDGMENTS

The list of people who made essential contributions to the writing of this book is so long that it makes me wonder what I contributed. I feel extremely fortunate to have received so much help, advice, and feedback.

I want to begin by acknowledging the enormously helpful contributions by people whose names I cannot mention because I want to protect their anonymity. Some are featured players in case stories; others, employees at a company whose identity I don't want revealed. But not explicitly recognizing them causes me heartache, for these people deserve major credit. Without them and their willingness to reflect aloud about their personal lives and difficult-to-face situations and to react to the provocative case descriptions I wrote about situations involving them, this book would lack a critical dimension. There were many instances where their getting "into it" with me made me feel like little more than the scribe. In the process, some wonderful relationships were built.

Mary Culbert, my wife, and Scott Schroeder took the journey with me from inception to completion and were always available when I needed them. Mary is an attorney and professional mediator who really knows how to get to the crux of matters. She's tough with her criticism, and believe me when I tell you that if I didn't need tough-mindedness, I would have taken an easier route. But her critique and commentary were so essential that, as always, I found her irresistible. She was always generous with her time and spirit. Putting myself in her shoes, I don't think that I would treat "the other interest" nearly as well as she treated the "manuscript," benevolently ignoring my sincere promises that she and the family would have my entire focus just as soon as the manuscript was completed. Of course she's heard that one before.

Scott Schroeder is the Gary Cooper type, who would never use a paragraph when a few words would suffice. Working as my doctoral student research and teaching assistant, Scott became a valuable colleague on research projects that yielded important data for this book. His discussion, counsel, enthusiasm, and generosity in reading and rereading drafts were invaluable in getting me back in touch with the forest at moments when I was consumed hacking away at a tree. Scott has a way of holding on to the big picture and his comments advanced my thinking a great deal. Both Scott and I would like to acknowledge the research support he received from UCLA's Institute of Industrial Relations.

I discovered an invaluable resource when Carolee Dodds interviewed me for a university project. It was at the end of a long writing day and, reflecting back, I was used up, minimally social, and couldn't have been very coherent. Two days later she brought her copy by for my review and I discovered that I was sitting opposite an incredibly talented writer. Very fortunately she agreed to be my editor. Her fine touch is on every page of the book you are about to read.

Guess what happens when people find out that you're writing a book about giving advice? You guessed it—they give you advice. Although not all of it was usable, I did get a great deal of dead-on advice from dear friends I always seek out and rely upon for insight, support, and candor. Warren Bennis always found the time, and his extraordinary talents in contextualizing and providing world-view perspective were particularly helpful in my recognizing the distinct and novel areas being mapped. Other dear friends who, like Warren, were always "there" to help in any way needed were Herb Kindler, Oscar Ortsman, Max Elden, Bob Tannenbaum, Mort Lachman, Walt Nord, and Ilene Kahn. All but Ilene are gradually aging and all are becoming my "old-boy network." Reflecting on their contributions makes me think that a book is a work by many for which one person steals the credit.

Herb Addison, my editor at Oxford, provided valuable paragraph-by-paragraph reactions. That's terrific treatment to get from someone at his elevation with his talent and hectic schedule. With one exception he's been dead-on. The exception came at lunch one day when, cacophonously to my ears, he made the mistake of introducing Harold Roth as "Sam's agent." Harold and I have worked together for over ten years and, as I pointed out to Herb, "I'm one of his authors." Hal is a distinguished former publisher, who, as an agent, gives exquisite guidance and representation.

There are many others who volunteered advice that proved particularly helpful. Mentioning these people fills me with trepidation, for as I age I find myself suffering from a "recency effect." I seem to remember only those who helped in the last three months. They include Charlie Norris, Lisa Barron, Kim Kurtzberg, John and Rhoda Novak, Patrick Obertelli, Bob Foster, Bill Hicks, Gar Culbert, and my computer expert, Charles Culbert. Then there is the love I received from my family, the aforementioned Mary, Gar, and Charles, as well as Samantha and Spencer, whose enthusiasm for basketball added spirit to my effort. If you are one of the people who gave earlier advice, please forgive my absentmindedness. And if your name is Jack McDonough, please read the Preface.

Publisher's Note

Workbook

Mind-Set Management is ideally suited for use in management training and executive education, including both in-house and university-based programs. To facilitate its use, the author has collaborated on writing a workbook that is keyed to this book. The workbook provides exercises and a process aimed at helping readers apply the powerful ideas in *Mind-Set Management* in their own lives. For more information on the workbook, including prices for bulk orders, please contact:

> The Center for Effectiveness in Leadership
> (310) 459-6052
> (310) 459-9307 fax

CONTENTS

Part III   Matching Advice with the Need
and the Capacity to Receive It

Part IV   Applications and Conclusions

I

The Problem and the Required Insight

1

The New Management Models: What They Say and What's Needed to Pull Them Off

If you think you can run this organization in the next five years the way you ran it in the last five years—you're crazy. We've got to disturb the present.

Roberto Goizueta, Chairman and CEO,
Coca Cola Co.

The stream of progressive new management models appears to be flowing open-endedly. Almost every day brings something new. Each of the models is aimed at changing the way that you function so that you can survive and prosper in an organization world that's rapidly becoming unlike anything you've known before. To this point you should know the merits of total quality management,[1] the importance of leadership that empowers,[2] the imperative of a critical "fifth discipline" with a focus on organizational learning,[3] the possibility of quantum leap transformational change,[4] the need for "reengineering" corporate functions[5] and "reinventing" government,[6] the importance of constructing an organization that learns,[7] the essential utilization of diversity,[8] the possibilities of changing the internal culture,[9] and the list goes on and on.[10]

Each of the new models has been field-tested. Most are conceptually credible and the result of common sense and imaginative practice blending with theory. Even some of the ones that, on the surface, sound a bit far-out and use strange terms like "fifth discipline," "reengineering," "stewardship," and "skunk works" have merit if for no other reason than they serve the important function of jarring you out of your current thinking and extending the boundaries of possibility.

Almost regardless of the model, the principles are the same. They have emerged from a revised set of beliefs about what's needed to propel corporations ahead: total organization teamwork, thoughtfulness and flexibility at the customer contact point, sensitivity and quick reaction to marketplace changes, the importance of everyone having the big picture, leadership from within the ranks, attentiveness to the human element, constructive politics and trusting relationships, a dedicated and informed workforce, globalized thinking, and strategic input by everyone involved in the execution and implementation of company action.

These principles ought to work. They are terrific and you need to learn about them and use as many as you can. Read the books and choose the model that appears to work best for you. A model will give coherence to your actions. It will guide you to work systematically to make your organization a success. Even picking and choosing and eclectically piecing together your own model may work. If you find that it is not the right time to get others in your company to agree on a model, then choose your own and practice it until others grasp the possibilities and take a complementary track. Don't delay acting just because you don't currently have a top managerial assignment or because others haven't gotten started yet. Your success in job and career depends on your getting it right regardless of whether your hierarchical superiors or the people around you do.

There's a problem

So far, it all sounds straightforward. You merely read the books, have the conversations, plug into a model or two, regroup, and keep on rolling along. Right? **Wrong!** In order to make them work, you've got to change *your* mentality. If you don't, the new model will quickly transform into just another version of the old. But, given your training and indoctrination in former* models, changing your mentality is something you're ill-equipped to do.

While in theory the new models ought to work, in practice you'll

---

*What we attribute to the time period "former" actually describes the majority of *current* practices and managerial actions. However, in order to make the point that current practices are obsolete, we decided to use the term "former."

find them disorienting. They are so intellectually attractive that they can lead you to believe that you have taken a critical step forward without having left the spot you are on. The reason can be stated quite simply. You'll think that you are enacting them because you are behaving differently, but that's not all that they require. They require that you actually think about people differently—about their nature and motivations at work, and about how to go about influencing them. When you employ new models using the former mentality, you may, in fact, be in the boat, but your oars won't be in the water. The new models require you to do some things with people that reasoning in the former mentality won't permit.

You've got to relinquish control

When it comes to implementation, the new models will challenge you to the hilt. That's because they all require that you, and the others in your organization, learn how to expand your influence and, at the same time, relinquish control. They all instruct you to push decision making and operational flexibility as far down into the organization as you possibly can, and to leave it there for keeps.

This contrasts with the mentalities that the previous generation of models required. In those models, involvement and participation were primarily tricks used to get people to buy into decisions made by higher-ups and to commit to courses of team action that, without group pressure, people might not otherwise want to take. Power and decision may have been delegated, but the delegation was under constant review. Input from lower levels was energetically solicited but, despite the window dressing, upper management's front-end commitment was only to listen passively.

Some of the new models advocate management relinquish control by reasoning that a company can't compete on quality and service without authorizing people who do "frontline" work to break from precedent and make decisions on their own. Proponents cite numerous compelling and dramatic examples of people in the ranks deviating from standard practices to take actions that satisfy a customer or capitalize on a marketplace opportunity. Cited examples clearly illustrate what individuals who are in tune with the corporate strategy can accomplish by applying thoughtfulness and ingenuity when responding to local situations and circumstance. While these accomplishments don't necessarily leave a trail of tangibles, they inevitably show up on the bottom line.

Some new models advocate relinquishing control by contending that hierarchical domination and top-down decision making create a docile, insensitive workforce and a corporate intelligence that's limited to the insights and experiences of the top executive team. These models also come with numerous illustrations of lower-level people in the field making market-sensitive responses that refocused the corporate effort in a profitable way. Frequently cited are the legendary accomplishments of Japanese automakers who, through decentralizing authority and encouraging worker participation in decision making, were able to bring innovative new car models to market in half the time that it took their American counterparts working within the hierarchical system of top-down management control.

Some new models advocate relinquishing control, reasoning that when it comes to control, the most you can possibly accomplish is to get everybody thinking and communicating in the same broad framework. Their proponents argue the folly of attempting to control people beyond orienting them to the corporate mission, getting them versed in the same broad business strategy, and having them recognize the intangibles against which their work will be judged. Such models assume that, in order to be effective, people need the freedom to utilize their distinctive resources and skills. These models contend that the organization works best when as many people as possible function with latitude of action and real, not illusory, empowerment.

Your corporate nightmare

In contrast to former models, the new schemes really mean what they say. They seriously advocate pushing control and authority downward, with management review after the fact, not before. Herein lies what's about to become your corporate nightmare. How are you going to sleep nights knowing that people who aren't as competent as you, who aren't as well versed in the corporate plan or the economics of the global marketplace as you, who, on paper, look like they should be reporting to you, are taking actions that could undermine your credibility and the quality of the production that you are responsible for overseeing without your having the last word, or perhaps even any word, yourself? For example, when President Clinton came to office, didn't he immediately have to stand accountable for the mismanagement of the White House travel office, then the mismanagement of firing allegedly incompetent or possibly dishonest personnel, and then the mismanagement of calling in the FBI to investigate the alleged mismanagement, no matter how much authority and responsibility had actually been channeled down? Was it a case of then Chief of Staff Thomas (Mack) McLarty, or another executive-level presidential assistant, actually taking the authority that came with his job, and exercising it by acting independently, totally on his own?

The "former" models offered you far more protection. In them, each level of management could reasonably stand accountable to the next because their subordinates were required to keep them in the decision-making loop. In them, individuals, groups, and even entire departments could limit their responsibilities to doing what was "right" for their immediate operation without being constrained by having to worry about the functioning of the company as a whole. The former models made it possible for people and work units to succeed while adjacent operations deteriorated and failed. In these models, people could aggressively compete for budgets, priorities, and personnel without having their advocacies compromised by the thought that an adjacent unit might need those resources more.

New assumptions

But the new models are based on other assumptions. They begin with an appreciation of an increasingly competitive marketplace and a realization that no individual's fate is separable from the corporation's performance as a whole. They insist on a logic of total system maximization that makes it difficult for any unit to persuasively argue for resources irrespective of the other uses that might be made of them. They define team spirit and team play in ways that make it difficult to value the technical contribution of any person whose impact on the people working directly with him or her, or even on related or remote operations, is not positive. In the new models, even a "normal" amount of political infighting and internal competition will no longer be tolerated when it's seen as detracting from the total effort.

The new models are based on recognition that we're in an era where markets and technology change daily and where no individual remains on the technological cutting edge for an indeterminate length of time. Over the long run, the most that you're going to be able to accomplish is to maintain yourself as technically relevant and conversant with the new technology. In the new models, the tests for successful functioning and keeping your job will be conducted on nontechnical grounds—those of team-worthiness, trustfulness, positive impact on others, and such intangibles as contribution to the well-being of the corporation as a whole.

In the new models, leadership is not expected to come just from the top. Everyone is expected to lead. Creating the corporate "vision" becomes a joint effort. Fine-tuning and adjusting to meet the demands of a shifting, globalized marketplace is everyone's responsibility. Every operation and business activity becomes part of everyone's business and no individual's incompetent performance or disorientation is exempt from anyone's scrutiny. Everyone has an opinion to register, and everyone is expected to jump to an urgent situation to pitch in as needed.

In the new models, the words "team" and "teamwork" take on new meaning. No longer is a team merely a collection of individuals working on the same task. No longer is teamwork merely playing one's part in the group effort and performing it well. Suddenly, the team expands to include the entire corporation and teamwork expands to encompass doing whatever is necessary to help the other guy operate effectively, in ways that build the corporation's success.

In the new models, management becomes a mind-set technology in which managerial work entails helping people to harmonize their personal and organizational commitments so that, at any moment, their reasoning, decision making, and actions have integrity for the institution as well as for themselves. The new emphasis is on people seeing themselves as system resources, not partisan, turf-oriented, unit advocates or freewheeling, individualistic performers. Managers who don't succeed in helping "their" people make these transitions are going to have a great deal of difficulty distancing themselves from performers who fail. You're going to see a lot more of these managers being cast out along with "the people who couldn't be fixed."

As the requirements change, you'll find that only those whose presence enhances and empowers others will be treated as valuable team assets. And you can expect the cast of "others" to become an increasingly large circle of individuals and organizational units. In the new models, people who formerly circumscribed their relationships and responsibilities, perhaps primarily to maintain focus in the areas that were directly chargeable to them, are going to find themselves confronting unprecedented challenges to extend their spheres of influence.

The challenge to you

In requiring that you expand your responsibilities and exert more influence, the new models threaten to bury you. If you're like most of us, you are already working at 110 percent and barely have the time and energy to take care of commitments that are directly chargeable to you. Wherever do you expect to find the time to give others more focus and to get more involved in their activities? If you're going to expand your impact, you've got to find ways to do so efficiently.

The key to your having the time and energy to involve yourself in other people's areas, especially those that are remote from your primary unit, lies in limiting your involvements to assisting others to execute their responsibilities more competently. In their domains, this makes you a helper, not a doer. This contrasts with what you are expected to accomplish in your own domain. There you are expected to be a doer and to receive help from others—help you may resist.

The new models require you to perform simultaneously two functions that, given your experience in former models using the former managerial mentality, you will probably find a contradiction in terms. Using the former management models, when you needed to exert influence, you did so by taking more control. But the new models require you to exert even more influence and, at the same time, relinquish control. This is all well and good in theory, but how are you going to pull it off?

Relinquishing control, increasing your spheres of impact, and getting involved influencing people over whom you have no formal authority requires that you find persuasive ways to make your viewpoints known. How can you intelligently push power and decision making down to the customer and marketplace contact points without being able to influence the people you are empowering to act on your company's behalf? How can you accept responsibility from upper-level executives without your having the ability to convincingly explain what caused you to improvise and deviate from what they thought they had good reason to expect? And how can you tolerate your dependencies on cohort functioning if you can't tell others what you see and how you think their operations might function even more effectively than they currently are?

The core technology is advice-giving

When it comes to influencing people you can't control and making the new models operational, or even working in former models and avoiding the use of directives that rub people the wrong way emotionally, the core technology is advice-giving. We're talking about telling people what you think when you lack a basis for insisting they follow suit. We're talking about offering advice, providing feedback, giving your reactions, and doing whatever is required to help others learn from your thoughts and feelings about their actions when you can't insist that they listen. We're talking about influencing the actions of others when you lack the authority to direct them and have to content yourself with influencing the perspectives, thought processes, logic, and strategies that give rise to their subsequent actions. We're talking about having your ideas respected, your motivations trusted, and your opinions recognized even when they are not solicited. We're talking about your eliciting receptiveness and open-minded thinking in people who may not even see themselves needing the advice and influence you want to give. That's the new form of participation and leadership that the new models are depending on you to accomplish.

The advice and influence we're talking about your asserting pertains to how other people think and behave at work—about what the company needs, the effectiveness of their operations, the problems they solve, the roles they take in getting work done, and their styles of responding to situations and interacting. And the data that you get, which provide the basis for your advice-giving, come from noticing imperfections in how these other people work and your thinking about what will allow them to function more effectively. Basically, we're talking about your asserting lessons that others should have already learned from their experience but, thus far on their own, either have failed to learn or have learned the importance of performing but have yet to figure out how to implement. In either event, there obviously is some block.

But giving advice is a radical suggestion

When you stop to think about what needs doing, you'll see that, easy as it seems on the surface, what we're talking about your doing is really quite radical. You want to talk with work associates about what you have learned from observing them and listening to how other people critically interpret their actions. You want to share perspectives and lessons that they need to know but thus far have not been able to learn on their own. Of course this isn't radical in terms of what you have been trying to do up until now. Every day you're out there trying to open someone's eyes to some fundamental, but overlooked, "truth." What's radical is that we're implying that you might actually pull it off.

In fact, giving advice, sending feedback, openly sharing your reactions, fears, opinions, and thinking are activities that almost everyone practices ubiquitously today. At work, no set of activities consumes more time or drains more emotional energy than the giving and receiving of feedback. You constantly react to work associates, and the situations you find yourself in with them, and you spend tremendous amounts of time searching for the means to make your re-actions known. And you don't need to be reminded about how often you come up empty-handed or worse—with more problems than you had when you began. Given your positive intent and the time and energy you're inclined to expend, it's difficult to see how any management activity is predictably less rewarding and less efficient than the giving and receiving of advice and feedback.

If you're like most people, reflecting back on your advice-giving experiences quickly becomes an exercise in revisited frustration. Retrospectively you see a stream of situations that, in your mind, were relatively straightforward and in which you should have been far more successful than you were. You see others, whose effective-ness is crucial to your organization's success, and whose personal well-being is a source of genuine concern to you, functioning ineffec-tively, and you see yourself futilely trying to help them succeed. You see disoriented people pursuing priorities that don't match the orga-nization's; you see people misperceiving situations and making invalid assumptions about events and what they need to do to perform effec-tively in them; you see people repeatedly embroiled in interpersonal clashes, having their energies drained by avoidable conflicts, while operating with little sensitivity to their role in creating the dynamics that repeatedly ensnarl them; and you see people acting in ways that you generally consider self-limiting, self-defeating, fate-sealing, and organizationally dysfunctional.

Reflecting back, you also see how predictably and systemati-cally your best efforts to give advice and feedback were thwarted. You wanted to warn people about the limited and self-defeating course they were taking, and you wanted to redirect them so much further than you were able to. No doubt there were some instances where you thought you did get through. But probably, even in those instances, you found yourself failing to achieve the full impact you wanted to make. While you wanted to help someone learn how to deal more effectively with a class of situations, you see that all you accomplished was forcing that person to deal more effectively with the specific issue at hand. You see how those same lessons will need to be recommunicated when the inevitable happens and the next sim-ilar situation comes along.

Perhaps by now you realize that we're heading straight for for-bidden territory. We're not just talking about your giving feedback when you are the boss and the other person is your subordinate, and time has been earmarked for performance and salary review. We're talking about your giving feedback and advice to people who don't really have to account to you, and at the very moment when they are attempting to accomplish something they think is important and maybe even out to get you to agree that the course they are taking is correct. These are precisely the moments when another person's every inclination is to act as if all external influences are barriers that can be overwhelmed by some combination of force, cunning, and perseverance. These are the times when another person is likely to experience your goodwill as just another obstacle. What begins as a well-intended action on your part all too readily gets perceived with suspicion.

Once you start giving advice, others will immediately raise questions about your motives. Whether explicitly or implicitly, the "What's in it for you?" question will leap to the minds of just about every individual you seek to advise. For this reason, the issue of motives will follow us through a great deal of this book. However, for the meantime, assume that your motives include enough of the other person's well-being to make it in his or her best interests to open up to your advice. In short, until we comment differently, assume we're talking about the benevolent and good-spirited advice you want to give in the service of adding quality and effectiveness to another person's efforts.

Of course the ultimate benevolent motive is to help the other person avoid what you perceive as impending failure. We hate thinking about the number of times we've seen people who were headed for major trouble, life setbacks and career-turning disasters, who could not be deterred from the self-defeating path they were on. And then, almost immediately, after adversity struck, after the horse was out of the barn so to speak, we watched them respond by seeking out and embracing the very advice that they had ignored, defended against, and strenuously rejected right up until the end. People whose projects failed, whose proposals were rejected, who were disappointed at promotion time, who were sued, who were fired, whose spouse walked out, whose teenager turned to drugs suddenly lowered their defenses and embraced the very advice and feedback they had rejected, which could have prevented the disaster that had just befallen them. And we're not talking about "gun to the head" openness. At work, people are amazingly resistant to advice even while staring down the barrel of a gun. We're talking about an openness that takes place only after the gun has been fired and the damage is irreparable. Only then do people reliably open themselves to feedback and self-improvement learning.

But adversity is not the condition that you or anyone else wants to rely upon for "successful" advice-giving outcomes. When it comes to giving advice, the objective is to help someone as far up the line as you can before the situation reaches an adverse conclusion. People need to know about flaws in their basic outlooks and orientations to avoid significant setbacks. We're also talking about giving advice aimed at helping people function closer to their potential.

You're going to find your advice-giving and feedback-sending dilemmas exacerbated by the requirements of the new management models. More than ever they require others to see you as helpful, team-worthy, trustful, interested in their well-being, and working for the corporation's success. However, by and large the models don't offer much in the way of help in how to transform your positive intentions into actions that other people will see as assisting them. And you'll find that you immediately get yourself into trouble, embroiled in time-consuming negative politics, whenever others experience you and your advice differently.

Once you start giving feedback and advice, you run the risk of being seen as meddlesome, intrusive, and controlling. Such a perception can launch you on a course of win–lose political machinations where your credibility depends on proving that the people you are trying to "help" were wrong and where their credibility depends on proving that you are off-center, working a self-interested agenda at their expense. Such situations take you far off the track of helping others and making the company more effective.

Using the new models, you couldn't be more off track than when you are in a situation that has you energetically involved documenting other people's failures to prove that the advice you are giving is not an instance of your being overly controlling or meddlesome in an attempt to take the suspicion off yourself. Once that happens, the relationship and trust issues entailed in switching back to the positive, helpful track become extraordinarily difficult, perhaps impossible to renegotiate. The only efficient course is to start off on the effectiveness-enhancing track and stay on it from the beginning.

To this point we've painted a picture of the new management models emphasizing a set of activities, advice-giving and feedback-sending, that, to date, no one performs with much success. What is going to allow you to perform these activities competently, given that you've never had much success with them before? How are you going to relinquish control and develop enough influence to get others to open-mindedly entertain your ideas? How can you be sure that these so-called progressive new models aren't your one-way ticket to corporate oblivion?

With respect to these questions, we've got some bad news and some good news. The bad news is that there is no way you can succeed attempting to influence people you do not control using the mentality you're accustomed to using. The good news is that there is a fundamental insight that can equip you for your new assignment. From it you can develop the skills and perspectives for engaging people differently and the mentality required for you to operate the new models effectively, notwithstanding the degree of resistance you will encounter based on how people have been experiencing you and your control-oriented mentality up until now.

The insight that can make the new models work

There's an insight that holds the potential to turn your mentality around. It states: **"Organization Is an Artifact of The Mind That Views It."** It's an insight based on the idea that each organization event, activity, and action is endowed with meaning that is an artifact, or production, of the specific mind that views it. This means that, just like the rest of life, nothing is anything until it is viewed and portrayed in someone's mind. It's *Rashomon** and more. It's *Rashomon* because it states that people with different self-interested motives actually see the same situations differently and live individualized realities. It's "more" because it states that people, who naturally see the same events differently, eventually catch on that there are conflicting views, and through collusive interaction invent group-expedient meanings and interpretations that they agree to observe when working with one another.† Through this process of social and political agreements, group-lived realities are created.

Management is a psychological science

Regardless of the basis for the reality lived, the beginning point for managing and influencing people is the same. Your success depends first on your ability to work back from what another person does to comprehend what that person actually thinks and sees, and then on your ability to engage that person in a mind-set conversation, even if that conversation has to be conducted indirectly. The bottom line is that **management becomes a psychological science instead of just a manipulative art**—because now your thinking about the other person's actions are tied into the view of the world that the other person actually lives.

---

*This is the 1950 film described in the Preface.
†This is Berger and Luckman's "social construction of reality" thesis and it is also Cyert and March's "theory of coalition advocacy." See endnotes for citations.

Case in point

Here's a situation that clearly demonstrates the essentiality of relating to the mind-set that's lived by the person you are trying to influence. It conveys the importance of doing so whether you are working in a former model or a new one. As with each case presented in this book, it doesn't just illustrate theory, it presents it.

Our case revolves around an interaction we had with Marty, the operations vice president of a development company that builds and sells about $200 million a year in luxury homes. Marty is an intelligent guy who likes to think of himself as "good-willed" and "people-sensitive" although he's quick to add, "Last year I was also tough minded and results oriented to the extent that, in addition to my salary, I earned nearly a quarter of a million dollars in bonus." In light of the scope of his operations, the issue we were discussing was almost humorous. It would have been outright funny if it were not for the fact that this executive, in using the former mentality, was on the brink of creating workplace carnage and wasting a corporate asset. Apparently we got to him just in the nick of time.

The conversation we want to relate came up almost by happenstance. We were getting coffee and merely asked, "How's it going?" Lightheartedly, Marty replied, "We're doing swell except I have to fire an $80,000-a-year manager because he can't screw in a lightbulb." As we started to laugh, Marty interrupted, "Wait a minute, you gotta hear the entire story." Then ushering us into his office and closing the door he continued, "In many ways it's a shame, because Al's exactly the type of new blood we need to cultivate here."

Continuing, Marty said, "At Luxury Homes we pride ourselves on producing houses that are error-free when released for customer move-in. Two weeks ago, while Al and I were walking the thirty-unit extension of our Country Club Estates development that I gave him to run, I noticed a lightbulb missing in the entrance chandelier of a home he was getting ready to release. I said, 'Al, there's a lightbulb missing, please take care of it.' He replied, 'No problem.'

"But it started to become a problem when three days later I was out with the marketing people walking the development and stuck my head in that unit and saw the bulb still missing. I mentioned it again to Al, and he gave me another 'No problem.' Then a couple of days later I asked my assistant, who was going out to the tract for another purpose, to check on the lightbulb. He, at least, was smart enough to say, 'I'll take along a bulb and make sure it's in before I leave.' I said, 'No, that's not the issue. If it were, I would have put one in myself. Just tell me if the lightbulb is in.'

"Well he came back and said it wasn't. So this time I put a message on Al's voice mail. Two days later it's Friday afternoon and I'm walking the tract and I see that it still isn't in. Catching Al at another unit, I asked him, 'Is the lightbulb in?' Looking me square in the eyes he assures me it is, as if I'm a dummy for asking such a stupid question. With the weekend coming I decided not to agitate myself. I figured I'd give him until Monday to cover his tracks. Then Monday morning I swung by early on my way to the office. Can you believe that dumb son-of-a-bitch still didn't have the bulb installed! Here we are selling a half-million-dollar house and the first thing the new owners are going to see when they walk through the front door, with stars in their eyes ready to experience the dream they've worked so long and hard to realize, is a goddamn missing lightbulb!

"To me this lightbulb thing is entirely symptomatic. I invested all this money recruiting and moving this guy in from out of state to discover that he can't take simple directions and, on top of that, he lies. To my way of thinking it's time to cut my losses and send him home before he does us in on something big."

We asked, "Is it possible for us to talk with Al before you send him packing?" Marty said, "Of course you can, but it won't do any good." Then he placed a call and said, "Al is just now jumping in his truck to bring his time sheets to the office. When he's here he'll be dropping in."

Thirty minutes later, a big strapping guy walked through the door, pulled up a chair, and cracked a most engaging smile. Marty said, "Al, I've got these professors here and they asked to meet some of my headaches. Of course I thought of you." Hesitantly Al laughed. At this point our job was to learn what kind of thinking processes led to the neglect and dissembling that Marty described. When Marty asked if he should leave, we said, "Absolutely not."

Our conversation lasted twenty minutes. We covered such important topics as the Chicago Cubs, for whom we are perennially optimistic; Al's diligence in paying rent a week ahead of time to make sure he's never late; his social and recreational life, which, at that time, was nonexistent due to the twelve- to fourteen-hour days and weekend time he was putting in learning his new job; and, very important, what Al likes best about construction.

After Al left, Marty said, "What d'you think? Should I fire him?" We replied, "No way. He's a great find!" Laughing as Marty shot us a cross-eyed look, we continued, "The problem is the way you are thinking about him. *Your* expectations and *his* mind-set are not matching up. This is not a man who feels he's accomplishing anything important by taking care of 'minor' details. The two of you may have been talking a lot but it doesn't seem as if you have communicated."

Continuing, we said, "Take a look at who Al is and how he thinks. He's a new employee who's out to impress you. He's going to show you that he can build complete houses from the ground up in four months or less. From what you've previously told us, that's the type of accomplishment that is going to make you and the company a lot of money. When you said 'new blood,' we thought this was what you were after. And his ability to pay attention to details that mean something to him is documented by how he pays his rent.

"On the other hand, Al doesn't seem to really know your customers. In his mind they are merely the people who come out to 'ooh and ah' while he and his Goliaths are knocking out majestic circular staircases and beautiful marble floors. We'll bet you five bucks that if you face him down on the lightbulb, he'll tell you six stories of heading over to that house, lightbulb in hand, and being diverted by a major problem. And we'll bet you another five bucks that, when he told you the lightbulb was in place, he had one in his pocket and was thinking he could beat you back over to have it installed prior to your walking in." We must have been convincing because Marty reached in his pocket and pulled out a ten-dollar bill as if to signal that the lightbulb in his head had just turned on. Leaving the ten dollars on the table, we just laughed.

What's to learn?

This story illustrates the importance of mind-set matchups and learning how to read people's actions in a "psychologically" sensitive way. Given Marty's customer-pleasing mind-set and control-oriented mentality, Al was a ticking time bomb that the company could well do without. Given Al's mind-set, he was a star in the making. He was building high-quality units in record time. Consciously Al was willing to respond to Marty's directives, but no one can do that very well when the directives clash with his internal priorities and mind-set. And the situation wasn't very complicated. Marty was using a former management model with no "progressive" twist.

This story reflects deficiencies in managerial training that were present even in the former mentality. Clearly Marty's behavior and thought processes reflect the quality of training he received. The little psychology he studied in school was academically focused and never prepared him for what he was encountering here. The psychology he picked up in bits and pieces through daily living, reading popular magazines, and watching TV talk shows was mostly directed to his thinking about himself and the personal situations he faced.

Nevertheless, Marty is anything but an incompetent manager, and even from this conversation you can see that he rates fairly high on the "concern for human beings" scale. But he was viewing events though his own mind-set rather than Al's. He was not asking the searching questions the new mentality directs him to answer. Marty needed to find out why an otherwise competent person like Al, who was good enough for him to hire, was not responsive to his directives and not giving enough attention to details. Locked inside his own mind-set, he could see only that Al was doing a lot of things wrong.

Marty was expecting Al's priorities to mirror his own. This is not to say that the company didn't also need the details covered, and clearly it was Marty's responsibility to ensure that people understood their jobs well enough to make sure the details were. But at this point Al couldn't see the importance of small items like lightbulbs, especially in the scope of his other priorities. From the standpoint of what the new mentality requires, it was important for Marty to recognize that Al was another imperfect performer giving the company a lot of what it needed, with the potential to give it even more, who was not yet living up to the company's customer-pleasing creed.

The help we gave did not require deep psychoanalysis. In fact, to this day we don't think Al even knows whether we are really professors, or what we are professors of; nor do we think he feels like we had him reclining, let alone laid out on the couch. He probably thinks of us as ardent Cub fans, reconciled to our annual losing fate.

What we did was no more than you could do if you came equipped with a model that told you what you needed to learn and what to make of it. We were out to learn what was important to Al and how it tied in with the company's objectives. It was something Marty couldn't see until we showed it to him. We know he eventually saw it, because he's not the type to put down ten dollars without a struggle. To us Marty is the archetype of a manager who can commit organization mayhem due to insufficient psychological training, exactly the type of manager most people were trained to be. Marty is as well-intentioned and kindhearted as they come, but he doesn't know enough psychology basics. Nevertheless, he's the boss, which means that left uncorrected, his way of seeing things and reasoning are likely to first become the organizational "truths" but eventually the traps that cause his obsolescence.

In this instance we weren't out to change anybody, although to the best of our knowledge Marty and Al are working well together today. Understanding Al's reasoning proved to be sufficient for changing Marty's mind-set, and by now maybe Marty has changed Al's as well. We knew that you can't conduct a fair-minded assessment of questionable actions without inquiring into the acting party's motivations, self-concept, and skills. We also knew that, at work, people often get so caught up in power dynamics that they readily slip into judging one another's actions without taking the time to "crack the code." They evaluate the other person using their own mind-set as the standard, as if it were a valid way of measuring what the other person set out to do. Of course the Artifact of Mind insight tells us that this way of judging is ever fraught with error because each person's mind-set is going to be distinct. People with different personal agendas and different ways of seeing organizational events and reasoning about them confuse one another by speaking the same language with different personal logics that impute different meanings to the same words.

We think that having Al more accurately in his sights gives Marty more control. Now he knows what to work on in developing Al's thinking and what experiences can help accomplish that. Perhaps he'll give Al a training assignment in sales and customer contact. Certainly the lightbulb incident exposes the downside of using discipline in trying to get someone, Al this time, to change his behavior when this person actually sees things a different way.

In subscribing to the Artifact of Mind insight we must quickly point out that we do not believe that everyone's viewpoint has the same organizational value. Some actions are clearly more correct than others and some people are better stationed—by virtue of experience, information, ability, and intent—to act in the organization's best interests. Nevertheless, we also believe that everyone operates with a distinctive mind-set that must be considered when you require their participation or when you are trying to anticipate how they are likely to respond to initiatives you are about to take.

Mind-set management

Mind-sets are the distinctive viewpoints, needs, and agendas that determine how an individual engages events at work—what that individual actually sees and what that individual is inclined to do in response to what he or she sees. The Artifact of Mind insight leads directly to the most basic advice-giving tenet: **Until you know how the other person is inclined to see events and think about them, management and advice-giving are nothing more than power plays and manipulative acts.** Only after mind-sets are comprehended can management become a nonmanipulative activity

where straightforward statements evolve into candid exchanges so
that accuracy and clarity of communication eventually replace reciprocal deception.

Mind-Set Management asks you to face up to a fact in your
organization life that you already know from the rest of daily living:
**People experiencing the same events live entirely different
realities.** Only when you have this fact internalized, so that it is
central in your thinking all the time, can you begin to appropriately
view people and the actions they take at work. This is different from
viewing their behavior primarily in terms of how it fits with your
motivations—which, in most cases, will not be what others intend.
People may act as you would, but seldom will they do so for the
same reasons. And if it is an action about which you feel moved to
critically comment, you can count on the fact that their reasoning will
be different from yours. All these statements derive directly from
what the Artifact of Mind insight instructs.

Actually, the Artifact of Mind insight is a series of insights that
provides the beginning points for a comprehensive education in managerial psychology. In stating that every individual functions with a
distinctive mind-set, it makes a fundamental point: **Mind-sets are
the origination points for all workplace behavior.**

Then, by stating that the actual meaning an event or work situation holds for an individual is determined primarily by the mind-set
that individual uses in perceiving it, the Artifact of Mind insight
makes two additional points: **What another individual perceives
will not necessarily be an accurate reflection of what you
did or of the intentions behind your act; how that person
decides to act, based on what he or she perceives, will not
necessarily be what you desire or have a "rational" reason
to expect, given what you did and how you would act if you
were in that person's position.**

Finally, the insight states that individuals working together are
subliminally aware that their experience of events is colored by their
own needs and motivations, and instinctively sense that everyone
else's are too. But rather than reveal these differences and risk
exposing the idiosyncratic bases of their perceptions, people spend
their time together inventing "meanings" that allow them to talk and
work efficiently and productively with one another. This leads to another fundamental point. **When people use the term "organization" they are actually referring to man-made, political,
agreements, constructed for purposes of attributing meanings to events and actions that are reciprocally convenient
to the people making the agreements.** This is the basis of "or-

ganization." That is, organizations are the production of people with different mind-sets striking agreements about what to produce, how to organize to produce it, what performance is to be valued, what is expected in the way of work process, output, and marketplace results, and everything else.

This book teaches managerial psychology

This book probes the Artifact of Mind insight to derive a series of psychological tenets to orient your attempts to influence people and give them advice. Its aim is to advance your skills and perspectives in the intelligent and disciplined practice of managerial psychology.

Mind-Set Management explains what you need to know to read the mind-sets that others use in viewing events and taking action. You can tell people what you think is going on and what they need to do to operate effectively until you are blue in the face, but the only way to know what people are actually inclined to do, and that which they might be inclined to do differently based on your counsel, is to understand their mind-sets before you interact with them. Until you do, you'll find yourself in one situation after another trying to get what the company needs in the way of output while the person you are advising is hung up with you—frustrated that you don't appreciate what he or she is already contributing and how he or she wants to go about it.

Of course, comprehending the mind-set that is at the root of an individual's behavior is just the beginning. You must get it accurately, you must communicate to the other person that you have it straight, and you must actively relate to it **prior to formulating your advice.** Otherwise the advice you give will be aimed at solving problems that, in the other person's mind, either don't exist or exist in a different format than you are pursuing. All of this requires a model to cue your search and sensitivity. It also requires a model that helps you understand what you can influence and what you cannot, as well as a process for testing your determinations. In this book, we take up these assignments.

The theory and advice-giving perspectives advanced in this book are directed toward enhancing your leadership, management, and influencing activities with just about everyone whose performance is essential to the successful functioning of your company. Chartwise, this means up, down, and all around. Everyone needs to hear from you. And we're going deep-sea diving in contrast to the usual surface swimming, where probably you are already quite proficient but lack impact. We're going out to engage problems arising from how an individual sees and thinks about events, not just from what an individual does or fails to do. After all, how a person sees a situation and thinks about his or her motives is the origination point for behavior. The rest has to do with skill, self-discipline, and judgment.

In preparing you to appreciate the value of the Artifact of Mind insight, we have to give you fair warning. This insight is so deceptively simple and logical that you're going to have problems internalizing it. That is, it's something you've always known and that your experience has validated a "jillion" times. However, based on twenty-five years of teaching and consulting, we believe that, in every instance, you are fully capable of ignoring it because it runs counter to the rational and objective logic that characterizes most of the models you have been using. Yet the new management models require that you embrace this insight and use it in sizing up every situation you face. If you don't, the models will sweep by you with your head nodding "they are right" but without your actions reflecting them.

Fortunately there is a litmus test to which you can submit your thinking when you are out to influence someone and have competence-enhancing advice to give. Do you experience a compelling need to first get more understanding about the person and how the "mistaken way" he or she has been proceeding makes good, logical sense to that individual? This is the test. If you say "yes" and really mean it, it's entirely possible that you are, in fact, already on the mind-set management track.

Now it's time to extend this introduction to mind-set management with a more thorough exploration of the underlying and guiding principles that constitute the Artifact of Mind insight. After covering this in Chapter 2, we'll give you a quick overview of what's in the rest of this book.

Notes

1. W. H. Schmidt and J. P. Finnegan, *The Race Without the Finish Line* (San Francisco: Jossey-Bass, 1992); W. E. Deming, *Out of the Crisis* (Cambridge, Mass.: MIT Center for Advanced Engineering, 1986); P. B. Crosby, *Quality Is Free: The Art of Making Quality Certain* (New York: McGraw-Hill, 1979).

2. P. Graham (ed.), *Mary Parker Follett: Prophet of Management* (Boston: Harvard Business School Press, 1995); W. C. Byham, and J. Cox, *Hero Z* (New York: Harmony, 1994); T. J. Peters, *Liberation Management*

(New York: Fawcett Columbine, 1992); W. Bennis, *On Becoming a Leader* (Reading, Mass.: Addison-Wesley, 1989); J. F. Vogt and K. L. Murrell, *Empowerment in Organizations* (San Diego: University Associates, 1990); C. C. Manz and H. P. Sims, *Superleadership: Leading Others to Lead Themselves* (Englewood Cliffs, N.J.: Prentice Hall, 1989); P. Block, *The Empowered Manager* (San Francisco: Jossey-Bass, 1987).

3. P. M. Senge, A. Kleiner, C. Roberts, R. B. Ross and B. J. Smith, *The Fifth Discipline Fieldbook* (New York: Doubleday, 1994); C. Argyris, *Knowledge for Action* (San Francisco: Jossey-Bass, 1993); P. M. Senge, *The Fifth Discipline: The Art and Practice of the Learning Organization* (New York: Doubleday, 1990).

4. D. K. Banner and T. E. Gagné, *Designing Effective Organizations: Traditional and Transformational Views* (Newbury Park, Calif.: Sage, 1994); T. A. Kochan, *Transforming Organizations* (New York: Oxford University Press, 1992); B. Nanus, *Visionary Leadership* (San Francisco: Jossey-Bass, 1992); R. T. Pascal, *Managing on the Edge* (New York: Simon & Schuster, 1990); N. N. Tichy and M. Devanna, *The Transformational Leader* (New York: Wiley, 1986); F. J. Govillant and J. N. Kelley, *Transforming the Organization* (New York: McGraw-Hill, 1995).

5. J. Champy, *Reengineering Management* (New York: Harper, 1995); M. Hammer and J. Champy, *Reengineering the Corporation* (New York: Harper, 1993).

6. D. E. Osborne and T. Gaebler, *Reinventing Government: How the Entrepreneurial Spirit Is Transforming the Public Sector* (Reading, Mass.: Addison-Wesley, 1992).

7. W. Bennis, *An Invented Life: Reflections on Leadership and Change* (Reading, Mass.: Addison-Wesley, 1993); E. Lawler, *The Ultimate Advantage: Creating the High Involvement Organization* (San Francisco: Jossey-Bass, 1992); P. F. Drucker, *The New Realities* (New York: Harper, 1990); T. J. Peters and N. K. Austin, *A Passion for Excellence* (New York: Warner, 1985).

8. D. Cantor and T. Bernay, *Women in Power* (Boston: Houghton Mifflin, 1992); D. Jamieson and J. O'Mara, *Managing Workforce 2000* (San Francisco: Jossey-Bass, 1991); M. Loden and J. B. Rosner, *Workforce America: Managing Employee Diversity as A Vital Resource* (Homewood, Ill.: Irwin, 1991); R. M. Kanter, *When Giants Learn to Dance* (New York: Simon & Schuster, 1989); B. Zeitz and L. Dosky, *The Best Companies for Women* (New York: Simon & Schuster, 1988).

9. H. S. Astin and C. Leland, *Women of Influence, Women of Vision* (San Francisco: Jossey-Bass, 1991); T. J. Peters and R. H. Waterman, *In Search of Excellence* (New York: Harper, 1982).

10. J. A. Thompson, *The Portable Executive* (New York: Simon & Schuster, 1995); J. O'Toole, *The Executive's Compass* (New York: Oxford

University Press, 1993); P. Block, *Stewardship* (San Francisco: Benett Koehler, 1993); E. C. Murphy and M. Snell, *The Genius of Sitting Bull* (Englewood Cliffs, N.J.: Prentice Hall, 1993); S. R. Covey, *Principle-Centered Leadership* (New York: Simon & Schuster, 1991).

11. P. L. Berger and T. Luckman, *The Social Construction of Reality* (Garden City, N.Y.: Doubleday, 1966); R. M. Cyert and J. March, *A Behavioral Theory of the Firm* (Englewood Cliffs, N.J.: Prentice-Hall, 1963).

2

The Artifact of Mind Insight

To this point we've described how the progressive new models require you to influence an increasing number of people, in directions that you see as critical to the effective functioning and productivity of the overall corporate team, without the capacity to control them. Now it's time to probe the Artifact of Mind insight for how it can be used to help you accomplish this. It's the critical insight for teaching you the psychology that will enable you to implement what you're being asked to do. The new models require a new mentality, and that means thinking about people differently.

In most organizations the way to influence people when you lack the capacity to insist that they actually use your advice is through one-on-one discussions and group meetings. Hypothetically, these are the forums for voicing your opinions, giving your reactions to what people are doing, and declaring what others ought to be considering when making decisions that are theirs to make.

However, operating within the former mentality, discussions in which you are supposed to "say it straight" rapidly become tedious exercises in "saying it oblique"; meetings ostensibly called to "kick ideas around" quickly turn into defensive encounters and misguided exercises in "consensus seeking" and "group decision making." Instead of the process yielding new ideas and keen insights, it produces reductionistic thinking that lacks the insightfulness of anyone's initial thinking. Too often the meeting you attend with high expectations becomes a "group grope" in which discussants search less for the best solution and more for solutions to which no one will object.

While the people involved hate to acknowledge this, too often the emphasis is on compromise and concession leading to lowest-common-denominator thinking.

Likewise, in one-on-one meetings, most people who would like to candidly say what they think and give directive advice are inclined to soft-pedal their ideas. They feel a strong need to remain within the realm of the politically acceptable so as not to damage their relationships. They send out trial balloons and make watered-down statements that give others the option either to read between the lines and to "get it" or to "play it dumb." The underlying idea is to avoid a clash in viewpoints or sharp conflicts in views.

Reciprocally, the people who are the targets of the advice are less inclined to experience advice as valuable counsel and more inclined to see it as resistance and self-interested and agenda-biased opposition to how they want to proceed. Fearing that forthrightly engaging disparate advice might lead to resentments and explicit opposition, they also soft-pedal their ideas. Oftentimes they do so by drifting into a cat-and-mouse process of trying to figure out what is minimally acceptable to the advice-giver. In the process, the character of everyone's thinking is compromised. What is done in the name of being "open-minded" and being seen as a "team player" results in a consensus-seeking search in which basic issues are broken down into piecemeal decisions, in which each person gets some of what he or she wants, producing end results that lack character and integrity.

We've found it the exception, not the rule, for people to leave a meeting room feeling that an advice-giving exchange has been a useful expenditure of their time. Using the former mentality, too many meetings are conceived on premises that are more fraudulent than real. They follow from such ideas as "participation ensures buy-in," "more heads are better than one," and "seeing all the pieces will cause people to maximize the interests of the whole." Unfortunately, in actual practice these become disorienting assumptions. When they pan out it's great. But in terms of percentages, your organization would be far better off if everyone assumed they never did. Practically speaking, you would be a lot less confused and there would be a great deal more coherence and efficiency in everyone's efforts.

The advent of new management models threatens to make meetings the blight of your organizational existence. New models inevitably mean more influence-exchange meetings, and more meetings hold the potential to waste more of your time while producing outcomes that may not be as good as anyone's going-in ideas. In fact, when new models are implemented, it's not uncommon to hear people complain that they run from meeting to meeting without having time to do their work. When this happens, it's usually the result of someone attempting to operate a new model using the former mentality.

Case in point

We encountered an extreme example of an individual complaining about meetings when we were consulted by an executive of a company that had gone to lengths to develop and institute an imaginative new management model in making the change from high-tech aerospace and defense to space-age technology and communications. The executive complained, "I now spend so much of my time in meetings that I have to work twelve to fifteen hours a day and on weekends merely to stay afloat."

In describing the model he said, "The original solution was a good one. We got rid of hierarchy and created autonomous business units. Initially we were so busy getting our systems in place that we didn't have time for many meetings. Our communications were spontaneous, efficient, and straight. Since that time we've grown, and our profitability has skyrocketed. But now we spend our time holding ridiculous discussions in which it's not clear that anyone says what he truly thinks."

He explained, "During the reorganization, each functional unit was reformulated to become an independent business. We created an internal marketplace in which we bought from and sold to one another. For example, my unit manufactures 'zibits,' which the 'Space Marketing Unit' buys from us and then sells to commercial customers. But 'Space Marketing' retains the prerogative of buying 'zibits' from our competitors and, hypothetically, will do so if they can make a better deal. And we're supposed to do the same when purchasing component parts. Likewise, when we can charge premium prices, we're permitted to sell our 'zibits' to a competitor's marketing company. Until now we haven't because we're far exceeding our profit goals, and in the process we're getting recognition for making heroes out of everyone else."

He told us that his problems stemmed from the organization chart created to facilitate the company's new business strategy and the surreptitious use of power. He explained, "Residing at the top is a sector president and four senior vice presidents. All the rest of us are called various things. Inside the company I'm called business unit leader with the acronym BUL, which, when you view what I'm dealing with, you'll see is only half a word. Outside, I'm called anything from sector director to division president. I use whatever title seems appropriate to the situation.

"On the surface I'm told I have 'absolute power' to run my business however I see fit. Of course I also recognize that the sector president has overriding absolute power which he uses all the time but which, because of the model, he wants us to pretend he never uses. He thinks that once he gets heavy-handed the new model will no longer work. But my real problems come from the senior vice presidents who don't have any business units directly under their control. In concept each has advisory responsibilities for each business unit's profitability and production and for the operation as a whole. In addition, each performs nominal oversight of one or more staff functions such as accounting, human resources, legal, and public relations, which all of the business units share."

Continuing, "The way I see it, the senior vice presidents are relatively young men who are each bent on becoming the sector president. Each appears to be constantly striving to have his ideas recognized and be seen as important value added. When they come over to talk one-on-one they usually realize I'm not about to be a part of their campaign so, generally, they have relatively little to say. But when we have sector management meetings, which can be three full mornings a week and even more often, it's a horse of a different color. Then they are out on the campaign trail, vocally advocating one self-inflated scheme after another.

"Most of the other business unit leaders, and many of what are called staff leaders, have learned to deal with such discussions by going limp. Few of us are envious of the senior vice presidents' jobs so we don't see much to gain by entering the discussion and risk getting between a senior vice president and his latest advocacy. On the other hand I can't stand listening to vanilla statements that lack substance and don't go anywhere. Occasionally I say as much. When I do everybody nods strong agreement but then, two minutes later, acts as if what I just said was spoken in Chinese. So here I am running a 100-million-dollar-a-year business that, in mega-areas, I run autonomously, listening to a forty-five-minute group discussion in which four senior vice presidents get all worked up debating my proposal for an eighteen-hundred-dollar student summer-hire! Not only do I go limp but it makes me feel a little dirty.

"Last week I went to the president and said, 'this happy horseshit has got to stop.' I begged him to pull my business unit out and make it a separate company. I told him it would be a slam dunk to come up with a business plan that, with nominal capitalization, could diversify our product line, triple our sales, and quadruple profits three to five years out. He knows that I could damn well do that, and he also knows that what we're currently doing so profitably could drop off the cliff at any moment. We can't predict market saturation because a technological breakthrough could change our business entirely. Yet he sits there rolling his eyes telling me he'll give my request consideration when I know he has no such intention."

Concluding, he said, "Of course I realize that the politics of the situation makes his agreeing to my request impossible. How can they spin my group out without telling others who might also want to make their situations more sane that they aren't good enough to be independent? And how can they deprive the senior vice presidents of the campaign grounds they need to get ahead?! But I don't know what's going to get our Sector management out of this compression and I'm sure our president doesn't know either."

The new models require straight talk

To us this is a clear example of high-level executives and managers bringing a former mentality to a new management model. Proceeding this way is guaranteed to deny a model's full potential. From this executive's account, there is no question but that the new model is a powerful one that has allowed the company to make valuable progress. He made the model sound creative, functional, and profitable. It decentralized authority, created an efficient utilization and sharing of staff resources, promoted light-handed leadership and a spirit of corporate-level teamwork that caused unit leaders to continuously reflect on how their operations and business involvements were affecting company profitability. And it had what all the unit leaders considered to be a very special innovative feature—an internal marketplace that simulated what the company faced externally. Nevertheless, there was a process problem that had at least one highly-thought-of executive feeling trapped and, apparently along with many others, inefficiently mincing words.

But using a new model with the former mentality, people were not adequately positioned to straightforwardly state what was on their minds or to make direct responses to what their associates were saying. Blocking them was the inability to deal forthrightly with the sector vice presidents, who, while relinquishing control, had retained the need to be seen as having an important value-added impact on the performance of each business unit. Subsequently we had the opportunity to ask executives in other parts of the company how they saw this situation, and their comments corroborated the picture the frustrated business unit leader had related. Thus we concluded that despite the sector's implementation of a new model, with its resulting business success, the use of the former mentality was causing the company to lose out on even more success.

The underlying psychological principles

The Artifact of Mind insight is highly relevant to understanding the dysfunctional bind each of these executives found himself in. In stating "organization is an artifact of the mind that views it," this insight portrays what, in the aforementioned story, became an irrefutable but undealt with fact: **Self-interests and personal, work-related effectiveness agendas significantly impact—even wholly determine—how people see events at work, and ultimately how they think to operate given those perceptions.** This insight states that what people talk about when they say "the company," "the corporate way," "the strategy," "the operation," "the function," "the unit," "the right team composition," "the business plan," "the organization chart," "the structure," "the culture," "the appropriate style," "the right response," "the appropriate motivation," "the expectation," "the effective approach," "the right way to manage," "the profit picture," "the bottom line"—the you-name-it— is a blend of what's inside them personally, what's outside them and thought to exist "objectively" in their environment, and what they have been talked into believing, authentically or conveniently, by the people with whom they interact. Of course, what people believe is outside them and "objective" and what they have been convinced by others is "objective" are colored by their perceptions, which, in turn, are also partially a function of what's inside them.

Saying that "organization is an artifact of the mind that views it" is a straightforward extrapolation of a well-known psychological principle: motivation determines perception. Recall the old experiment where researchers measured the size of the coins drawn by children who were shown pictures of quarters, half-dollars, and silver dollars on a screen. The kids from poor families drew the coins larger than the rich kids drew them. Also recall the sociological principle that reality is socially constructed, which is the underlying explanation for the tunnel-vision/group-think phenomena that lead a given piece of information to cause the price of a stock, in a single day, first to go down 3 points and then, as a new explanation is thought up, come back 3 and then rise 10. In other words, what people perceive and genuinely experience to be "reality" or to be of "value" is a mixture of self-interested personal needs, including work-related competency and productivity agendas, and social processes in which people in groups decide the meaning of events and determine the value of actions in those events. In other words, people, alone and in groups, "manufacture" conceptual categories that they later use in interpreting the meaning of events and evaluating their own and other people's performances in those events.

To illustrate, we're reminded of the apocryphal story of the tailor who was asked if he could accurately describe the man who robbed him in a dimly lit alley. He answered, using the conceptual category in which he thinks, "Of course I can. He's a perfect 42-short." Also illustrative is the often-told story about a conversation that took place between a newly hired manager and the president of a large, industry-leading paper company. The manager asked, "What's the dress code here?" The president answered, "That's a ridiculous question. Wherever did you get the idea that we had one?" The manager replied, "Certainly there's one. For one thing, you and everyone else around here wear only white shirts." In response, the next day the president wore a blue shirt. People now say, "That's the day the dress code changed, but shirts with stripes are still out."

Thus everything that an individual refers to when talking about the company, the marketplace, or even another person's effectiveness has a highly subjective, local-culture, synthetic component that derives from a combination of self-interests and work-team agendas. Every perception has an indestructible and distinctive self-interested dimension that cannot be determined independently of knowing the specific individual involved. This is the essence of what is meant by "organization is an artifact of the mind that views it." What an individual sees "out there" is a function of what is going on inside that individual to an extent that it becomes impossible to ever fathom out "true objectivity."

The Artifact of Mind insight instructs us that what people think at work, what they see at work, and how they decide to act in any work situation is determined by their needs to size up and frame work situations for their effective and competent participation in them. It is not that people are capricious or corrupt. It is that their prime motivation is to perform competently. And the competence they seek is a dual-function competence. On one hand it is related to self-satisfaction, self-esteem, and how they feel they need to conduct their affairs to live their lives with personal meaning. On the other hand it is related to their need to perform their organizational work competently and to gain recognition for their contribution. People automatically and authentically frame work situations according to their needs, motives, and desires to perform effectively. And none of this can be prespecified independently of knowing the individual.

Most of the new management models recognize that self-interests are a given that need to be engaged as a critical variable in staging a situation for organizational effectiveness, but they don't go far enough. These models lead managers to plan retreats and team-building meetings aimed at getting each participant to see the same situations comparably, as if a strong model could redirect how different individuals are internally programmed to think and act. The goal is to achieve a group mind-set that influences how people think, not just what they do. In our minds such attempts to get people's thinking to converge on a common plan cannot become realistic as long as essential, governing variables that actually control what an individual has to do to look out for his or her well-being are unavailable for consideration and discussion.

Although most of the new models get to the point, they don't quite take the right step forward. They contrast well with former models that addressed personal mind-sets as self-interested bias and resistance to be partitioned, controlled, and overcome. Viewing personal mind-sets as mentalities that require managerially specified re-focusing certainly is a step forward. Nevertheless, both instances contain at least two assumptions that fail to square with the Artifact of Mind insight. The first is the implied belief that the idiosyncratic, self-centered biases and limitations that exist in people's perceptions can be circumvented. The second is that you can get to the point where everyone in the organization views critical events and operating modalities comparably and "correctly," with "correct" corresponding to the directions in which top-level corporate executives would like to head.

In one company where a progressive new model was being used, we heard executives enthusiastically portray the process by saying, "At Acutron we force conformity down, and pull clarity (of that conformity) up." When we asked how that works, they explained, "All proposals for action have to be linked and justified to established corporate objectives before they get a hearing." While we could see the benefits, we also saw problems. To us their situation sounded reminiscent of the escalation of American troop commitments during the Vietnamese war. Once the American generals figured out that their boss, Secretary of Defense Robert McNamara, had a penchant for letting the numbers dictate the decision, they began manufacturing and selectively feeding him the numbers required to get the "right" decisions made.

We see the Artifact of Mind insight taking the personal dimension a significant step further than the "refocusing" premise used in many of the new models. It acknowledges and accepts as immutable fact that people operate from distinctive personal equations, and it directs you to engage people in conversations to discover how they actually see things. Then, after true beliefs are uncovered, the conversation can move to the search for confluence between the course the individual is following and the directions that "the organization" needs to take. In this mentality, the prespecified "plan" may need adjusting to fit the realities of the people involved. Using the former mentalities, regardless of new or old model, management is merely looking for the manipulation that will get people to follow course.

The Artifact of Mind insight says, **"Wait a minute. You've got this whole thing backward. If you want to manage effectively, stop trying to get people to be what you want them to be. Engage them where they actually are."** Until you do so and have earned their trust because you're actually listening, you are going to have trouble getting people to form internal bonds with the evolving and changing joint effort.

In other words, when you eventually hear people out and comprehend the basis of what they are thinking, saying, and feeling, you might change how you think and reason, especially when it comes to understanding what constitutes an effective performance for the person to whom you are listening and your ability to influence that person.

That is to say, and this is radical, **if you want to know what people are going to do, don't content yourself with telling them what they ought to be doing.** Instead, on Day 1 tell them how you see the situation and what you would like in the way of results from them. Then, on Day 2, ask them what they intend to do and how they plan to operate. And don't just settle for abstractions. Ask them, "How does that (what you just said) translate into action?" Insist on getting the visuals. Then once you understand how they actually see things and their ideas for operating given those perceptions, consider whether what you have planned still makes sense or whether it's your plan and expectations that need revising. You need to calibrate people realistically. **Sometimes "relinquishing control" merely entails facing up to that which, under no circumstance, you could ever control.**

While many of the new models continue to proceed as if organizations and organization structures are entities that exist outside the individual that views them, the Artifact of Mind insight specifies organization and structure as entities that exist inside the mind of each individual. This is not to say that nothing about the corporation or the work structure exists outside the individual. This is simply to say that everything on the outside receives a highly personal interpretation, spin, filtering, slanting, prioritizing, and refocusing. And in every instance, the spin relates to the individual's need to structure "reality" in a way that meshes what's demanded internally with what's demanded externally in living a personally competent, meaningful, and productive life at work.

The Artifact of Mind insight instructs that if you want to find out what the organization is, you have to ask the people who live and work in it, and the picture you come away with will not be independent of the motives of the individuals with whom you consult or of their constituent interests. Likewise what you conclude is going to be filtered through your interests, work agendas, and the objectives that underlie your inquiry. And when you ask people what they are trying to accomplish and why they are proceeding as they are, pay attention to Chris Argyris's[1] warning: The explanations that people espouse for what they do, and sincerely believe are true, may not be the same as the explanations that are implied by scrutinizing their actual practice.

The marketing guys almost have it right

Sales and marketing people *almost* have the right angle on the Artifact of Mind insight when it comes to dealing with customers. They know that you can't accurately predict what appeal will work best with a customer until you know how that customer prioritizes needs. Among salespeople there is an established maxim: "Until you know the territory, you can't make a sale." Enter the marketing discipline that proceeds on the assumption that consumer research precedes the formulation of customer appeals. And the research they conduct is aimed at articulating the mind-sets that products engage. With this articulation they proceed in two interacting ways. First, they consider modifying the product to better fill a need. Second, they engage the customer's mind-set to reshape the need to better match what they are selling.

It's fascinating to note how quickly people learn to apply the sales and marketing orientation to the thinking and perceptions of a variety of people who are external to the firm. When dealing with outsiders, whether they be suppliers, customers, government regulators, or others, they readily acknowledge the presence and legitimacy of biases and self-interested agendas. Marketeers automatically ask "What's the customer's perception?" and "Which of their needs are the most central ones?" And when questions are raised about how the market works, the answer is usually some variation of "It works the way the customer thinks." Sometimes marketeers go so far as to say, "If it doesn't exist in the mind of the customer, it doesn't have reality." And, inside advertising agencies, we've even heard people say, "Reality is not what you want it to be, it's what the customer wants." In short, when it comes to dealing with outsiders, people readily understand that these outsiders can't be accurately engaged without appealing to the self-interested and emotional agendas that drive their actions.

But the same people who take the Artifact of Mind approach when dealing with outsiders think and act quite differently when dealing with people inside the firm. Instead of acknowledging the presence of self-interests and personalized work agendas, they stubbornly push what others **ought to think,** how they **should operate,** and what others **have to be convinced of and sold** without engaging in the inquiry they would automatically utilize in dealing with outsiders. They treat their "teammate's" insider status as entitlement for force-feeding viewpoints irrespective of how the other person actually views events and the self-interests that person has at stake. But the Organization Is an Artifact of Mind insight contends that you should be treating everyone as if he or she were an outsider operating with a distinctive self-interested agenda that must be understood and engaged prior to expecting any behavior. We would go so far as to assert that before you go out "to sell" anyone on how he or she might perform more competently, you first need to perform the necessary "market research."

Certainly there are factors from which you can derive some general expectations about how people perceive and relate to events at work, and the opportunities they see for performing competently in them. Knowing how people generally see the system working, using such information as the mission statement, the marketing strategy, the financial picture, the incentive system, the business plan, and the targeted numbers, allows you to formulate some reasonable expectations. Any or all of this information provides a sound departure point for appreciating how people intend to operate and how they are inclined to interpret work situations and events for their competent performance in them. But without knowing the distinct individual forces, which are unspecifiable prior to researching the way a specific individual is inclined to frame and interpret reality, you're likely to find yourself operating with an incomplete set of givens that leads you to expect behavior you might not receive.

The phenomenon that we're referring to is well known in the

artistic and literary disciplines but only occasionally finds its way into the scientific disciplines. Artists and writers clearly understand that everyone lives a distinctly different reality. They know this immutably. In fact, many draw explicitly on the gap between their perceptions and the established social order to derive their creativity. However, in management, the technical and intellectual analysis and design that creates work and management systems has been overextrapolated to obscure the art and science of effectively managing people. The desire to control, direct, order, and program people irrespective of the personalities and uniquenesses involved has been overdone to the point of systematically disorienting management.

Of course there are generalizable principles of human behavior that are valid regardless of the unique individuals involved. These principles can be implemented through systems and human resources design. But with any system, you inevitably reach the point where you have to deal with a specific individual, and the Artifact of Mind insight tells us that this cannot be done appropriately without first comprehending the distinctively personal equation that directs that individual's orientation. Thus when you're talking management and progressive new management models, you're probably on safer ground to add "the art form of management" as a component element of your model to prevent people from misconstruing it as a rationalistic human science.

To operate any new management model effectively you need to make the personal subjective dimension an important element in the management approach you are using, otherwise you will not apply it with the appropriate mentality. Until you do, you'll be stuck expecting that the same job given to five different people is going to be interpreted and effectively performed the same way by each. Until you do, you will be stuck expecting people to understand what you are saying simply because you communicated it clearly. Until you do, you will be stuck thinking that you can influence another person without first conducting extensive personal "market research." Until you do, you will expect that people are more governed by their adherence to the organization's paradigm than their own internal one. All of these expectations are false and misleading. Yet they are held almost universally!

To know what you "said," you have to ask people what they heard

At work people reason with different self-interested and need-generated systems of thinking—mind-sets—that determine the meaning they assign to events. These mind-sets act as personal paradigms, determining what each individual actually hears and sees and how he or she rationally acts in relation to what is heard and seen. Thus **when it comes to understanding people's behavior in organizations, you can't begin to be objective until you understand the subjective personal interests and work agendas that underlie what a specific individual sees as competent production for him- or herself and others.** Herein lies the key in applying the Artifact of Mind insight to the optimization of the new management models. Internalizing this fact, in contrast to acknowledging it but not constantly utilizing it, means that you are convinced that good management never involves top-down strategizing and specifying without a great deal of conversation with the people whose actions are being orchestrated. Yes, it is management's job to provide the vision, direction, and leadership. What we're saying is that you don't know what version of the vision or game plan has been received without knowing the mind-sets of the specific individuals to whom it has been given.

Likewise, the Artifact of Mind insight instructs that there are limits to what you can achieve by getting people together in groups to plan actions that a "standard," "normal," "rational" group member is then supposed to take. At work, **people who don't operate as you expect are a lot more rational than you think.** People are rational in being focused on their self-interests. They are rational in trying to operate in ways that they think allow them to be effective given all that they are balancing that you don't know about. However, when you don't know how specific others view their individual competencies, or don't know what they see as the personally appropriate way to maximize their organizational performances, or don't know the self-interests and work agendas that are central in their minds, or feel you do know but "objectively" are convinced that they ought to be different, others will not appear rational. They will appear irrational, self-interested, egocentric, biased, emotional, competitive, and political. While these attributes are to be expected, they are experienced and phrased with inappropriate negativity.

Self-interests never go away, even when you play ostrich

Only after you internalize the Artifact of Mind insight can you see personal motives and different work agendas as legitimate and intractable dimensions of corporate participation. No discussion about the most effective and appropriate course of organizational action should take place without engagement of the interests and motives of the specific people that you're counting on to carry them out. People don't have to tell you specifically what they are balancing internally; they may barely know themselves. But if you ask them how they see what you are asking them to do, they are likely to tell you about their resistance and the obstacles they face and provide the data you need to be realistic about what you can actually get from them.

It's not necessary that you know each individual's self-interests precisely, although the more you know the better off you are. **What is fundamentally necessary is that you understand that distinct interests and motives exist and are the driving force behind people's participation and that these are neither known to you nor under your control.** You should indelibly recognize that the self-interests of performing competently are fused in every idea an individual speaks in advocating what's required for the corporation to move ahead. Cognizance of this bond is required before any management discussion can reasonably proceed. But in the former mentality, personal self-interests and corporate pursuits are discussed separately with self-interests viewed as a dimension that needs to be, and can be, manipulated and controlled.

Most of the new management models rely on a seamless bonding of personal effectiveness interests with the productivity interests of the corporation as a whole. The idea is that individuals should take actions that simultaneously promote the long-term success of both. This is the sought-after mentality for optimizing corporate resources. And teamwork requires that everyone's distinctive and individual bond with the corporation points in the same basic direction and that performance goals not put "corporate resources," a.k.a. "teammates," in competition with one another. In fact, in the new models, complementing the other person's skills, and helping him or her to function more effectively, is the only long-term strategy that can propel both you and your corporation ahead.

Case retrospective

With the Artifact insight introduced, it's instructive to briefly revisit the story of the executives in the space-age technology company and the plight of the one who complained about meetings. In that executive's mind, the self-interested pursuits of the sector vice presidents were straitjacketing the system. We would say it differently. It was the use of the former mentality that made it impossible for the sector team to make self-interested pursuits a valid dimension of the corporate equation. It was not the presence of self-interested pursuits per se that was impeding the executive group's functioning and effectiveness. It was the inability to make attention to self-interests a legitimate discussion topic that was confounding their logically derived process for managing.

Apparently everyone recognized the vice presidents' situation, but because of the reigning mentality, they didn't know a constructive intervention. So the situation deteriorated to the point where legitimate career-progress concerns created a need for group meetings on topics that compromised the new model's decentralization of authority and control. As we see it, the vice presidents' behavior was highly predictable and rational. But as the dynamic evolved, rational behavior turned out to entail daily competition over inconsequential scraps of influence in an effort to gain image and progress in one's career.

The vice presidents were swept along by the former mentality in which self-interests and internal political concerns exist but are seen as negatives. Hidden or expressed, their existence detracts from the optimal application of any progressive management plan. Assuming we know what they were doing, and we don't because we didn't interview them, the vice presidents' natural desire for a personally meaningful assignment, one which would allow them to make value-added contributions and to progress in their careers, put them in competition, creating an unfortunate state of affairs that had these professionals who ran five $50 million to $100-plus million businesses feeling the need to debate the wisdom of an $1,800 summer hire.

A mentality derived from the Artifact of Mind insight could have made the difference. With it, people would have addressed the vice presidents' self-interested pursuits and held discussions that searched for more constructive ways to realize their personal objectives. Without this mentality, however, there was no departure point for considering the counterproductive force the vice presidents were playing in the conduct of sector work and meetings. Our executive suggested, "There should be a rule that none of these guys can succeed the sector president. Then everyone's self-interests would be served by limiting each of these men's promotability to either elsewhere in the company or in the marketplace outside the company. The vice presidents would be more externally directed, and they'd have a need to conduct themselves more efficiently within the sector. At the very minimum, they wouldn't have the time or inclination to discuss the fine points of summer hires." "Not bad," we thought, "Not bad at all!"

Major lessons

We want to conclude this introduction to the Organization Is an Artifact of Mind insight by stating some unequivocal points that are essential considerations in influencing others with advice, feedback, and reactions to what they do at work.

1. At work, and in organizations, it is not what exists or what happens that counts, it is how what exists and happens is perceived by the various individuals involved.
2. To understand what someone perceives, you need to understand that individual's mind-set.
3. Understanding an individual's mind-set entails in-depth understanding of how that individual sees him- or herself performing competently, both in relation to life in general and to his or her work in the company.
4. Given how people differ from one another, the only thing you know for certain is that almost every event and conversation is going to be perceived disparately by someone in the group—even at times that you are certain that you have total agreement.
5. Whether or not a difference in perception is materially important to competently dealing with the issue at hand, or to any other issue essential to running the company, cannot be determined prior to engaging the mind-set of those holding the differing perception. Only then can you determine the implications and significance of that "deviant" perspective. Only then can you determine how to go about teaming up with that person and envision what the two of you might accomplish together.

Looking ahead

With the principles that derive from the Artifact of Mind insight introduced, we're ready to sequentially engage the body of this book. In Part II we're going to cover the mind-set fundamentals that you need to understand and have consciously in mind whenever you attempt to influence people and give them advice. Then, in Part III, we're going to take up the practical issues of matching up levels of advice given and sought, and what you need to understand when giving deep-level advice that you think can systematically improve the quality of an individual's effectiveness at work. How to get through with "breakthrough" caliber ideas, ones that reach behind surface actions and verbalized thinking, to impact the underlying assumptions another individual makes, is a goal that we think you pursue far more often than you let on to yourself. Throughout Parts II and III we'll be commenting on the new mentality and the mind-set transitions required to embrace it. Then in Part IV we're going to put the new mentality to work. We're going to consider some valuable applications that you can make of this material when operating in the mentality that the Artifact of Mind insight leads you to assume.

Note

1. See *Reasoning, Learning, and Action* (San Francisco: Jossey-Bass, 1982).

II

What You Need to Know Prior to Giving Advice

3

The Outsider's Perspective or "If you're from out of town, you must be an expert."

The preceding chapter illustrated some of the problems that arise when implementing a new management model using the former mentality. Note that we've merely scratched the surface in describing what can go awry. We saw that to avoid problems, new models require a new mentality and the Artifact of Mind insight provides the foundation psychology on which the new mentality is built. This insight provides the key for engaging any of the progressive new models that you and your company decide is best.

However, as we said, mere familiarity with the Artifact of Mind insight won't be enough. You've got to internalize it. You've got to ingest it to the point where it adds a critical dimension to everything you see. When someone says or implies "This is how it is," having the Artifact of Mind insight internalized will cause you to think, "What this person is telling me is not how it is; it's how this person sees it." Once you naturally start interpreting people this way and reflect, "But this isn't how I see it," a world of possibilities arises. Instead of thinking "Oh my god, I've got to set this person straight," you'll be scratching your head, wondering, "What's causing this smart-enough person to see things so differently?" With this line of thinking and questioning you're off and running. You'll automatically be searching for the thought processes and inclinations, the mind-sets, that lie behind the actions the other person takes. This is the essential first step in successful advice giving.

What makes you so smart?

"What makes you so smart?" is the first question that comes to the minds of the people you attempt to advise. And given the amount of advice you would be providing if you thought you could get away with it, it's a valid question for you to consider as well. Certainly if you didn't feel that you had something useful—even insightful—to contribute, you wouldn't be going to the trouble. Your experience must have already taught you that giving feedback and advice can readily become quite a hassle.

How do you answer the "What makes you so smart?" question anyway? That is, why do you think you are so consistently able to spot important competence- and effectiveness-enhancing opportunities that the bright people, whose situations, styles, and abilities you are commenting on, don't themselves appear to see? Certainly demonstrating their competence and performing effectively are issues that they spend a considerable portion of their day thinking about. How is it possible that you, as an outsider looking in, can observe people for a relatively short period of time, or sometimes just talk to them briefly, and almost immediately identify major oversights and faulty assumptions that allow you to offer personal-effectiveness advice? In addition to your basic intelligence, what do you think is the source of your insights? What makes you so smart is the topic of this chapter.

Case in point

This is precisely the line of questioning that occurred to us when we got sidetracked in a business discussion with the newly recruited and well-paid vice president of "fiscal planning" of a business that was grossing $150 million a year. It took a five-minute conversation to convince us that this guy was screwing up and only a few minutes longer to figure out exactly what he needed to do. And when you examine the situation he faced and how he was handling it, you will see that our insights didn't require the brains of a rocket scientist or the deep insights of a Freudian analyst.

We had been talking with Ralph about his inclination to over-commit, both himself and his department, and the tensions that arise from tackling ambitious workloads. Noticing that even our conversation was becoming intense, we were looking for an opportunity to break the tension. So when Ralph mentioned that his two young sons were coming out from Minnesota to spend their annual summer month with him, we jumped at the opportunity to lessen the pace by asking what he had planned. His answer astonished us. On the face of it, we couldn't see how a bright and apparently capable performer like Ralph could have reasoned himself into a bigger jam. And as we got into it with Ralph, we quickly learned that the topic was still Ralph's management style.

Ralph said he planned to take the first week off to spend with his boys and then go back to work. His parents would fly in from Illinois to care for the boys the second week. Then, for the last two weeks, he planned to enroll the boys in day camp with wraparound child care provided by a college student. As a package this would provide child-care coverage from 6:30 in the morning to 7:30 at night, the hours when he was off at work.

The Artifact of Mind insight instructs "ask for background factors" when people's actions fail to compute with common sense, and we've got that down pretty pat. In such situations much more is usually involved than what is apparent on the surface. The way to find out is by asking questions aimed at uncovering what the individual sees him- or herself facing. Experience has taught us that learning a critical detail or two can often cause an action that we initially saw as misguided, or even irrational, to make perfect, reasonable sense. However, in this instance, when we asked Ralph "How did you arrive at this plan?" the story we got made his plan sound even more misdirected and self-defeating.

We learned Ralph had been divorced six years earlier and that he experiences considerable guilt about the effects of the divorce on his two boys, now eleven and twelve. He feels he let them down by moving to California and leaving them in Minnesota with their mother who, he said, harbors bitter feelings, disparages him as an absentee father, and lives a more materialistic life than he wants the boys to have. He related how weekly phone conversations with his boys always feel stilted and that he counts on their summer month together as the time to reestablish communications and to bond. Ralph added, "Very importantly, it's my opportunity to instill the values I want my boys to have."

Ralph explained that, as a first-year employee, he receives only two weeks' annual vacation and that he needs to reserve one week of it for his girlfriend, with whom he shares a house. Painfully he related how, last year when the boys visited, she felt "pushed out." He emphasized how unfortunate this was since they have a loving relationship and he's upset when she feels slighted.

Next Ralph described how he spends as much as four fatiguing hours on the road each day commuting from his home on the southern outskirts of Los Angeles to the company's office in north San Diego. He explained that his commute reflects the compromise he and his girlfriend worked out in dividing the driving distance between his new job and the location of the professional school she attends on the other side of Los Angeles where she is completing a counseling psychologist degree.

Ralph told us that his girlfriend has two grown children, and that while she well understands the attention his boys require, she is very sensitive to the fact that his focus on the boys comes directly from the meager energy he has available for focusing on her, given his demanding job and long commute. He said, "Last year when the boys came for a visit her feelings of neglect added such pressure that just thinking about what's coming up makes me feel a bit overwhelmed."

We asked, "Are you sure you can take only one week's vacation? That sounds very minimal considering the connection you and your boys are looking to establish." This prompted Ralph to consult the policy manual, which revealed that, despite his short tenure with the company, as a corporate officer he was actually entitled to three weeks. Realizing this he mentioned that taking two weeks of vacation would constitute an uncomfortably long absence given that, at the time of his boys' visit, one of the two departments reporting to him would be deep in the process of a major systems changeover and the other would be in the middle of the annual audit, which required his personal supervision.

We asked whether his boss Jerry, the chief financial officer, might fill in some of the gaps. Ralph replied that he was reluctant to let Jerry get too involved because the system he was revising was one that Jerry had instituted when he had Ralph's job, and the audit would be uncovering practices that he could best explain. Ralph wanted to avoid the possibility of straining their relationship.

To us Ralph's portrayal sounded like a priority scheduling nightmare in which he was guaranteed to lose on all fronts. No matter how good the camp or how loving the grandparents, Ralph was vulnerable to his boys feeling shunted off to caretakers and resenting him for, once again, being an absentee father. Looking ahead, we pictured Ralph arriving home exhausted, as we always were when we drove round-trip to work in San Diego for a day, finding the boys tired from camp, frustrated from lack of interaction with him, and requiring dinner. And we could picture his girlfriend feeling neglected and seeing herself relegated to the role of baby-sitter and cook. With this schedule and pressures, we could see that for Ralph, finding unpressured, quality moments with the boys and his girlfriend would be an extraordinary challenge.

We also had concerns about Ralph's vulnerability at work. Clearly Ralph was one of those self-sacrificing employees who normally focus on company needs first with personal needs coming second. But the month he wanted to use for making his boys his number-one priority was exactly the period when late workdays and weekends were required. He experienced himself on trial at work just like he experienced himself on trial at home. Besides, he had told us, "I've been working hard to overcome the morale problems I inherited from Jerry's tenure. The people are just beginning to trust me. I have to be careful not to abandon them at the moment when the plan my guys and I spent months creating for the divisions encounters resistance and implementation problems."

Reflecting on the situation Ralph was about to face, an alternative came to mind. We suggested, "How about spending the day-camp money on an apartment with a pool in San Diego for the month?" We suggested that being in such close proximity to his office, he could work six-hour mornings, and reserve afternoons and evenings for his boys, who were at an age where, with some minimal help from a college student, they could sleep late, swim, and manage on their own until he came home from work at lunchtime. Moreover, his girlfriend could drive down and visit when she had a break and on weekends. In this plan, the dailyness of his involvements with the boys would create more natural relationships. And, conceivably, Ralph would have more energy, focus, and enthusiasm for his girlfriend when she arrived. What's more, many work pressures could be alleviated by his ability to meet daily with his staff and, with his new proximity, he would always have the option to run over and deal with problems and questions when something significant came up.

Ralph surprised us by accepting each significant feature of our suggestion. Not knowing him very well, we figured that more of what we were suggesting would not fit the details of his actual situation. Of course there were some modifications, but these were inconsequential adjustments having to do with the details of his parents' visit. The basic plan he adopted was the one we suggested.

The perceptual powers of the "outsider"

Later on we thought about the suggestions we made, reflecting that nothing we said required an expert. In fact, as we were having the conversation we merely thought of ourselves as interested outsiders motivated by empathy and friendship. We didn't think there was anything special in what we came up with and felt that almost anyone having the same conversation with Ralph would have raised problems and made suggestions more or less like the ones we were making. Only later did we begin "psychologizing" about Ralph and what he was doing in his life at home that reflected the types of traps he set for himself at work. But this wasn't part of our consciousness when we were giving him the other advice.

When we think about why we were on-target with our advice, we think about the power of being an outsider. Unlike Ralph, our objectivity wasn't hampered by absentee-father guilt or an overly responsible, heroic mind-set. This is not to say that our "objectivity" wasn't hampered by our own personal biases and shortcomings or to say that if we were in his situation we might have made comparably important but different oversights. The point is that the "reasoning trap" that ensnared Ralph was structured to ensnare someone making precisely the assumptions and misassumptions that Ralph typically makes. It's Geoffrey Vickers's point: "A trap is a trap only for the creature that cannot solve the problems that it sets. . . . The nature of the trap is a function of the nature of the trapped. To describe either is to imply the other."[1]

It was clear to us that, left to his own devices, Ralph could have spent hours, even days, fine-tuning the details of his plan without coming up with a solution that extricated him from the trap in which he found himself. On the other hand, there was nothing special about our reasoning. Our capacity to find a solution of a different ilk than Ralph could come up with on his own was due to our not being limited by the same type of guilt and unrealistic self-concept.

But, apparently, Ralph's girlfriend was caught up in a set of assumptions that complemented Ralph's. Only by engaging in a comparable self-sealing logic could she, as his cohort and confidante, not reason Ralph and herself out of a situation that she—especially with her interest in people—would readily spot in the lives of friends and the people to whom she provides apprenticeship counseling. From her inability to help Ralph reason beyond the solution he was pursuing when we got involved, we saw her assuming an "insider's" status similar to Ralph's.

It would be incorrect to conclude that we saw Ralph's situation more objectively than he saw it merely because we were "outsiders" who had nothing at stake and were not involved having to justify and defend our course of action. All we can accurately say is that we saw Ralph's situation differently enough to place us in a different category. The Artifact of Mind insight instructs that everyone views events through a lens of self-interests and personal agendas and that no one's perceptions are entirely independent of his or her immediate inner motives and work objectives. An "outsider" is an observer who, because he or she makes substantially different assumptions than those made by the person who is transacting with the situation firsthand, sees the situation differently. Conversely, "insiders" are people who, either because they live a situation firsthand or because of similar enculturation, personality, self-interests, work responsibilities, or whatever, make sufficiently similar assumptions as the "actor" to disqualify them as independent-thinking advice- and feedback-givers.

For purposes of clarification, we should quickly add that our definition of an outsider doesn't necessarily mean someone from outside the company. It could be anyone whose viewpoints and assumptions are dissimilar to the person who is living the situation firsthand. Depending upon the issue and the assumptions that are being made, an "outsider" can be someone in the same work unit or even the advice recipient's boss or a subordinate. Likewise, being from outside the work unit or the company does not, in and of itself, create outsider status. It depends upon the issues, stakes, and types of assumptions that the person is making about the situation being addressed.

Outsiders with agendas

While outsiders are defined as people who operate with different underlying assumptions that cause them to see events and situations differently, their advice does not necessarily come without systematic self-interested bias. In fact, there are many people that the person living the situation would call "outsiders" but whose particular self-interested motives and partisan work agendas disqualify them as objective advisers and/or sources of helpful feedback. Our term for this outsider category is "agenda-biased outsider." Ralph's concerns about his boss Jerry's attachments to the former system demonstrated that he had Jerry placed in the "agenda-biased" category. Because of this Ralph showed no inclination for expanding Jerry's knowledge of the personal equation driving his summer work schedule and vacation plans.

Agenda-biased outsiders contrast with outsiders who are not perceived as having a self-interest pursuit that overrides their concern for the effectiveness and well-being of the advice recipient and whom, as such, the advice recipient is inclined to call "objective." While at the time we were giving our advice we thought of ourselves as "objective," the important issue was that Ralph thought so. Here the situation becomes circular. Because he saw us without a competitive agenda, he saw us as "objective." Because he saw us as "objective," he freely revealed all the variables that were key in his planning, including his guilt and penchant for taking responsibility and overcommitting. Thus he openly divulged the information that we needed to know in making our advice relevant to the total situation he faced. Had he withheld one or more key variables, it's likely that our subsequent advice would be lacking to the point that Ralph could not use it.

Outsider "objectivity"

Perhaps by virtue of not having one's perceptions colored by the emotions produced by firsthand involvement, an outsider is, in fact, "more objective." On the other hand, when an outsider is not working with all the variables that the advice-recipient is facing, an important element of objectivity is subtracted. Thus the advice-giving issue is less "What's objectively correct?" and more "Do I know enough about each of the variables that are key to understanding what this individual is facing to formulate advice that is valid in relation to the reality that this person lives?" According to this line of reasoning, the issue of objectivity reduces to the perceived and practical usefulness to the person you seek to advise.

The aforementioned discussion of "objectivity" leaves out an important stakeholder, one that is crucial to the use of the term "objectivity." It's the *organization* and its need for competent performance and productivity relevant to its business goals. Whereas advice-recipients often get consumed with the question of "What's 'objectively' best for me?" the people who advise them often emphasize "What the organization needs and what's 'objectively' best for the company." Their focus on organizational consequences articulates a critical dimension required for a feedback recipient to achieve a balanced perspective. Certainly no one's self-interests are independent of the company's success or of having others perceive you as an essential corporate contributor. Being seen as an essential contributor to the company's success is one of the bedrock premises from which all the new management models emanate.

Case retrospective

In the case of Ralph, the success of our advice-giving was not due to the fact that we were "objective" in pushing what was right for the company. The key was that we came up with a solution that covered most of the essential variables in the equation that Ralph was trying to optimize, which included what was needed by the company. Our suggestion allowed Ralph to accomplish his multiple personal and organizational goals. Simultaneously it dealt with each of the key variables in the personal equation he was trying to solve. It covered time with his boys; a girlfriend who needs focus; the people he leads; his image as a team leader; and his credibility with his boss Jerry, based on his participation in the audit and his oversight of an important systems changeover. Had our proposal omitted any one of Ralph's multiple, high-priority concerns, Ralph probably would have rejected our suggestion, no matter how valid a view of reality it reflected.

Notwithstanding the usefulness of our advice, Ralph continues to have an underlying vulnerability. We don't believe he learned what he needed to learn most about overcommitting and his tendency to deceive people by convincing them that he, in his overcommitted state, gives their needs sufficient priority and focus. No doubt Ralph is well-intentioned and his words are eloquent in stating this. But at a deeper level, something, probably personal insecurity, appears to be driving him to a life pattern of saying "Yes" when he really doesn't have the time and energy to come through as they might reasonably expect.

The advice we provided allowed Ralph to successfully plan a summer month that was responsive to the needs of all interested parties. But in this conversation, and in subsequent ones, he never appeared to advance beyond the heroic thinking that produced the solution he initially related to us. The fact that we made different assumptions about what Ralph could reasonably accomplish, and how he might best go about it, set us apart from him and his girlfriend as well. They were both acting as if he should be able to pull the situation off as initially planned even though we find it hard to believe that either of them ever thought it could actually be accomplished with the commute he had to make.*

In relating this story we've implied that almost any open-minded outsider who took the time would have spotted Ralph's self-defeating assumptions and, if that outsider were so motivated, could have come up with an alternative plan that appreciably improved on what Ralph was contemplating. This assertion sets up the next question: "How is this done?" What methodology do outsiders, ourselves this

---

*Not that it's particularly relevant to the issue we're discussing here, but at one point we thought that the girlfriend's "myopia" might be caused by her unconsciously staging a "Prove that you really care about me" showdown fight. If that were the case, she might be better described as an "agenda-biased outsider."

time, utilize to produce insights about what another individual needs to do to improve his or her effectiveness? Certainly more has to be involved than merely not being stakeholders whose objectivity is impaired by how his or her behavior affects us. Precisely what is it that allows outsiders to penetrate the biased thinking of the insiders who actually live the situations, and to come up with suggestions that improve upon what the insiders were planning and doing?

Case methodology: pluses and minuses

For us the natural laboratory for researching "What's the source of the outsider's insights?" is the MBA classroom with its case-discussion format. Here, in a relatively short period of time, say thirty minutes to an hour, our student outsiders "tackle" and "crack" case study problems that perplex and bewilder the people who are featured in them. And the people in the cases are not just "Joe Average" guys plucked off the street. These people are professionals and managers who, by and large, are at least as well educated as our students, and whose professional work experience can exceed theirs by as much as fifteen to twenty-five years.

To "crack" these cases our students inevitably gravitate toward a methodology that instantly provides deep insights, which they unabashedly offer as objective paths to effectiveness for the people in the cases they are studying. It's probably the same methodology that you instinctively utilize when analyzing the performance problems and areas of apparent ineffectiveness in the people with whom you work.

Our students use what might be called "ends–means analysis." They begin by figuring out what they consider to be a reasonable statement of the organization's goals. Then they figure out the rational and logical sequence of actions that will cause the people featured in their case to work most effectively toward those goals. By hypothesizing an efficient path, they figure out the "means" for accomplishing the desired "ends." Comparing what they figure ought to happen with what is actually taking place allows students to recognize limitations in the direction that case participants have taken and what needs to be done to get them all functioning effectively.

Standing back, applying ends–means analysis, provides students a bigger and more complete picture than the people depicted in the case tend to formulate for themselves, for their experience tends to be on an episode-by-episode basis. Themes and contradictions leap out at them. It's as if students are equipped with polarizing filters that allow them to see through the fog that clouds the vision of the people who are the subjects of their cases, to focus on what is most essential. In this context it's relatively easy for students to speculate about business imperatives and the types of interventions that might rationally motivate and redirect case participants to think and act more effectively. At face value, this appears to be an entirely reasonable track for students to take.

However, we find that our students' analyses are more logically coherent than practically correct. The gap is caused by students erroneously assuming that the case writer has included all the information that's essential to an accurate understanding of the problems faced by the people and organizations described in the case. We find it rare for students to ask for more information or to state that they cannot talk conclusively based on the limitations of the data provided them.

Instead, students circumscribe their analyses to the facts at hand, which leads directly to reductionistic thinking. They identify a limited number of organization effectiveness variables, usually three, four, or five, and attempt to develop an "equation" for optimizing organizational payoffs using these variables. Then they critique the various courses that managerial action might take in directing people in their pursuits of these variables.

However, invariably the people in the case are working with performance equations that include more variables than the relatively few depicted in the snapshot case write-ups. We think that the absence of these variables in the equations that the students are solving reduces the observable IQ of the people depicted in a case anywhere from ten to fifty points. Moreover, some needs like "ambition" and "desire for upward mobility," which students almost always assume, may not necessarily be givens despite the case presenting that impression.

In many instances, the omitted variables are precisely the ones that cause the case participants to behave ineffectively. If the people in the case were merely dealing with the same limited number of variables that the students were considering, in most instances they would have, on their own, escaped the limitations created by their insider status, and there would be no case for the students to solve.

But in most instances, the actual determinants are not limited to what's rational and objective or independent of the specific mindset that views a marketplace, a financial statement, a strategic plan, an organization chart, or a management situation. As the Artifact of Mind insight emphasizes, personal, subjective, and self-interested considerations are critical factors in leading people who work together to view the same situations differently and to assume distinctively different orientations to their jobs.

Few case descriptions include these variables, so students can't really be faulted for neglecting them. On the other hand, even if the students could interview the people in the case, in essence conduct their own case-study research, we doubt that they would identify these variables and/or accurately calibrate the extent to which they contribute to the problems and contradictions at hand.

Our doubts stem from the fact that actual access to case participants would essentially put students in real-life situations like the ones we watch our clients wrestle with daily at work. We seldom see them collecting enough data of the kind that we're talking about here. That is, whether we're talking about students performing a case analysis, or your analysis of another person's problems at work, we believe that many of the most important variables and facts required for understanding the apparent ineffectiveness and short-sightedness in another person's performance, or even an entire unit's operation, are not being assessed.

For example, let's say a case researcher decided to write a case describing the system's changeover problems faced by the "fiscal planning department" headed by Ralph, the manager in the previously described story. And let's say that we hadn't gotten involved and he was running "thin." Chances are the researcher would know nothing about the problems created by Ralph's boys arriving at precisely the time his department was changing systems and going through their annual audit, not to mention the pressures of a neglected girlfriend and the ninety-mile commute. That person would be oblivious to the issues that caused Ralph to avoid weekend work and to leave early while all the key people reporting to him worked late. The case, then, would be slanted to show the morale and attitude problems created by an insensitive and inaccessible boss when, in fact, the problems were created by a highly sensitive and guilt-ridden boss who was inundated by behind-the-scenes priorities to the point where he could no longer tell the difference between an impossible situation and one that he, and most other people, attempt to handle by exerting more self-discipline and energy and a little deception to cover over missed commitment gaps.

Advice-giving pointers

By using the Artifact of Mind insight, several points can be derived from this discussion that you should have in the back of your mind when giving advice and feedback.

To begin with, the "outsider's" status is all but guaranteed to provide you a continuous stream of insights and ideas for improving the effectiveness of the people with whom you team and work. What makes you think you are "so smart" is a combination of what you can see that the other person doesn't see, and what you can't see because you don't sufficiently understand the actual situation with which the other person is coping. Figuring out which is which will be your constant challenge.

Of course being outside the system in which another person is working, reasoning in a mind-set that uses a different personal paradigm, immediately makes you aware of issues that the insiders systematically size up differently or just plain overlook. It's an experience likened to traveling abroad. Your home culture provides a different angle on daily experiences than what the insiders are able to see. It's a matter of bas-relief, figure–ground contrast, internal sensitivities, local politics, and people living with cultural blinders making assumptions that aren't second nature to you. It's all these things plus the inevitable trappings of any paradigm that a group of people agree to use.

The pressures to cope and adapt to the requirements of any paradigm cause insiders to dismiss the obvious. That's why every writer needs an editor, every artist needs critics, and every dancer needs a master class. That's why each of us needs a true-confessions friend. And that's why every drunk needs a philosopher-bartender and why every one of us needs a barber or hairdresser who, in being the recipient of our straight talk, inner truths, and personal confessions is able to ask "simple-minded" questions and say the "dumb-obvious" that make profound statements that far outstrip their education and psychological training.

When considering someone's behavior and what in your mind needs righting, your bias will be to think that what is "off" is caused by the other person's faulty reasoning, and often this is the case. However, there will be many times when you haven't read the other person's situation as accurately as you thought. Some of these times will be due to important considerations not being revealed to you and some of these times will be due to your having missed the meaning of factors that were explicitly expressed but aren't that visible when viewed against the backdrop of your mind-set–driven view of the world. Thus there will be many times when the problem your advice is attempting to address is primarily a function of what you don't seem to know.

Notwithstanding the relevance and accuracy of the advice you have to give, there is another issue that you need to consider in making yourself credible to the person you intend to help and advise. It has to do with some predictable sources of bias. The first source derives from your own mind-set inclinations, which are rooted in your own self-interested pursuits. Mind-sets give focus to our perceptions but they also distort. There will be times when, in your mind, you'll be out to help another person but where, in your advice recipient's mind, the person that you are helping most turns out to be yourself.

At some level self-interests are always involved when anyone decides to give advice or feedback. Perhaps it's just the self-interest of being a good guy or a smart person that is involved. This doesn't mean that you don't have an altruistic bone or that your advice isn't totally aimed at improving the other person's situation. It simply means that before you give advice you need to check in on your motivations, because—you can bet your last dollar—before the other person lowers his or her guard, that person will be checking you and your motivations out.

The second bias has to do with your propensity to think something is "off" because the other individual takes actions that fail to maximize the interests of the organization as a whole. This is the ends–means bias that our students often use. From this vantage point your reasoning is sound, although from ours, it often turns out to be simplistic. Using it you reason that "this person maximizes his or her personal interests by doing what the organization needs done most." If, in the other person's mind, this were the case, then that person would be sleeping restfully having devoted his or her focus exclusively to making the organization effective. He or she would be thinking that all residual personal-effectiveness issues would automatically take care of themselves. But, in all likelihood, this is not the way the people you are trying to assist will be thinking and acting when it occurs to you that they require your advice. In fact, their thinking the opposite way will be precisely why they need your advice and feedback. They don't see how to maximize their personal gains by operating competently doing what the organization appears, in your mind, to need most from them. For you, then, the missing dimension is what they feel they need in order to be personally effective and feel secure.

The third source of bias derives from a line of thinking in which everyone engages from time to time. It takes place when you think that your suggestions are sufficiently compelling to be straightforwardly expressed and that, besides, there isn't sufficient time to conduct a detailed preliminary inquiry. The result is that you shoot from the hip, saying what you think the other person needs to know, counting on your good intentions to serve as a "no-fault insurance" bond. While agreeing that there are times when this mode of thinking and conducting yourself is reasonable, we have to caution that most of the time you are far better off delaying your feedback until you can find the time to investigate the other person's situation more thoroughly. The risk you take by proceeding precipitously is not just the risk of being wrong. The risk is possibly injuring your relationship and losing your chance to openly engage in a dialogue at a time that is more opportune for the other person.

Most of these predictable biases can be handled with a basic Artifact of Mind fact. While knowledge of the specifics with which the other person is dealing is important, it is not nearly as important as your knowledge that meaningful unknown factors exist. That is, the most important assumption you can make is that you don't know all the motives that underlie the misdirected actions you perceive.

Recognizing that you may not know the most key concerns that drive another person's actions adds an essential perspective to how you should go about framing your advice for another person's acceptance. It provides a reason for you to search further when you don't know what to make out of someone's seemingly ineffective behavior. Reciprocally, it tells you that solutions that seem logical and rational to you will not necessarily compute in the mind-set that the other person uses, which, when that person uses it, produces actions that you see as misguided. Yes, you will often be correct when you observe another person missing the organization mark. But the Artifact of Mind insight instructs that merely hitting that mark does not account for all the variables the other person has been attempting to address with what you have been viewing as ineffective action.

The Artifact of Mind insight instructs us to resist imputing motives to another person's behavior, especially when, in our minds, that behavior makes no apparent sense. It tells us that we are far better off thinking "I don't get it" than we are speculating using a low-probability hypothesis that is almost guaranteed to be inaccurate. It cautions that someone else's behavior does not speak for itself; it can only be understood against the backdrop of the logic and motives of the individual who is initiating it. The Artifact of Mind insight alerts us that what people do or resist doing at work is seldom a response only to those events that we, as outsiders, see taking place. Given that people's ways of being competent are so different, even the same behavior manifested by different people is likely to be directed toward somewhat different personal and organizational pursuits.

You are making progress when you treat behavior that you see as blatantly self-defeating and organizationally dysfunctional as a clue to understanding an individual's reasoning. The more far-out the behavior seems to you, the better chance you have of identifying assumptions and variables that have escaped your analysis.

At work, personal and political considerations usually appear in camouflaged form. They are disguised as rational imperatives of what the corporation needs accomplished most. Some of the time the camouflage will result from people fearing that being up-front with their motives will provide you and/or others grounds for discrediting their positions. Some of the time the camouflage results from people not being conscious of the motives that are actually driving their behavior. Early socialization has taught people not to let emotions and subjective attachments show at work. This adds to people's difficulties in recognizing their own motivations, especially when, in order to be successful, they find it necessary to engage in activities that are self-unacceptable.

You'll seldom find outreasoning or outarguing someone to be a sufficient technique for getting that person to change his or her behavior. In fact, you can count on people resisting advice that runs against the grain of any variable in their personal success equation. Your attempts to intimidate and aggressively show the merits of a "superior" logic will, in most instances, merely create the grounds for deception. Keep in mind that when you get involved this way, you are placing yourself in a politically adversarial position.

You'll find that your problems in influencing people will be compounded by the fact that people seldom partition their responses at work from the rest of their personal needs or from the rest of their lives, no matter what story they tell or how organizationally focused they portray themselves to you.

Thus when somebody acts in a way that doesn't mesh with your rational and logical expectations, refrain from offering advice until you discover the logic and considerations that person is acting upon. If you feel that these dimensions are not discoverable, then you ought to frame your feedback accordingly. For example, you might simply say something on the order of, "I get the feeling that I'm missing something here." Or, "I need more understanding of what you are dealing with to be of help to you." Or, "Obviously something is wrong here. I can't see the reason why you need to act as you do. Based on what I know, I can't figure out the issues you are responding to that cause your actions to, in my mind, appear suboptimal." From the vantage point of the Artifact of Mind insight, these statements are not just diplomatically smart; they are precisely correct.

Keep in mind that people seek synergy of effort. They try to make their responses at work simultaneously serve the entirety of their lives. The former mentality was based on the false assumption that, most of the time, personal life and work life existed separately in people's minds and that some combination of moral rectitude and self-discipline would prevent leakage. The only time that people think this way today is when they think about intimidating other people whose attachment to their life outside of work is screwing things up for them. And of course, no sensitive person ever thinks this way about his or her self.

We think that most people intertwine the entirety of their lives with the organizationally competent actions they take at work. That's the instructional importance of considering situations like Ralph's. People attempt to make their lives seamless. They do so by developing work orientations that integrate personal meaning and life effectiveness considerations with their desires to be competent, productive, and valued in their work.

Being seen as objective and credible

To this point we've been proceeding on the Artifact of Mind logic because we believe that when it comes to describing and evaluating organizational events and people's actions in them, there is no real objectivity. All discussions about real objectivity converge to different self-interested perspectives. Nevertheless, there is a posture that, when authentically assumed, can make the feedback and advice an outsider offers sufficiently credible to the point that insiders call it "objective." Of course whenever we use the word "objective," we're talking about relative objectivity.

When you are an outsider, advice-recipients will consider you "objective" only after they perceive you utilizing an ends–means analysis that includes the important variables that they see as essential to their well-being and not having a self-interested agenda that can override your concern for their success. Their attribution of "objectivity" will be further enhanced when they perceive you approaching their situation strategically, thinking ahead about how steps taken today affect the requisites and relationships required for their success tomorrow. And, most important, at the process level, they will only see you as "objective"—deserving of their trust—when they see you open-minded to the possibility that, given their mind-set, they might have a legitimate reason to act differently than what, on the face of it, seems logical to you.

Tactical advice versus strategic impact

This means that when you have been endowed with "objective outsider" status, advice-recipients are assuming that you are thinking strategically with respect to their effectiveness. They see you placing their long-term objectives over their immediate advancement, their relationships and reputations ahead of today's outcome, and taking the time to engage their views of the world and how they think before you begin giving advice aimed at helping them get what they immediately want today. Along these lines, it's here that we were blocked by Ralph. He was so intense in solving his immediate problems, and so engrossed in basking in his short-term success, that we weren't able to get him to focus on the foundation, personal identity, and mind-set orientation issues that we saw him needing to revise.

Our advice was useful only to Ralph having a successful summer, and we felt very good when we heard he did. However, by the time we got back to raise the more far-reaching issue of how he sees himself and reasons that get him into messes like this, his anxiety had subsided to a level where he couldn't quite find the time to meet. In fact, he never was able to make meeting with us to address what we had framed as "our deeper level concerns for him" a sufficient priority.

We felt we did our best to put Ralph's hand to the stove, but he was past his crisis and not interested in feeling the heat. Moreover, he saw us operating as concerned "friends," not business associates having problems with his effectiveness. We lacked the organizational context for going further. There was no work-effectiveness imperative that we could point to in making the argument that he change. Thus despite Ralph's saying all the "right words" and taking the "right actions," we never felt he got the deeper level lessons that could have changed his orientation, both in his personal life and his assumption of responsibilities at work.

In summary

Being an outsider who is interested in the effective functioning of every aspect of your company's operations is going to bombard you with opportunities to give advice and feedback. Keep in mind that, no matter what you see, you're seldom going to be working with the whole equation. Talking about what the organization objectively requires may win you public acclaim but it won't win you the hearts and minds of the people who need your counsel. You may influence their behavior but you'll never get them to change the way they reason and think.

When you attempt to influence how someone reasons, in contrast to how that person behaves, you need to relate to the personal equation that drives the reality that person lives. To do this you are going to have to learn how that person sees him- or herself and the situation at work and the variables that are key in his or her life. Moreover—and this is very important—you will need to understand the organizational politics that person faces in creating the circumstances to operate at his or her best and in getting people with competing needs to value his or her efforts. These politics are ever-present considerations an individual needs to take into account. Politics is the next topic we address.

Note

1. G. Vickers, *Freedom in a Rocking Boat* (New York: Basic Books, 1968).

4

Giving Advice and Feedback
Are Inherently
Political Activities

The tack we've taken has been primarily psychological. Now it's time
to emphasize the political. This is another area where people have to
develop skill and sensitivity before they can operate any model, especially a modern one, successfully. But just like psychology, it's a
specter that most have been doing their best to avoid. It's almost as
if people treat organizational politics as a low-grade virus infection,
hoping that if they ignore it and think positively it will go away.

We've long been baffled by the illogic in this thinking since we
see organizational politics as a natural result of people, with different
self-interested agendas, attempting to manipulate meaning in an effort to structure work situations for their accomplishment and success. What we know, and we think too few people realize, is that
while politics are a given, there are different ways to play the game.
Some ways lead to positive outcomes and others lead directly to the
type of competitive dynamics and corporate infighting that give politics a bad name.

This chapter probes the nature of daily organizational life to explain the political issues that, subliminally or explicitly, are inherent
in every work event, and in every one of your attempts to influence
and give advice, generally and specifically. To be an effective advice-
giver you need to know what the person you are engaging is out to
accomplish fundamentally; otherwise all you have to go on are that

person's actions. To understand, you must also have his or her political concerns in mind. Then you need to consider how the influence you are attempting to exert plays within the sphere of those concerns. You can't hope to be an effective advice-giver without anticipating political consequences, for all advice has a political dimension. Certainly you don't want to be perceived as politically threatening, especially at moments when your intention is to help.

What is politics?

The Artifact of Mind insight takes you directly to the core of organizational politics when it asserts that, ultimately, everything that takes place in an organization is a matter of perception. It leads to seeing "organizational politics" as the interpersonal dynamics initiated when people (with somewhat different organizational agendas, and different ways of being competent, who naturally perceive all events opportunistically) attempt to persuade others to go along with their self-interested ways of perceiving and structuring events to ensure their competent performance in them. These dynamics are joined and extended when others experience newly proposed shifts in meaning to be threats to their own self-interested staging of those events for their competent performance. They, in turn, feel the need to reassert perceptions they believe to be more consistent with their needs to perform effectively and to be seen that way.

In organizations, self-interests and organizational agendas determine mind-sets; mind-sets determine how people perceive events; and perceptions determine what people think are the actions required to deal competently with events (Figure 4.1). Thus the political goal of people with different personal and work agendas, who as individuals have different needs and distinctive personal qualities to emphasize, is to get events and problems framed "properly" in other people's minds—in ways that require and value the actions that they can competently take to produce outcomes that contribute to

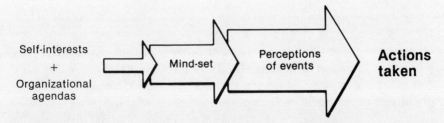

Figure 4.1. Schema for how an individual deals with organizational events.

the corporate effort. And the situation is further complicated by the fact that, at work, behaving is one thing, but having others view what you're up to as productive is quite another. People not only have to produce but they have to convince other people about the value of their production. **Any action that one individual takes in the service of establishing the conditions to be personally productive and in getting others to value his or her production is political.** It's political because such efforts may inadvertently cross up what others have in mind for their own well-being. Such actions constitute an open-ended invitation for the conflictual and aggressive work dynamics that people refer to when invoking the scourgeful term "internal politics."

Don't get us wrong. We're not implying that every perception and every organizational action is self-focused at the expense of what's optimal for others and the organization. We don't believe that at all. We believe that most people, almost all of the time, also want what's best for everyone concerned. But we also believe that, not coincidentally, there is always a tremendous overlap between people's ideas of what's best for others and the company and what's best for themselves. Internal politics come into play when advice-recipients fail to grasp this fact.

Even when people take action that an "objective outsider" sees as nonconstructive, or even organizationally destructive, at the time of acting they almost always believe their actions are serving the longer term interests of the firm. We'll be continuously referring to and expanding this point as we go along, for the people doing this include many of the well-intentioned individuals you would like to influence and advise. Along these lines, everyone we've spoken to who has had difficulty implementing a progressive new model has laid the blame on "internal politics." In our minds, this translates to other people not seeing the connection between what's proposed in the new model and the advantages that doing things differently hold for them. Lacking the mentality to think about people any differently, they are at a loss for the skills required to implement the model and realize personal benefit.

"Organizational politics" come into play whenever people negotiate—discuss and argue—how events are to be perceived, the "meanings" attributed to certain outcomes, and issues as basic as whether a situation is an opportunity or a threat and what actions are called for and when. They are created whenever people attempt to identify "the problem" and its cause—that is, who did what, or failed to do what, and whether disappointing outcomes result from overly ambitious goals, unforeseen marketplace changes, or insufficient human performance—or issues as basic as what production is required

from each unit and what resources are needed for that unit to operate as planned. Of course, none of these conversations is finite. Most
take place open-endedly in the form of innuendo and spin inserted
into any and all subsequent conversations and actions.

Why do we call these moments political when, from strategic
and problem-solving perspectives, they constitute an important set
of basic discussion topics? Certainly these are discussions that must
take place. It's because each resolution is a matter of interpretation,
with stakeholders vying to get their self-interested views cast as the
dominant, reigning "organizational reality." And while arguments are
advanced on the grounds of what's objectively required for the organization's success, you can count on most advocacies coinciding with
the self-interests of the people espousing them.

The stakes

The stakes in organizational politics parallel those in public politics—
power, stature, and money. However, in organizations the terminology used is far more subtle. In fact, the stakes are often stated in
process terms. They include individuals establishing the conditions,
contexts, and images required to perform effectively and for gaining
other people's support for their efforts; individuals accumulating sufficient power and credibility so that others, who hold conflicting organizational perspectives and personal agendas, are forced to take their
interests seriously; and individuals achieving acknowledgment and reward for efforts expended and contributions delivered. And just like
public politics, we're talking degrees of personal power, organizational stature, and monetary success ranging from stock options to
pay increases to curtailment of responsibility to being out on the
street.

As a means of setting the stage to explain some basic tenets of
organizational politics, especially as they bear on advice-giving, examine with us a political situation we encountered several years ago
when we were called upon to settle what was framed for us as an
"internal political dispute." It's a situation that allows us to illustrate
both the politics that people face every day in their jobs and the
politics you face when attempting to give advice, convinced that it is
valid. Stand beside us as we struggle with the politics inherent in
attempting to exert influence and give **great** advice.

Case in point

We were hired by executives of a major metropolitan bus company
who, after five years of watching internal morale and finances sink

progressively deeper in the red, decided it was time to ask for "expert" help. They asked us to figure out what could be done to improve cooperation between two long-feuding departments—the one operating the buses and the one that purchased the buses, whose ongoing responsibility included keeping them clean and mechanically sound. We were given carte blanche to interview anyone in the company whose perceptions might help us to see things accurately and conceive the proper fix.

When we were finished we produced a draft version of the report we were inclined to write. It focused on what we saw as a problematic assumption residing at the foundation of most of the company's management practices. We also described an alternative assumption that we thought would lead to every sought-after result: a lessening of internal politics, more effective management, empowered employees, better operational performance, more satisfied riders, and greater public confidence leading to a usage level that would put the company in the black.

Before finalizing our report and "officially" releasing it to management, we held individual and then joint discussions with the two department heads. We asked them how they felt about our conclusions and whether they would be able to support them. Individually and jointly they said they could and urged us to run them by their (common) boss. In that conversation, the boss enthusiastically put his ace on the table. He said nothing less than, "Your analysis is exactly the shot in the arm that we need." While his comment was a little vague, we certainly thought the department heads would derive a lot of support from it. After all, they were the ones who would have to get out in front implementing our suggestions. Supported by these conversations, we finalized our report.

That report described how, as things currently stood, each supervisor, manager, and executive up and down the line came to work daily focused on a single, politically inspired thought: "How can I please my boss?" Before people thought about what was actually needed to ensure effective operations, or what was the right way to approach an issue, they were inclined to think "What does my boss want?" Our report alleged that everyone saw his or her primary job as empowering the boss, even though in many instances empowering the boss came with the cost of disempowering one's self. We included lists of examples to document the prevalence and dysfunctionality of this assumption and to show the central role it played in causing interdepartmental political conflict.

In recommending a switch in assumptions, our report conceptualized what we termed "basic service units." Our formulation envisioned cross-departmental teams in which the goal was to produce a happy driver, a mechanic who took pride in his or her bus, and a clean, mechanically sound bus that operated on schedule. All the changes we advocated were in one direction. They were all aimed at causing supervisors, managers, and executives to come to work each day inquiring, "What actions can I take to support and help those reporting to me to do a better job of supporting 'basic service units'?"

In essence we were drawing from the progressive new models to recommend changes in the management system that would turn the bus company's hierarchy and daily politics upside down. Instead of subordinates assuming that their job was to empower their boss, our report was advocating that the bosses empower subordinates. We wanted bosses asking, and subordinates volunteering, how the "boss" could help the "subordinate" to play an increasingly positive role in making basic service units more effective. "Empowering subordinates" was our suggestion for the changed assumption that could turn their troubled operations around. We even suggested that they make the slogan "Support B.S.U." (the basic service unit) the company's internal motto.

In response, the department heads thanked us and praised our report. They held several meetings to paraphrase it to lower level managers and supervisors down through their ranks, and they made several joint statements agreeing that following our simply phrased conclusions offered a successful route to turning operations around. Each individually told us that he or she was totally committed and would like our assistance with the follow-up. But after several weeks, when no one had called, we started placing calls of our own. However, we could never get beyond platitudes and surface-level conversation.

It didn't take long for some of the people who had served as our informants, and who subsequently had read our report, to call asking when the system was going to change. In fact, one person sent us a copy of a memo she had written to her department head listing four recent examples of management being on the wrong side of an opportunity to improve company effectiveness and interdepartmental cooperation. She included a recent newspaper article detailing how service and revenues were further on the decline. We felt terrible, but we didn't know exactly what else to do.

The first law of advice-giving

If we've told this story to our MBA students once, we've told it thirty times. And in those thirty or more times, we can't remember a single instance of students finding the substance of our conclusions inappropriate and we can remember only a few who expressed surprise in hearing that we got nowhere pursuing them. Thus, right off the top, this story illustrates what might be called the "first law of advice giving and feedback sending." It is: **Accuracy of your perception and profoundness of your insight do not ensure that the feedback you send will be embraced, taken seriously, understood, paraphrased accurately, listened to, or even heard.**

If you react to this "law" by thinking it isn't very profound, we won't give you much of an argument. Its importance comes from your understanding that the principle that underlies it is 180 degrees away from what you expect to accomplish when you decide it's time to give someone feedback and advice. By the time you've reached this point you've probably decided that the accuracy of your perceptions and the aptness of your insight should be compelling. If you didn't believe this, why would you be going to the trouble? But, as the "first law" implies, the quality of what you have to say does not, in and of itself, determine the open-mindedness of the hearing it receives.

After we tell our students the bus company story, we typically withhold our commentary, feeling the need to first get students to focus on and expose what they think they would have done in our shoes. Discussing a disappointment, rather than a success, causes them to expose their ideas, which allows us to see inside their thinking. Neutrally we inquire, "What do you think went wrong here?"

In response, some students criticize our before-the-fact failure to extract an implementation contract, as if such an agreement were ever possible and as if we didn't think we had received ironclad assurances when we took our draft report around for preliminary viewing. Some comment critically about the internal politics involved and management's vested interests in not having their power base usurped. Others speak disparagingly about the people who would work for a "Neanderthal bus company"—as if to emphasize that these "bureaucrats" are a cut below them and their MBA classmates and that the "sophisticated" companies, where they plan to work, operate quite differently. Students also conjecture about the trickster machinations and power politics we could have used, such as attempting to force adoption of our conclusions by leaking our report to the press.

The second law of advice-giving

When it's our turn to comment we tell students about the first law and then go further into the politics inherent in this case. This leads us directly to the "second law of advice-giving and feedback sending": **All advice-giving and feedback-sending comes with an inherently political dimension that, when unsuccessfully negotiated, can impair open-minded consideration of the current message as well as of any subsequent ones.**

In order to cover the politics entailed in influencing people and advice-giving, we take students through the fundamentals of organization politics. This entails a microanalysis of the situations people face at work that make daily politics a necessity. It's at this point that we back up to describe the personal and political dynamics that result from the former mentality and the culture of deception that results.

A culture of deception

Using the former mentality, people are reluctant to acknowledge that they are viewing events self-interestedly and are constantly in the position of having to pretend that their perceptions and viewpoints are unbiased. They fear having their viewpoints discredited on the grounds that they are self-serving, power-seeking, and thus personally involved and not objective. Their reluctance creates a culture of deception in which they try to cover up and play down the fact that self-interests are involved. It's as if people feel pressured to wear contacts, not glasses, in order to conceal that, when it comes to "objectivity," their natural vision is not 20-20. The motivation for this deception is relatively benign. The intent is not to harm others; it is to politically posture for credibility.

Of course, the Artifact of Mind insight instructs that these self-interested perceptions aren't premeditated or even deliberate. They occur naturally. They result from unconscious processes that automatically organize and configure how an individual views situations for his or her competent and personally efficient performances in them. Self-interested focusing is based on what a competent performance means to a specific individual, the demands that person experiences from external sources, and the capacities and limitations that person sees him- or herself possessing. Thus in addition to focusing on distinct opportunities to perform competently, these natural processes include self-protective behavior and resistance to situations and organizational structures that hold the potential to disempower.

Are people conscious of deceiving you?

While people don't consciously set out to organize work situations self-interestedly, they usually are aware that they are doing so. Most people recognize that they operate with "sensitivities," that they have "biases," that they focus more on "certain elements," that they systematically give events a "self-interested twist," that their responses to people and situations are made with "hidden constituencies" in mind. Most people appreciate that they get insecure, overwhelmed, and defensive in "certain types" of situations, or on "certain topics." Most become aware that they have "blind spots," that they systematically "misinterpret," and that they repeatedly make the same "self-serving" assumption when others point these actions out to them. Most people know in advance that there are certain types of people with whom they have "good chemistry" and certain types of situations in which they react "emotionally" to the point that they probably "lack objectivity," although at the time of their reaction they are not precisely sure what is setting them off.

Level 1 deception: the pretense of objectivity

Even with all this self-awareness, it's not with any forethought of purpose or intent to compete or to manipulate that causes most people to configure situations self-interestedly. In fact, at the viewing level, there's no deception intended. People honestly report what they see and that's where the bias comes in. A relatively benign deception takes place when they feel the need to impress upon you that their reactions result primarily from their making an "objective" response to what the situation or external event requires, as if that situation or external event would be seen the same way, and evoke the same response, from just about anyone else performing their job.

When we use the Artifact of Mind insight to refer to the self-interested ways people naturally see and structure the world, we don't intend to include intentionally corrupt or selfishly exploitative behavior. We are simply referring to the self-interests entailed in people viewing work events opportunistically. This is the source of their creativity, the essence of their efficiency, the source of their personal power, and thus the basis for their political posturing. What's more, in most instances this isn't even a conscious activity. People automatically and naturally see and structure events in ways that meet their needs to perform competently. Likewise, they automatically and naturally employ defense mechanisms that protect them from vulnerability and cause them to resist organizational structures they find disempowering.

Level 2 deception: the self-interested staging of events

However, maintaining the pretense that one's view of organizational events is "objective" necessitates a confounding deception that, in practice, is usually more conscious and less benign. To be convincing, an individual has to pretend that viewing organization events objectively is the ordinary state of affairs. This necessitates pretending that others are also viewing events objectively, which everyone absolutely knows is not true. The motivation to maintain this pretense persists only as long as the self-interests involved in another person's views and actions don't become "too" discordant with one's own.

The result is a self-subliminal and implicit collusion in which people cast all of their organization actions in a rationalistic logic of doing "what is 'objectively' warranted by the situation," "what is 'objectively' best for the business," "what is 'objectively' called for in following the organizational strategy and the company's business plan," "what's 'objectively' in another person's best interests," and so on. Justifications that might reveal the presence of subjectively determined perceptions, and self-convenient action, are replaced with ones that argue that the individual was merely doing what the organization needed done most.

Using the former mentality, a political game gets established in which whether one individual decides to challenge the objectivity of another person's self-interested portrayals depends on two factors. First, it depends on whether one notices the hidden self-interested bias and distortion, which of course can't happen if the person is an "insider" reasoning similarly to the person advancing the "objective" portrayal. Second, it depends on how raising an issue of self-interested bias and distortion, and discrediting someone's alleged objectivity, stacks up with one's own self-interested pursuits. When it's in their best interests to go along with a ruse, most people are only too happy to do so. They realize that when they object they instantaneously provide the other person with a motive to look for and point out their biases. At work, everyone understands that the first stone cast is not going to be the last one thrown.

Using the former mentality, people can pretend that they view organizational events objectively only if others don't notice, or notice but decide that it's in their best interests not to challenge a particular brand of nonobjectivity. And if someone does decide to challenge, his or her objection doesn't have to be thunderous. It might be as gentle as "I see it a little differently," or "But did you notice that . . . ," or "Yes, but in this instance. . . ." Whatever the level of challenge,

the basic dynamic is the same. The interaction revolves around people attempting to self-interestedly frame and manipulate how situations are going to be portrayed, responded to, and perceived.
Whether the political objective is pursued light-handedly or heavy-
handedly, it's the same: to stage organizational situations for one's
own self-interested pursuits and personal well-being and success.

The conduct of political advocacies

In our classes, with tongue in cheek we explain that, within a company, organization politics are supposed to be conducted in a straightforward, candid, fair-minded, aboveboard manner with people putting
all their self-interested issues on the table so that their work associates can come to trust them all the more. Then, provocatively, we
ask students, "This is the way people in the companies where you
have worked conducted their political advocacies, isn't it?"

Our question typically elicits laughter and irreverent comments,
the sum and substance of which reflect our students' inclination to
see organization politics as a type of guerrilla, or trench, warfare.
Their experience, in what we term the former mentality, is that people primarily deal with political events through behind-the-scenes manipulations. We then attempt to list some commonplace forms of political manipulation, which include people controlling access to
information, giving one-sided accounts, highlighting certain problems
and playing down the importance of others, framing organizational
events self-conveniently, selectively critiquing personal competencies, lobbying those in important positions, buttering people up,
building alliances, intimidating, trading support, and all the other activities that people associate with the negatives of public politics. In
fact, there was a memorable instance where a student drolly one-
upped us. With a straight face, he told us, "You guys got it all wrong.
At the company I work for, we practice clean politics. We never get
stabbed in the back. We get stabbed in the chest!" Of course, in
most organizations none of the aforementioned behind-the-scenes,
manipulative activities are carried on too blatantly. The emphasis is
on subtlety, camouflage, and deception.

The new basis of power

The Artifact of Mind insight comes with a slant on organizational
power that's considerably different from how people using the former
mentality typically think of it. It conceives of organizational power as
the congruence between how an individual self-interestedly sees and

structures organizational situations and events for his or her competent performance in them and how key others either actually see
events or are willing to allow them to be structured. That is, the
more that key others—coworkers, evaluators, and opinion leaders—
see events and situations that are important to an individual's effective functioning as that person sees them, or are willing to go along
with that person's competency-driven, self-interested framing of
those events, the more that individual is likely to feel empowered.

In organizations, the people with the power are those who get
to name what a situation is called. We're talking about the organizational equivalent of the allegorical story about three umpires sitting
in a New York City bar, bragging while they down a few beers. The
first says, "I call 'em the way I see 'em." The second says, "I call
'em the way they is." And the third says, "They ain't nothin' till I
call 'em."

In organizations, there are many daily parallels to the third um-
pire's quip. Whether an event is called a business opportunity or a
threat, whose opinion or decision is required, whether someone's
performance is deficient or demonstrates potential, what a job demands, how an innovation is judged, whether progress is being
made, and even whether or not we're in the "black" are functions of
people's self-interested perceptions and the labels they assert and
can get others to use in sizing up a situation. In today's organization,
the extent to which you can get others to endow your viewpoints
with credibility, go along with the meanings and labels you attach to
events, and view your activities as value-added production constitutes the basis and value of your power—regardless of your rank and
position in the hierarchy.

Thus in the new management models the critical political activity—and new basis of power—is an individual's opportunistic framing
and staging of situations to require the special brand of competence
that he or she can self-confidently deliver. As the Artifact of Mind
insight instructs, it's not just what one does that determines that
person's value; it's how others think about what that person has done
that determines it. This is the organizational parallel of Bishop Berke-
ley's question about whether a tree falling in a woods makes a noise
if there is no one around to hear it. We ask it differently. We ask,
"Does a gun shot in the woods make a sound if there is no one
around to hear it?" While the person who pulls the trigger is convinced it does, it becomes a political issue for the rest who weren't
there.

This is not to say that the political processes of naming events
and framing situations to require the type of competence an individual

can deliver is necessarily corrupt nor is it to say that the value of what that individual is delivering never gets reflected against some "objective" standard. We'd like to think that eventually the inherent checks and balances of the same performance being judged similarly by many people with diverse self-interests combined with the truth-test of the marketplace generate a valuing system that approaches objectivity.

Certainly the goal of every fair-minded, institutionally concerned participant is the use of objective standards in measuring performance. Nevertheless, up until the point that a situation or work effort gets demystified, there can be a great deal of support for an effort that doesn't ultimately prove to be valid while perfectly valid contributions go unappreciated and criticized. Most of us could fill a book with examples in which "smoke and mirror" bogus contributions and "spin-doctoring" of results brought employment, income, and status to noncontributing performers.

Along these lines, we'll never forget the image of Maurice, the highly touted director of computing services, staring out through small, Coke-bottle-thick, Italian-styled eyeglasses, performing his routine update at his company's quarterly management review meetings. His explanations were always long-winded and entertaining. Using "computerese" and fractured English, they interspersed simple statements of goals to which everyone related with technically complicated explanations of what needs to be done next to "finally go where we want to get us." His logic always sounded convoluted but because he was the "resident genius" and all the top guys said "we're lucky to have him," it made no difference that the punchline was always the same—another "final piece" of exotic equipment or software was required to finally get what we need from the system. Two and a half years later Maurice and his crew still hadn't gotten it straight. The reaction to the report that finally sprung the trapdoor under him was memorable. When he left the room all the executives turned white in the face with bewilderment. Then they turned red in the face with laughter as the big boss wisecracked, "Our computer center has to be IBM's most profitable research laboratory." The next day both Maurice and the IBM sales and service representative were gone.

Case continued

To illustrate the importance of reading the politics of a situation and comprehending the basis of people's resistance to advice, we ask students to once again reflect on the bus company case and the reactions our report received from bus company managers. With respect to the personal-competency motive, we entered the realm of organization politics the instant we presented advice that people weren't sure they possessed the skills and support to carry out. Apparently the progressive new model we had recommended made many people insecure.

Recall we had recommended reversing the direction of the hierarchy's focus. We wanted everyone to revise his or her orientation, which had implications for every interaction and conversation. More question asking and less answer giving would be required. "Here's what I want you to do" statements would be replaced with "How can I help?" and "What do you need from me to do your job more effectively?" The power dynamics would be dramatically changed.

It wasn't that we were totally naive about the resistance our report would generate; rather, the commitment we got for top management's backing unraveled behind the scenes. We were expecting considerable support from the top. And we thought we had been politically savvy in reframing the management assignment in unassailable terms; "empowering the people who report to you." We thought, "Who in their right mind would want to get caught taking a public stand opposing such an action?" In our minds, doing so would be politically self-incriminating.

Despite all the head nodding and acclaim our report received, the fact of the matter is that our recommendations were permanently tabled. People colluded in passively resisting and making our report a forgettable event. The resistance took place even among those whose immediate situation would have been dramatically improved. Why would these people resist, why wouldn't they make more of a public issue out of top management's mothballing of a recommendation by the very experts they had hired to help them remedy a situation that was clearly out of control? If we assume omnipresent self-interests, what self-interests could possibly be served by allowing our report to die from inaction?

In retrospect we see two ready explanations. First, those who were involved apparently weren't confident that they possessed the mentality and skills to position themselves to empower the people reporting to them. Their actions portray them preferring organizational ineffectiveness to relinquishing control and having to face challenges that might expose them as inept. Their inaction caused us to think that they were made personally insecure by the prospect of being evaluated for their ability to help and empower the people working for them.

Second, and more important, the department managers who

had assured us and one another that they would be out front leading the charge "chickened out." Months later we were able to corner them. They fell for the old "free lunch at the Faculty Club" routine. We asked, "After we snapped you guys the ball, what on earth possessed you to punt on first down?"

They responded by telling us they felt forced to "punt" when their boss decided to launch a campaign for the vacant CEO spot and began indicating that any action on their parts that could be interpreted as weak management would not be tolerated at this time. They said, "Frankly he was in scoring position and we were scared of lining up off-sides." This explanation reminded us that these managers were still operating in the old system in which they needed a boss to say that changing their mode of operating would be a "please your boss" act. To this day we think we did what we could. We see ourselves having been foiled by political circumstances over which we had no control.

We had always intended to take up the issue of "empowering subordinates" training with the bus company executives, but we didn't want to combine it with our report. We didn't want to have our recommendations compromised by appearing self-promotional. Were our self-interests involved and were our tactics political? Of course they were. Once we got involved advocating a course of management improvement, we were transformed from "objective" to "agenda-biased" outsiders. Instantaneously we became stakeholders. We knew what needed to be fixed and our egos were involved in fixing it. And we reasoned like any advice-giver can reason. Our self-interests were unimportant; our driving concern was the improvement and productivity of the institution.

Successful advice-giving requires win-win-win politics

By now we hope you are convinced that all organization behavior has a political dimension. Understanding this, you quickly see that the important issue is not how to avoid but how to conduct politics in a conscious, maximally constructive and minimally deceptive, nonmanipulative manner.

In discussing politics, our analyses have considered the interplay of three self-interested parties: the organization, the advice-recipient, and either yourself as advice-giver or the person transacting with your eventual advice-recipient. Now we can add that, before you can be convincing and trusted, advice-recipients must see you functioning with an accurate picture of their interests in mind.

Having them perceive you omitting any of these three sets of interests is likely to precipitate an unstable situation that eventually leads
to negative politics and reciprocal deception.

Thus no matter how "objective" and professional you believe
you are, politics are naturally present in all advice-giving. To carry
them out positively you and the person you are advising need to
agree on what comprises the three-party intersection of interests
and how to bring this condition about. Figure 4.2 depicts the categories of advice-giving created by various overlaps of three party interests.

But most advice-giving attempts are framed to emphasize the
two-party intersect of what's best for the advice-recipient and the
organization, leaving out the interests of the advice-giver. Of course
all this means is that the advice-giver's interests have not yet been

* If subconscious or mere oversight.
† If conscious or deliberate.
‡ Lead to competitive political dynamics.

Figure 4.2. Conditions created by various configurations of three-party
needs.

made apparent. But, reasoning in the former mentality, advice-givers avoid bringing up their self-interests because they fear that doing so will cost them credibility. They believe that, detected, their self-interests can become an overriding preoccupation that supersedes the value of any positive suggestion they make.

This practice is a direct contradiction of the Artifact of Mind insight. It instructs that when advice is given, of the three parties involved, the advice-giver's interests are the ones most likely to be fully represented. At a minimum, they will be represented in the framing of the organization's interests and the timing of the advice expression. Think about it: Why aren't advice-givers attempting to exert influence and micromanaging all the time? When are potential advice-givers most inclined to leap into action? Why would advice-givers risk the political consequences if they weren't personally identified with the outcomes? Certainly, what one advocates on the basis that it benefits the other person and the organization has got to make personal sense in the scope of the advice-giver's life as well.

In arguing this way, we do not mean to diminish the presence of benevolence, loyalty, and a deep and abiding commitment to the organization's productivity as well as basic work values. Certainly we think these values and the feelings of contribution they engender are present in our own work and good wishes toward others. It's just that from the practical standpoint of appreciating organization politics, one must not allow the presence of ideals to obscure your view of the role self-interests play in every perception and advocacy.

On the other hand, people who are receiving "helpful" advice keep a vigilant eye out for self-interested bias whenever they experience someone's influence. In fact, every instance of an advice-recipient not accurately hearing clearly formulated advice, let alone heeding it, should signal the potential presence of a mind-set, self-interest disparity. Disparities between the recipient's view of what the organization needs from him or her and how the advice-giver sizes things up are received as clues that the other person's interests are involved. Too often this instigates a search for what is not readily apparent and suppositions that cause significant relationship problems.

Using the former mentality, most advice-givers would like to convince themselves that their latent self-interests are not the cause of an advice-recipient's resistance. They would rather think that resistance is due to the other person not quite understanding the "correctness" of their advice. But whether or not a recipient understands may be less important than the fact that he or she is resisting and not attempting to draw out an advice-giver's ideas. At the very minimum resistance should serve as a clue that someone's well-intentioned at-tempts to help may be producing a political situation. Of course the politics may be internal to the individual, not external involving some-one else. Internal (to the individual) politics are the pressures an individual experiences when, to fulfill an organizational expectation, he or she needs to take an action he or she lacks the skills and confidence to render.

Using the former mentality, advice-givers are inclined to over-come resistance by arguing that by heeding their advice the advice-recipient meets the company's interests. The underlying logic, of course, is that being seen as meeting the company's interests ulti-mately benefits the individual. This is a logical line of reasoning when there are no buried competing subjective or political disagreements about what is the optimum way for an individual to contribute. Of course the Artifact of Mind insight would instantly classify this as a totally unrealistic theory.

There is one other possible two-party intersection of interests that warrants your consideration. It's the intersection of the advice-giver's and the advice-recipient's self-interests, to the neglect of what either or both parties, in a self-candid moment, actually believe is best for the company. When this takes place *un*consciously, this political dynamic is called **collusion.** When it takes place con-sciously, it is called **corruption.** Under either circumstance, when it involves you, and you don't know how to reverse it, our advice is that you read the want ads and call the headhunters. With the new focus on teamwork, activities such as succeeding while the people and the units around you fail will not go long undetected.

Implied in all of this is that, ultimately, the only stable advice and feedback-sending situation is a three-party intersection of inter-ests. This intersection has always been the teamwork goal. How-ever, in the former mentality, where self-interests get pursued in a hidden manner, the process for abating competition among these three interests is arduous consensus-seeking meetings in which the search for compromise too often leads directly to lowest common denominator solutions.

Capitalizing on the Artifact of Mind insight, the new mentality offers an alternative to lowest-common-denominator teamwork and excessive compromise. It takes the competence-striving motivations of all three parties as givens. No one needs to hide the fact that they have self-interests or needs to get involved in debates over whether self-interests bias their viewpoints. The goal is to give everyone as much of what he or she wants as long as the net result gives the organization what it needs to prosper.

Successful organizations are the outcome of satisfying as many of each of three parties' interests as is possible. Of course, required is a mentality that searches for the self-interested connections between perception and motivation and accepts that identified limitations and bias is a far more practical and desirable condition than interests that are present and hidden. The team-building strategy is to identify capacities, limitations, and areas that need bolstering and to redesign roles to be complementary. This replaces territoriality and people pretending to be fully functioning and fully capable. The new mentality acknowledges the presence of human imperfections and seeks a plan to operate realistically.

One more important perspective requires your consideration. Most managers operate with the assumption that their organization's interests are a given and that people and their personal agendas are fungibles and variables that can be modified. This premise is prominent in most theories of managerial motivation where, by definition, the motivator or advice-giver begins with what he or she believes the organization requires and then proceeds open-endedly to search for what's needed to get people to match that need with their performance.

Once again we find the Artifact of Mind insight instructive. It instructs that organizations are little more than the sum of social and political agreements that people have self-conveniently struck. When you see it this way, the organizational "program" becomes alterable and can also be seen as a variable, subject to interpretation and revision notwithstanding the fact that all modifications must withstand the criterion of marketplace success. Thus there are three variables to consider modifying when striving to achieve win-win-win resolutions.

Whereas the former models attempted to squeeze out self-interests, whereas the new models, using the former mentality, attempt to channel them, the new models, using the new Artifact of Mind–inspired mentality, proceed on the assumption that nobody really wins until the interests of all three parties are satisfied. That is, the former models featuring the former mentality featured "win-win" political dynamics in which each person negotiated for organization gains that, silently, were self-advantageous. But the new models require a new mentality in which "win-win-win" solutions are sought. Win-win-win results are possible only when all parties commit to finding ways of proceeding that maximize as many of the other two parties' needs as they can, with each party taking responsibility for maximizing the interests of the organization as a whole, while seeking to create relationships and conditions that allow both themselves and others to function competently.

As exemplified in the space-age technology company case described in Chapter 2, and now again in this chapter's bus company case, the presence of a progressive new management model and a positive intent are insufficient for changing an individual's orientation. Different models require different thought processes and these determine the needed skills. People who lack the skills either retreat from their new level of aspiration or delude themselves into thinking that they are performing with a new orientation while basically behaving as they always have. With the revived emphasis on "corporate team play," this is a frequent complaint that we hear people make about their work associates' behavior. In too many instances "politically correct" actions and politically crafted statements serve only to obscure the fierce internal competition that still takes place.

Concluding remarks

We conclude this discussion of organizational politics and the politics entailed in exerting influence and giving advice by emphasizing that, in organizations, it's a mistake to think that self-interests are typically expressed in discrete self-serving acts and conscious manipulations. The Artifact of Mind insight construes self-interests differently. It sees them ubiquitously ingrained in the very framework that an individual uses when perceiving events and responding to the actions of others. In this context, political dynamics are the result of people with different self-interests, competitively transacting with one another in an effort to get events construed and framed in ways that facilitate their individual contributions and personal and organizational well-being. Thus, in organizations, politics are a given. To be decided is how self-interests are going to be negotiated to produce win-win-win results.

The next chapter continues the exploration of self-interests and how self-interests that are seen as political liabilities can be renegotiated to produce win-win-win results. The inability to do so is what we think gives "organization politics" an undeservedly bad name.

5

Mind-Set Sensitivity: The Importance of Knowing How the Other Person Reasons and the Importance of the Other Person Knowing That You Know

We've taken several approaches to make the point that validity of feedback alone is insufficient to assure that your attempts to influence and advise people will be received. We have also described some of the minimal conditions necessary for getting them to consider taking your advice and feedback to heart. The minimal conditions require that (1) you learn the key component variables of the personal equation that the other person is working to maximize; (2) the other person sees you appreciating what he or she wants to accomplish long-term; (3) the other person sees you getting his or her assumptions and reasoning straight prior to your articulating the contrasting assumptions that underlie your feedback; (4) you identify and explain your own self-interested advice-giving motivations so that your recipient can independently assess whether your motives are compatible with his or hers; and (5) you clearly convey that you are taking the aforementioned steps. The last is essential to communicating your understanding and your ongoing commitment to tune in to the spectrum of the other person's concerns and interests. This person needs to see that, notwithstanding your own motivations, which are also present, you are out to help and not just to politically manipulate and co-opt.

The shorthand way of saying this is that prior to your attempting to influence someone, that person needs to see you functioning in the new mentality. Impressing the importance of this fact and your knowledge of the psychological tenets implied in it and illustrating how sensitivity to another person's mind-set is accomplished are the goals of this chapter.

In essence, we're advocating that all your attempts to influence people at work begin with a valid theory of how people perceive events and a model for comprehending the self-interests and organizational agendas ingrained in their perceptions. We're also advocating that all feedback and advice-giving begin with a searching inquiry into the competence-seeking motivations that underlie the behavior you want to influence and change. Of course, when the important variables are quite personal, the conversation can quickly shut down. On the other hand, when highly personal considerations are the primary determinants of the behavior you want to influence, you are better off knowing this than getting carried away drawing a wrong conclusion. If you don't know that they are, you're likely to frustrate yourself along with your feedback-recipient. This can be a systematic source of managerial and advice-giving ignorance. People jump to far-out, wrong conclusions because they limit their analysis only to those work events they have viewed. And most of the time when they do, the advice they give turns out to be experienced as diminishment, criticism, and put-down.

There are many ways to get yourself briefed on someone's actual motivations without the conversation becoming inappropriately personal. For example, you might simply list the key considerations about which you are aware and then inquire, either of the individual or of one of his or her close friends, whether there are additional factors that he or she is balancing. At this point, the other person has some choices. He or she can either tell you what they are, tell you they exist but he or she doesn't want to get into them, or tell you that there is nothing significant, in which case you will have to read the situation and the nonverbal cues to decide whether or not to take this denial at face value. In any event you are no worse off and, in the process, you have demonstrated an interest and sensitivity that might lead to a subsequent time when this person decides to tell you more.

Another systematic source of advice-giving failure and confusion emanates from the use of the term "objective." The Artifact of Mind insight is very clear on this issue, for essentially it says "perception is everything." Expecting feedback or advice to be objective implies that the data set the advice-giver is working from is sufficiently complete, that everyone who reads that data set will reach the same conclusion, and that anyone who reached this conclusion would formulate the same advice and deliver it in a comparable time frame. Perhaps this type of objectivity takes place from time to time, but we think not often enough for you to reason yourself into expecting it.

If it were practically feasible, we would ban the word "objective" from being used in any advice- and feedback-giving context because all viewpoints expressed, and all actions taken, have an ever-present, built-in, self-interested dimension that is anything but objective. However, experience in the former mentality has imprinted this word in everybody's thinking. Having someone interpret your feedback and advice as objective merely means that this person sees your reasoning as both organizationally constructive and sufficiently aligned with his or her well-being. It does not mean that your feedback is objective to the extent that any other observer would see what you see or draw the same conclusions.

Experience has repeatedly taught us the importance of someone not thinking that the advice you give has overlooked a concern that is critically important to him or her. Regardless of the importance of the advice you have to give, or of the extent of your real interest in that other person's well-being, you are unlikely to get through with your advice as long as your recipient hears you reasoning and speaking in a mind-set that is insufficiently related to the variables that are central in his or her reasoning. Thinking that you have overlooked something essential will cause an individual to focus on what you have omitted to the extent that he or she misses essential elements of your advocacy. The implications for influencing people and giving advice are very clear. To gain another person's confidence, you need to engage that person's mind-set and the other person needs to see you doing so. Absent either, your feedback will lack face-level credibility.

When another person is unable to make the bridge between what you are saying and the mind-set in which he or she is thinking and acting, the most you can expect are short-term accommodations in behavior. Even advice that is obvious and essential will be taken lightly and even categorically rejected. For example, consider the following case. It describes a situation in which an executive resisted a simple piece of advice that each of his teammates had tried to get across, to the point that the teammates were involved in a dangerous process that had them on the brink of doing in a capable peer.

Case in point

Ken was the first senior executive recruited from the "outside" to join Pacific Corporation's top management team. All the other members had spent years at Pacific and had worked their ways up from the ranks. Since arriving nearly a year and a half ago, Ken had displayed an irritating habit of prefacing his advocacies with "Here's how we did it at CDX." CDX was the prestige company in Pacific's industry where Ken had worked for twenty years.

Irritation with Ken was building. Each of the other executives was annoyed. Some said they were bothered because they saw the CDX reference as Ken's way of gaining added leverage in pressing the correctness of his viewpoints. Others said their displeasure stemmed primarily from the fact that CDX references seemed to place Ken above the fray and prevented him from assuming his share of the responsibility for decisions that were being made each day. For them, these references served as a reminder that, after a year and a half, Ken had yet to root himself in the company. These executives contended that by now Ken should either have bought in or gotten out.

Ken was well aware that his CDX references were grating on his teammates' nerves. Two executives reported that they had attempted to counsel Ken informally. One said he raised the issue of his discomfort at a dinner exclusively devoted to this topic.

With increasing frequency, explicit objections and sarcasm were expressed whenever, during a meeting, Ken made an "at CDX we . . ." statement. In fact, things had reached the point where Ken would occasionally catch himself in the middle of a CDX reference and, on the fly, recast his conclusion to avoid mentioning the three letters that provoked so much executive ire.

The executive with whom Ken worked most closely was particularly strident in giving Ken feedback and admonishing him for CDX references. This executive had a history of appearing competitive in issues involving his seniority and territory. Ken's CDX referencing grated on his sensitivities and provided ready ammunition for putting Ken in his place. Ken was saddened by this executive's aggressiveness, and when we overheard someone pointing it out, Ken replied, "I'm too much of a gentleman to engage in trench warfare." Several of the others mentioned that they appreciated Ken's turning the other cheek.

Despite efforts to correct himself and avoid conflict, Ken appeared fixed in a CDX frame of mind. The president, who played a major role in recruiting Ken, felt pressured to act as Ken's apologist. Periodically he reminded Ken's detractors, "After all, before coming to Pacific, Ken had spent almost his entire career over there." But he too was annoyed with Ken's CDX references and was expressing signs of frustration for the situations they were putting him in. Increasingly, the president displayed annoyance when apologizing for Ken and found himself needing to defend his inability to get through to him.

Bracing for two days in the room with Ken at the annual strategic planning retreat, which we had been asked to facilitate, several of the executives made carping CDX jokes at the congregating kick-off dinner. The next morning, true to form, at the opening buzzer Ken was quick out of the gate with two consecutive CDX references. Noticing the grimaces on the faces of his colleagues, and fearing a destructive confrontation, we prepared three pieces of paper. On each we wrote "CDX Coupon." After Ken made his next CDX reference, we handed him the coupons explaining that each "authorized" him to mention CDX and that his allotment was three coupons per day. In saying this aloud we took pains to keep the atmosphere light and not to make fun of Ken. Fortunately no one laughed.

Not only didn't they laugh, these executives were empathetic. Stunned by the directness of our feedback, their good feelings about Ken surfaced and the ensuing discussion was tremendously open and helpful. After thunderously "loud" moments of silence, Ken took the lead. He talked about being put off with the group's insular reactions to him and the ease with which they apparently discounted his expert knowledge. He went right to his desire to fit in but wanted terms that were more respectful than what he had experienced so far. When he finished, the others tripped all over themselves being apologetic and stating their appreciation of what Ken brought to the company and his gentlemanly way of dealing with their aggressive confrontations.

This became part of the company folklore as two years later people claim that Ken has yet to use even a single coupon. Something apparently shifted in Ken's way of thinking, because in talking with him one doesn't get the impression that abstaining from using CDX references is merely an act of self-discipline or a desire to avoid embarrassment. Those energies and motives were present long before we intervened.

In all likelihood CDX experiences continue to bolster Ken's thinking and advocacies. But more immediate in what he says today are his experiences at Pacific. In fact, the other executives now consider Ken an insider and sometimes refer affectionately to the coupon incident as "the moment Ken 'officially' joined the team." Even the executive who had given Ken a particularly hard time is respectful and has extended several friendship "bouquets," which Ken graciously accepted. Of course there are other frustrations with Ken, but there are also frustrations with each of the other team members. After all, we're not describing perfection; we are merely discussing a lifesaving lesson learned.

Ken's is a success story. But labeling it a success reflects a moment in time. Had we chosen to write about Ken prior to the coupon incident our story and conclusion would have been significantly different. We would have written about an executive who was so insecure and set in his ways that no feedback could reach him, no matter how constructive the approach or how essential the message to maintaining his job.

If it were not for the coupon intervention, or some feedback-sending facsimile, Ken's situation might have turned out quite differently. He might have become just another victim with an unmarked grave on the battlefield of fallen corporate warriors. Another capable performer who perished because he couldn't learn an obvious lesson that subsequent experience showed he was capable of learning. The point is that people have the capacity to live multiple versions of the same story, and they depend on us getting through with our feedback and advice before they reach the point of no return.

How did we know what to do?

Why did the people who sought to influence Ken and give him advice go a year and a half without successfully getting across a simple message that, eventually, Ken got in an instant, causing him to change dramatically? What qualities were present in the coupon incident that, missing in previous attempts to persuade Ken to modify his orientation, had caused well-intentioned others to fail? Could the learning process have been speeded up to avoid a year and a half of increasing resentments and crescendo-level frustrations?

A couple of weeks later we had the opportunity to ask Ken what about receiving the coupons had allowed him to break his pattern. From what he said we infer that he saw our intervention as a simultaneous act of support and confrontation. He said, "To be frank, at first I was embarrassed by your coupon approach but, even at the moment of highest embarrassment, I knew it was exactly what I needed. On the other hand, I'm sure it would not have meant the same if it came from one of the others." When we asked "Why not?" he talked about the trust and respect he developed in a long conversation he had with us the week prior to the team meeting.

That was a conversation Ken had requested. In it he voiced his frustrations with the group, his troubling relationship with a jealously competitive peer, and the "buy-in" pressures he was receiving from his boss. It was a candid discussion in which we thought he had discussed his personal insecurities, but only indirectly. He did so after we explicitly inquired about the talents and value-added attributes he saw himself bringing to Pacific and the formative experiences in which these were acquired and practiced. Then we asked what was unsatisfying and problematic about his work at CDX. This prompted him to tell us about areas in which he felt he had yet to establish himself personally and professionally, which we concluded were his reasons for leaving CDX and taking the job at Pacific.

As we recollect, we responded as we often do when people discuss their work effectiveness problems with us. We were guided by the Artifact of Mind insight. Primarily we were questioners and listeners trying to comprehend the distinctive mind-set in which Ken was reasoning. We were attempting to understand how he saw situations that others were telling him were problems. We asked whatever question came to our minds in trying to comprehend why Ken continued to illustrate his thinking with CDX stories. At this time our goal was not to influence him. It was to appreciate variables that were important in the personal equation he brought to his job at Pacific and the basis for his attachment to them. That's why we asked about the special competencies he developed at CDX and what he felt was incomplete in his professional preparation. And very importantly, because our motive was to understand, not to critique, we were supportive and accepting.

At the time we intervened, we felt our analysis was incomplete. Handing Ken the coupons was a desperate act to avert what we feared could turn into an ugly incident. We were consultants to the group, not just to Ken, and whatever we did needed to be perceived as even-handed. We had intended to legitimize Ken's framing things as he saw fit, and we wanted to indicate that we also thought his CDX referencing was excessive.

Not having formed a sufficiently supportive, mind-set–sensitive relationship prevented the others from getting through to Ken. Thinking they had, then acting confrontationally, only made things worse. Knowing Ken's abilities and credentials, none could conceive any rational reason for Ken to bolster himself with CDX references. And by the time they started looking into his mind-set and insecurities, so much water had passed over the dam that Ken had become suspicious of any conversation that inquired into the basis of his behavior or sought more understanding of his motives.

We have subsequently concluded that any magic existing in our coupon intervention came from Ken, for certainly there was no telepathy on our parts. Ken apparently felt we were "mind-set–sensitive," and he trusted us. Handing him the coupons was a "set-breaker," apparently provoking him to wonder "Why would these good guys, whom I trust and think are objective, be taking this course of action right now?" He intimated that he would have had a very negative reaction to any one of the others doing the same.

What would it take for you to do something similar?

What could Ken's peers have done if, from the beginning, their objective had been to relate to his mind-set to see how he was systematically inclined to view his role and position in Pacific Corporation events? If, for example, tomorrow you received a new boss or subordinate, how would you approach that person to learn about the distinctive mind-set he or she uses in viewing organizational events and thinking about what actions to take in them? In particular, how would you discover the disparities between how you frame events for your success in them and how this other person is inclined to frame them?

Well, first of all, it probably wouldn't occur to you to search for disparities. You'd probably be doing what most people do when they find out that they have to work together. They seek out similarities in styles and attitudes and focus on their "sameness" as a means of bonding. Most people spend their introductory time together vigilantly overlooking differences. Their practiced inclination is to smooth over conflicts and to ignore cues that indicate how the other person systematically is thinking differently from them.

The problem with a similarities approach to bonding is that by the time you and another person develop a compelling motive to comprehend the basis for minor differences in perception, examining them is likely to feel threatening. You're likely to feel as if you are putting your relationship in jeopardy by needing to examine what, in the context that finally inspires your inquiry, are a series of disappointments and betrayals of expectation. Under such circumstances, a conversation quickly becomes so charged that getting another person to openly and nondefensively disclose the presence of and basis for his or her biases and vulnerabilities becomes an extremely difficult feat to pull off. The other person fears the uses you'll be making of your knowledge and the possibility that there will come another time when you'll use what you learn to discredit his or her actions. No one wants to provide you or anyone else with grounds for dismissing their conflicting viewpoint as biased and nonobjective.

Build relationships before competitive agendas arise

The outcomes can be very different when you begin a relationship assuming the other person is going to see things differently and that you need to comprehend those differences and the impact they are likely to have. Such an assumption reconceptualizes the bonding process. The goal is not to fuse viewpoints, even though it will certainly include searching for common interests.

Most important, the goal is to build a relationship by learning about one another's mind-sets. You and your associates will be out to discover what dimensions are key in determining how each one reasons and precisely how each is inclined to view events. A productive way to accomplish this is to ask the other person what he or she sees as life accomplishments and counts as his or her special assets and strengths. Initially focusing on strengths will change how you look at shortcomings when the inevitable takes place and they become the center stage for your concern. Then your focus will be on a positive quality or a justifiable motivation that went awry instead of on a sheer exercise of self-indulgence or a total expression of incompetence. When you begin by reasoning that you've got an often good-enough performer whose limitations are in the way, you are not only correct but you have events staged to take up problems in a positive manner. You might approach the other person thinking, "Now it's time for this person to take the next step forward in how he or she thinks about ___(fill in the blank)___ and acts," or, as with Ken, "I've got an opportunity to help this otherwise capable performer whose insecurities have inadvertently been hooked, causing him to temporarily act out a self-defeating routine."

Relationship building is an unpredictable process that always is imperfect. But one thing is certain: it's a process that is much easier to carry out in a positive manner before performance problems arise. On the first day, when you are getting to know someone, we find that you can be direct and ask just about anything, even what was on the debit side of that person's last performance review, as long as you remember to smile, nod your head, and conduct your search from the angle of appreciating positives.

But when you broach the same personal style and background questions on the second or third day, after you've had some work engagements, you'll find that the other person is in the beginning stages of wondering "What are you up to?" and "Why are you asking me this now?" And after there's been a problem with a clash of viewpoints or expectations, you intuitively know better than to be too direct, for the other person will be suspiciously decoding your questions for ulterior motives, and with laserlike speed.

When we held our mind-set inquiring session with Ken, we assumed he had terrific strengths as well as a human amount of biases, blind spots, imperfections, and fears. Our motive was to understand him, not to get the upper hand. We wanted to learn how he thought and to help him succeed, so naturally we were accepting of everything we heard. At that point we had no personal stake in his changing and, sensing our acceptance, it was easy for Ken to be candidly self-revealing.

However, by the time we handed Ken the coupons, like any advice-giver, we had developed a potentially competing agenda. We had a stake in maintaining our credibility with the other executives. How would they value us as "facilitators" and "management coaches" if we couldn't help them with their biggest teamwork/communication problem? However, apparently because we had built a relationship based on appreciating Ken's strengths, Ken trusted us enough. He responded as if we were out to value him and our motives were to assist. Based on what we did, he could have easily made the case that our actions were hostile. On the other hand, we had developed "a feeling" for Ken that allowed us to take the risk.

The important thing is that Ken saw us appreciating his strengths and saw our interests aligned with his. And he was correct. We were interested in his competent performance, in the group's acceptance of him, and in a brand of teamwork that built upon Ken and his teammates' learning to respectfully engage different viewpoints leading to win-win-win political dynamics. Perhaps in this respect our motivation wasn't that different from anyone else's. The important thing is that we had built a relationship that allowed Ken to award us the benefit of doubt and give our advice an open-minded hearing.

But what if Ken had perceived our stake and agenda to be in conflict with his own—perhaps as consultants hired to figure out what was wrong with him and to be part of the effort to shape him up? At the point we met him, we thought that was how he was viewing his teammates and the president—in his mind they were out to control and "fix" him and he didn't feel "broke." From the standpoint of eliciting receptiveness to the feedback and advice we had to give, there would be no worse situation in which to find ourselves. Yet this is a very common situation to be in. There were his teammates, having feedback to give that they thought was crucial to Ken's successful performance, discovering that Ken did not see them possessing a sufficient appreciation for why he felt the need to operate as he did, and on top of that, saw them possessing a competitive agenda. These are the conditions that every well-intentioned advice- and feedback-giver wants to avoid.

Along these lines, not so long ago we encountered just such a competitively structured situation in which an entire group of advertising executives were under the gun to bridge broken relationships and to begin working together as a real team. It was a situation in which time was of the essence and the survival of their agency was at stake. They needed to smarten one another up, and they needed to transcend a blizzard of competing agendas. Viewing how feedback receptiveness was created illustrates how mind-set sensitivity can be applied to the type of teamwork problems managers refer to when they say, as we often hear them put it, "It's time to reassess how our group functions and to do some team building."

Case in point

Depending on how you count them, the agency had just received its third or fourth president in three years and, in the process, had suffered through several purges of executives and staff groups. To make matters worse it was a start-up agency whose reason for existence was a single major client with whom it had a rocky history and a reputation for delivering disappointing results.

All the executives were insecure, especially the ones that were there at the start-up, and who were battle weary from three years of hard-fought political wars. By the time the new president came in, the standard survival routine was set. Executives sought security by joining with dissatisfied members of the client's marketing organization to criticize the work performed by counterpart departments and, in the process, to get these clients to say good things about their own work and departments.

It was as if these executives were staking their futures on the client's defense of them, for their actions certainly were not going to build any bonds of loyalty internally. For example, the agency's national accounts executive was allegedly holding weekly discussions urging the client's marketing manager to require changes in media ads without discussing his criticisms internally with the creative department executives whose staff produced the ads. For example, the agency's special promotions executive was lobbying the client to insist that the agency spend less on print ads and more on promotions, also without any internal discussion. And the creative executives were lobbying for the firings of account executives whom they knew were not defending and selling the value of their creative campaigns and media ads. Overall, executives were behaving as if they could personally succeed while their clients grew more and more disenchanted with the agency as a whole.

There were at least twelve other major conflicts of this ilk, each creating waves of corridor politicking and daily lobbying and coalition shifting. Further fueling this destructive dynamic were members of the client's marketing organization, who were calling agency executives to tell them what their associates were saying behind their backs. Client functionaries were engulfed in the sport of fueling and watching backbiting agency dynamics.

Assessing the situation, the new president took his stand. He told his executives that he believed each of them was technically competent, that he didn't intend to fire anyone, for doing so would only serve to reinforce the current dynamic, and that he felt the agency was in a crisis situation and that it was folly to think that anyone could survive, let alone succeed, with so many failing teammates. He told them that he saw no alternative to their working cooperatively and helping one another to function competently and to succeed. He declared that the only way to build client confidence and a market-worthy advertising campaign was through a spirit of interdepartmental collaboration and integration of the entire agency's efforts.

The words and focus were right, but what was going to repair the deep rifts and feelings of betrayal that had fractionated agency executives for years? With a situation like this, what heroics could repair relationships and lead to internal teamwork and a reversal of cross-species bonding with clients in which rapport was built by executives joining their client's criticisms of agency peers?

It's at this point that the president called for team building and requested our help. We suggested that he form what he called the "agency executive group" (AEG) to meet on a weekly basis to address agency effectiveness problems requiring an interdepartmental cooperative effort. The president's job was to lead the discussion while we would monitor process and coach. We told the group, "Our job is to help you to constructively engage one another and to create the means for members of your departments to function effectively across departmental lines. Eventually this is going to require a concentrated period in which you reconcile philosophical differences and troubling relationships. But after all you've been through, you've first got to believe that there's a chance of actually turning this situation around. From what we've heard, merely believing that teamwork is required hasn't made a difference up until now." We explained that a greater semblance of order and rapport was needed before we could reasonably organize an off-site meeting devoted to feedback exchange and team building.

The weekly AEG meetings began at four in the afternoon and occasionally ran as late as ten. Typically pizza and salad would arrive around seven, with people eating at their places without taking a break. The president stuck to his commitment to require an integrated effort and was active in restating this when discussions got emotional and accusatory. For our parts we were active in pointing out where bad will and pent-up feelings were interfering with teamwork and the collaborative engagement of shared problems.

After the fifth meeting we began hearing isolated stories of how progress made was extending to staff interactions outside the meeting room. We took this as the signal that it was time to plan the off-site exorcising–team-building event. We pondered: How do we get people with a history of deceitful relationships to lower their defenses to open themselves to feedback from people they had seen undercutting them? And when we realized that they could devote only two days, we began to wonder whether this was too ambitious an assignment to take on.

The theory says for feedback to be effective you've got to put it in the mind-set framework of the recipient. But people with a history like these executives had with one another don't easily get inside the other person's shoes, let alone mind-sets and, in most instances, couldn't care less about trying.

Something extraordinary was needed. To clear the air and to make the transition from internal competition to collaboration these executives needed to exchange feedback and deal with their differences head-on. Yet we also wanted them protected from the harshness that severe feedback given in the spirit of "helping" people to function more effectively can bring. We understood that given past betrayals, feelings of ill-will, and misperceptions, it would be difficult to get them constructively relating to the unique mind-sets with which their associates were operating. Having a model of what needed to happen allowed us to come up with a plausible plan.

We decided to conduct a performance effectiveness survey and give the "feedback" to the participants prior to the off-site session. We requested that each group member answer four questions (listed in the appendix to this chapter) about the effectiveness of the other executives as well as the departments they head. We asked them to type their answers to make them anonymous. As a safety net we said that we would review each set of responses to edit messages that might sound unduly inflammatory and then, without making any additional copy, would sort the responses into eleven packets (each containing ten answers to four questions) and distribute them. At this point, people would only know the comments that were made about them and the comments they made about others. No one besides ourselves would have seen what was said to others and we would not retain any record.

People had a full week to review what turned out to be the totally unabridged feedback that we forwarded to them. That gave them time to reflect, to discuss with confidants, and to deal with their feelings about what they read. We requested that they come to the off-site meeting prepared to give a twenty- to thirty-minute report on what they thought about the feedback they received and how they would explain their actions. In particular we asked them to discuss how they thought they were being viewed, correctly and incorrectly, what others needed to know to better understand why they and their departments functioned as they did, what they were learning from the feedback, and what others could expect in the way of change.

We told the executives that after each presentation there would be an open-ended period for others to ask clarifying questions and then to comment and interact. We fully expected the interactions to be spirited, as people would have the option of associating themselves with comments others had made and to confront issues that they felt the feedback recipient had not addressed or had addressed erroneously.

Our process goal was to provide people who had come from a situation in which others were harshly critical an opportunity to contextualize their behavior for the critics by describing their mind-sets and reasoning. It was also to provide feedback-givers a way to gauge the impact they were having with the critical comments they made.

Because it was important to get the process off on the right foot we began with the president. We felt his attitude and acceptance of feedback would set the trend. While we told everyone "Don't hesitate to contact us if you need guidance in formulating your presentation," we made sure that we met with the president to review his reactions. That discussion was brief, and we really can't take any credit for what he eventually said. He gave the process a huge boost with his opening presentation and his candor during the ensuing inter-active discussion was received as "off-the-map great!"

Early presenters kept their self-reflection within the thirty min-utes allotted, but subsequent interactions were spirited and took more time. With subsequent presentations, self-reflections ran longer and the interactions, although spirited, were more efficient and took less time. The reason, of course, is that initial presenters were more inclined to manage the news with subsequent interaction used to "unmanage" the news and set them straight. But setting someone straight inevitably sparked a reciprocal exchange with in-creasing candor in which all parties involved expressed their inten-tions and reasons behind the misguided interactions that had taken place. Thus the self-presentations became longer as presenters added the insights that they were accumulating from the increasingly candid and open interactions that preceded their turn. In other words, the process fed on itself.

Feedback needs to engage the mind-set of the person receiving it

We could easily devote an entire book to describing the interesting and illuminating discussions that took place. To illustrate the process, we describe one amusing and mind-set–clarifying response. It was made by one of the most controversial and harshly criticized execu-tives. Yet he was also an executive who received feedback that praised him for possessing extraordinary talents and who, if he didn't bother people so much, could readily become an esteemed member of the team. He said, "I see now that you guys have taken your inability to influence me entirely too personally. What you need to know is that I don't react well to directives and there are times when I completely shut down. How can I be betraying you, when I don't even hear what you say?"

He went on, "To better understand what you are dealing with, listen to what happened to me last year when my parents went on vacation and asked me to stop by their house each day to take in the mail and water the plants. They had this rottweiler named Rambo who always hated me, but not as much as I hated him. Well, the first day, when I went into the backyard to water the plants, the dog was indifferent, which was just fine with me. The second day he was amazingly friendly. On the third day he was all over me with af-fection, and that's when it dawned on me that my parents might also have been expecting me to feed him.

"When they returned I told them the story of having to feed

Rambo and that he and I were now friends. Their response was 'Didn't you hear us tell you that feeding Rambo was our main concern?' Well the answer, of course, is that I didn't. Their list of directives caused me to shut down way before they got to the dog."

The executive used the story as a means of telling others not to take his nonresponsiveness too personally and that by virtue of the feedback and heightened consciousness produced, he intended to do a much better job of paying attention to their requests. He outlined how people might best approach him to ensure that he attends to what they need, which is his intent, and the backup tactics that he acknowledges are sometimes necessary. His humorous and candid self-reflection defused most of the heavy guns. We knew about those guns from previewing what people had written. In fact, during the interaction, the critics complimented this executive, expressing appreciation for the integrity he displayed in taking up their comments forthrightly.

"Correctly" framed, your criticisms become opportunities to explain mind-sets

The discussion and interactions served to make each individual's mind-set more explicit and thus more bridgeable, leading the way to teamwork agreements and a new integrated strategy. People who formerly had been entrenched adversaries, attributing hostile and aggressive motivations for such small "crimes" as another person abruptly excusing him- or herself in the middle of a meeting to take a client call, subsequently worked harmoniously and productively with one another. In fact their support of one another easily withstood members of the client organization continuing their mischief-making sport of exaggerating innocent comments to make them sound harshly critical and backbiting.

Included in the team-building results was action taken by an executive in response to criticisms she received about her unrelenting competitive behavior. The discussion clarified her difficulties with the agency's priorities, which she was now able to correctly interpret. The president said he wanted the agency to be "strong enough" in her specialty discipline, but *not* to feature it. In reaction to this clarification, she decided that her function was too subordinate for her career interests and she resigned to take a job at a different agency where her function would be more prominently emphasized. From the standpoint of talent lost, her resignation was a negative. From the standpoint of clarification of the strategic plan and conflict reduction, it was a positive. And of course from the standpoint of her own empowerment, the exchange provided her with the strategic information she required to intelligently manage her ambitions and career. She resigned with handshakes and hugs all around.

The "team" that left the meeting room claimed that they were significantly different from the collection of antagonistic individuals that entered it. They felt they had the consciousness and group spirit to become a big winner. They certainly had what it was going to take in terms of a common focus and commitment to teamwork. Remember we started with a group of people who were more interested in setting the other person "straight" than getting it "straight" themselves. Their distrust of one another had reached the point where each individual saw feedback sent his or her way as little more than a self-interested, politically inspired, manipulation and lobby.

The history and out-of-control dynamics at this agency required that feedback-senders receive protection, which we attempted to provide by invoking a process for anonymity. We don't think that anyone actually believed that all feedback sent would necessarily remain anonymous. There were many potential identity giveaways such as context, substance, processes of elimination, and what subsequent interaction might divulge. We even mentioned these in our written instructions. Nevertheless, apparently feedback-senders were left with enough feelings of protection to say a great number of things very straight, taking their chances with recrimination. And additional, often more subtle, issues were brought up and discussed as the conversation became constructive.

Contrasting mind-sets is the higher order opportunity that accompanies all feedback- and advice-giving exchange

"Feedback" derives from a contrast of mind-sets and personal paradigms. It involves much more than an exchange of pure information. It entails an exchange of *mind-set–interpreted information* in which a criticism or an improvement opportunity is expressed by an individual whose awareness was prompted by reasoning with a different orientation.

At face value, feedback is given so that recipients can upgrade the quality of their performance and function more effectively. However, we find that a substantial amount of feedback has a somewhat different impact. It serves to alert the feedback-receiver to problems in viewing events and reasoning that cause that person to perform suboptimally. Most people, ourselves included, rank this as the higher order objective. That is, identification and articulation of contrasting mind-sets is the higher order goal and opportunity that accompanies all feedback exchange and advice-giving. Of course whether or not either party can use the feedback exchange as a track to greater mind-set consciousness is an open-ended question.

Thus whenever feedback is exchanged there are two levels of personal-effectiveness upgrading opportunities. First, the face-level exchange of performance-enhancing advice may be used as a means of assisting the recipient to function more effectively. Second, the exchange may lead the feedback-recipient or sender, or both, to become more conscious of the mind-sets they are using and to evolve a more effective way of interpreting events and reasoning. We think it was the latter that provided the main team-building feature of what these advertising executives experienced with the survey and their subsequent discussion. In other words, what the executives learned specifically turned out to be less important than what they learned about the different mind-sets used in seeing situations generally.

Receiving feedback served as a prompt for executives to articulate the mind-sets that led them to act as they did. Their self-explanations paved the way for the feedback-senders to do the same. The spirited discussions following each feedback-recipient's presentation were alive with clarifications of how actions taken in one mind-set were being interpreted and experienced differently than intended because of competing personal and performance agendas and concerns. With these clarifications, and the emotions that were released, the team dynamics switched dramatically. All along there had been two realities, the reality of the actor and the reality of the perceiver(s). Now the search was for a third—one in which the concerns and interests of all the participants were known and in which accommodations were necessary to accomplish jointly held goals. The search was not for a consensus reality—people now understood that they would always see the same events differently. The discussion was how to work effectively to complement one another's contributions in the spirit of making the net organizational effort a success.

Left to their own devices, most people give feedback in the reverse order. First they give feedback, then they inquire into the reasoning behind the behavior for which they have already offered enhancement advice. You may even think that this is the way we proceeded in the aforementioned example. However, there was an important difference. We put the initial feedback under the control of the feedback-recipient in a structure that did not require the recipient to take the feedback literally. The feedback was primarily "a prompt" to get the recipient to articulate his or her reasoning and the mind-set that produced his or her behavior. We think the "actual" advice-giving feedback was in the conversation and exchange that took place after each prospective feedback-recipient had an opportunity to explain his or her mind-set. This is the line of thinking that continuously prompts us to advise, "Ask questions before you frame and express your influence and advice."

Our format never deprived prospective feedback-recipients of the power to explain their concerns and reasoning or to dismiss feedback they received on the grounds that it was based on inaccurate premises. At every moment recipients retained the right to interpret what they heard in the mind-set that made more sense to them. The format gave them a week to work through feelings engendered in reaction to hearing other people's harsh and out-of-focus complaints as well as time to check whether this was one person's or one constituency's impressions and whether their friends would see allegations of their flawed performances the same way. What's more, the format provided them the opportunity to gain personal credibility and to establish good will by acknowledging complaints that they themselves felt were deserved.

To their personal and professional credit, each of the executives responded in sterling form. Their openness to tough-to-face feedback engendered goodwill among feedback-senders to the point that the senders could release from their criticisms and proceed to focus on the mind-sets that the others were using. That's team building!

Feedback-senders learned what the recipients were actually thinking that led to what they were doing. They learned why the recipients felt their actions were necessary and how these individuals felt they needed to respond in an environment that everyone found intensely competitive. Early on, one executive quipped, "I'm beginning to think like Patty Hearst when she was captured by the Symbionese Liberation Army. I'm learning so much about these guys and their good intentions that I'm beginning to like them."

The situation at the agency was clearly one in which feedback, reports of people's experience of one another's actions, needed to be exchanged for purposes that went beyond merely improving one another's performance competencies. To save the agency, the emotional air needed clearing, relationships needed rebuilding, and people needed to strike some agreements about how to integrate their individual efforts. The way we proceeded circumvented a great deal of finger-pointing and eliminated the need for microprocessing events.

In advocating sensitivity to the distinctive mind-sets people use, we do not intend to diminish the importance of shared and common fates, visions, goals, and processes. Certainly each represents an essential constituent element for team effectiveness. Probably to a significant extent, these commonalities were present at the agency's inception. Nevertheless, their presence was insufficient to compensate for insufficient leadership producing widespread feelings of insecurity, in turn leading to internal competition and distrust, and the suicidal dynamics that greeted the new president. It was always clear that the agency would close if the account were lost. But feelings of being betrayed by one's teammates precluded people acting rationally.

Implied in much of this discussion is an important point that now deserves explicit recognition. Without mind-set sensitivity you won't be able to discriminate between an influencing–advice-sending–performance-upgrading conversation that fails for lack of technique, clarity of communication, or finesse, and one that fails because the feedback-recipient was personally and psychologically blocked. Lacking sensitivity to the mind-set in which a person conducts his or her organizational business may cause you to inappropriately blame the person you are trying to help.

Without mind-set sensitivity, even the best-intentioned attempts to influence and advise can readily degenerate into internal competition and political infighting. While for the most part the words were different, this is what took place at the Pacific Corporation among Ken and his teammates. So-called objective and valid feedback, initially given with the best of intentions, was experienced by Ken as self-convenient and more tailored to fit the needs of his feedback-senders than his own.

Once you and your feedback-recipient have established mind-set–sensitive communications, then modifying and changing behavior is relatively easy to accomplish. But when, due to mind-set insensitivity, you experience the two of you reasoning differently, where the same actions or events mean quite different things and you are at a loss to bridge the gap, then the complexity of the advice-giving actions you need to take is measurably increased.

The last two parts of this book, beginning with Chapter 10, are devoted to helping you determine the level of advice and influence you can exert and how to proceed once you have a situation scoped appropriately. We'll be explaining the difference between the type of advice that Ralph, the manager with a summer scheduling problem described in Chapter 3, was eager to take, and the type of advice we wanted to give but for which he could never quite find the time. That type of advice would have required Ralph to become more conscious and self-sensitive to the assumptions and ways of reasoning that repeatedly got him into the types of binds we saw him facing that summer. Backed up against the wall, so to speak, his only way out was to "cheat" on commitments he had made to everyone depending on him: subordinates, girlfriend, visiting sons, and himself as well.

However, prior to making any determination about the level of advice and influence that you can get the other person to accept, you first have to understand the specifics of the mind-set you are trying to influence. Providing you a framework for reading mind-sets, generically and specifically, is the topic of the remaining four chapters in this section.

Appendix: Questions on the Performance-Effectiveness Survey

Resources

1. What resources do you see (name of person) and the people in the (name of person's department) possessing that does, or could, add to your effectiveness and your department's productivity?

Problems

2. What needs to happen immediately for (name of person) and the (name of person's department) to function more effectively today?

Improvement

3. What needs to happen for (name of person) and the (name of person's department) to function even more effectively 3 to 6 months from now?

Ideal

4. What needs to happen for (name of person) and the (name of person's department) to function at optimal effectiveness some time in the future?

6

Understanding What Personal
Competence Means:
The Alignment Model
of Empowerment

Until you understand the mind-set of the person you are advising, you have no accurate way to comprehend the implications your advice holds for that person or how to position your advice for maximum consideration. Identifying the variables in the personal equations that direct someone, the background factors, self-interests, and organizational agendas that give rise to the mind-sets that determine how individuals specifically perceive events and reason in them, is the subject of this and the next chapter.

We've been using the term "personal competence" to depict the core ulterior motive for the self-interested perceptions people have at work. There are several reasons for selecting this particular terminology. Paramount is the belief that the need to function with personal competence accurately and efficiently strikes to the heart of people's motivations. Notwithstanding the need to earn "enough" money, the need to perform competently accounts for the self-interested spin that people put on everything that they perceive.

The term personal competence is a particularly useful one because it allows us to reference three key dimensions of self-interested perceptions simultaneously. First, people want to perform competently with respect to themselves. That is, to the extent that it's possible, they want each and every action they take at work to mesh with and serve all of their personal needs and style-of-life self-interests. Second, people want to perform competently in exercising the responsibilities that go with their jobs. They want to see themselves competently producing what they think the organization should be receiving from someone in their role and position. And third, people want key others to view them as performing competently. They want others to see them working in an effective manner, turning out value-added product that's essential to the corporate effort.

Another reason for choosing the term personal competence is that it allows us to allude to the natural self-interested, self-promoting, personal biases that characterize people's perceptions and inner reasoning without the inference that selfishness and corruption are the motivations. Semantically, personal competence provides a positive term denoting the high-quality, self-serving participation from which all organizations derive value.

Finally, personal competence is an expedient term for explaining an individual's self-interested pursuits. Using it allowed us to make progress mapping the Artifact of Mind thesis without getting bogged down explaining underlying vicissitudes. We wanted to avoid taking you through the details until your need to know more about the variables that underlie the perceptions and reasoning of the people you would like to influence and advise was sufficiently high.

The former mentalities led to some bankrupt approaches

There is nothing new about the need to discover the distinct motives that underlie a specific individual's efforts at work, whether those motives are called the pursuit of personal competence, self-interests, power and status, or money. Using the former mentality, people seek to identify and measure motives all the time. Practicing management as a manipulative art requires that managers make other people predictable so that they know the "buttons to push," the "incentives to use," and the "mazes to construct" in orchestrating and directing them. Of course since even managers who are reasoning in the former mentality are different, everyone goes about this distinctively.

We find that a significant percentage of managers are naturally empathetic and talented at reading people accurately; we find a greater percentage who are often able to read people accurately, but primarily at moments when it counts for them, not for the person who needs an accurate reading; we find a sizable percentage who are totally unskilled at reading other people accurately, and what they typically learn and conclude from their analyses seems to range between uninformed and downright dangerous; and we find a small but noticeable group who have such a difficult time reading themselves that reading others is totally impossible. In fact, over the years we've seen some very bright and successful executives and managers take approaches to understanding others that we think are so far beneath their abilities as to make them seem soulless. These people may be earnest in buying the management books but, judging from what we've seen, they're skipping too many pages. If they are reading from cover to cover, then the "former," control-oriented mentalities are even more disorienting than we ever imagined.

Notwithstanding the politically correct, new-model verbiage that managers using the former mentality acquire, we find that the dominant motivation theory practiced today features management's manipulation of rewards and punishments. We recognize it instantly— it's the same approach practiced by rat psychologists. Give your subjects an extra pellet when they take the right turn, and a little shock when they successively take two wrong ones. Then watch them shake with anticipation after they take one wrong turn when, from lack of reward, they begin to suspect what's in store when they fail to pick up on what their management wants next from them.

Not achieving results using the reward and punishment theory, a last-ditch theory is trotted out. This one features "anthropomorphizing" as if the other person's "species" operates just like one's own. This motivational scheme features the "motivator" anticipating that people will reason just like him or her and thus act like a "rational person." This way of thinking allows motivators to hold their thoughts and actions as the rational standard and to treat differences between other individuals and themselves as irrationalities that need correcting. The motivational treatment is a rational appeal and the laying out of logic and reason, subliminally giving off the message that, by definition, the motivator's scheme is "objectively" correct.

Both of these lines of thinking are carried out despite the fact that probably what signaled the call for a motivational effort was the other person behaving as the motivator never would, given his or her perception of events and "rational" reasoning. Clearly this is how Marty, the manager described in Chapter 1, had been perceiving his new supervisor Al when he extrapolated from a missing lightbulb to a permanently impaired mind-set. Too quickly his personal line of reasoning led to the conclusion that Al was deficient, inadequate, and broke beyond repair. For years the former mentality has allowed managers to bury their motivational mistakes. This won't be nearly so easy to accomplish when the new models take hold and raise the requirements for effective managing.

Becoming a mind-set researcher

Notwithstanding how you have been operating and the gaps in the psychology you have been practicing, we believe that you can become a capable mind-set researcher. To accomplish this you need three essential research tools. The first tool is a psychological theory that tells you about people's motivations and how motivations drive perceptions. That's what this book gives you through the Artifact of Mind insight and its derivative and constituent tenets.

The second essential research tool is a model that guides your search to understand an individual's motivations and provides a valid way for you to analyze personal data and to make good sense out of what you learn from any individual. We call this the Alignment Model of Empowerment and its explanation comes next.

The third essential mind-set research tool is a method and technique for eliciting valid data and conducting open-ended inquiry with a specific individual. That's the topic addressed in Chapter 7.

The Alignment Model of Empowerment

The insight that "organization is an artifact of the mind that views it" provides a natural introduction to the Alignment Model we use in thinking about an individual's motivations at work, which we have been portraying as a quest for personal competency.[1] Recall that the Artifact of Mind insight begins with the premise that there is an ever-present bias to each person's view of all organization events. In characterizing this bias we have risked using the term "self-interested." The liability is that self-interested is a term that's loaded with extraneous meaning. In organizations, it typically communicates premeditated and conscious distortion and selfish competitiveness.

The self-interests we're talking about, which constitute the motive to be personally competent, are *not* necessarily conscious, premeditated, intentionally selfish and competitive, or intended to distort. "Preconscious" probably describes the situation more accurately because most of the self-interests that lie behind an individual's biased perceptions can be raised to consciousness when people are asked to reflect on them. And "selfish" is not at all an accurate way of describing the interests to which we're referring, nor is the idea of getting ahead at the expense of others. "Opportunistic" and "self-protective" are far more accurate ways of describing the competence-seeking purposes we think they serve.

Keep in mind we're now talking about the self-interests involved in one's actual perceptions, based on natural, unabridged, honestly held beliefs and nondeceptive accounts of what an individual actually sees. We're not talking about the self-interests that take place *after* an individual discovers that others see a situation "incorrectly" and then attempts to set those people straight. Those self-interests have an entirely different character. They relate to the politics of persuasion, not natural perception. Those self-interests lead to consciously staged, calculated, oftentimes manipulative acts and statements that are full of self-efficacy spin and deliberately aimed at controlling another person's thoughts or actions.

The alignment model depicts personal competence as having two main motivational components—self and organization. The self-competent component pertains to the individual attempting to perform his or her work in a personally meaningful and successful manner with respect to all important aspects of his or her life. It recognizes that what is important to an individual at work includes the rest of his or her life along with the specifics of the assignment at hand, and that one's focus is, as much as physically and mentally possible, to attend to all life concerns and desires simultaneously.

The organization-competent component pertains to the individual's focus on performing his or her job in a manner that gets the organization the coverage, quality, and production it needs to receive from anyone occupying that job and having comparable responsibilities. Of course, each individual's beliefs about what the job requires are colored by his or her self-interested perceptions.

With the two components of "alignment" specified, we can add a third component, which, when added to the concept of alignment, makes the transition from alignment to "empowerment." This is the component of others in the company seeing and valuing what the individual produces and how he or she goes about achieving that production. Being valued and appreciated by key others enables an individual to take actions that, in his or her mind, are both personally and organizationally correct. That persons feels sufficiently supported, by external as well as internal valuing, to engage "problems" as opportunities for learning. That person is ready to take on the world as it exists, not just as he or she expects or wants it to be. Conversely, when others, whose opinions are important, fail to perceive the value of an individual's actions it becomes much more difficult for that individual to work effectively. That person's focus and energies are split between performing competently and lobbying and justifying to get meanings adjusted so that others are forced to recognize his or her contributions.

By including the reactions of others, the alignment model of empowerment raises the umbrella of organization politics over each individual's personal-effectiveness equation. Politics are involved in getting others to see work events as one needs them seen, in a way that requires the particular brand of competence the individual is poised to deliver. Politics are also involved in getting others to see and appreciate the value of one's participation in those work events. As stated in Chapter 4, the influence dynamics that evolve from these states of affairs are the core of what's commonly referred to as internal politics.

The model combines these three personal-competence components into a theoretical proposition of what it takes to achieve "empowerment at work." It states that empowerment is the result of an individual (1) believing that he or she is performing competently in a self-meaningful way, appropriately attending to all important professional and career concerns and life situations, (2) producing output that, as the individual views it, the company needs to receive from someone occupying his or her role and function, and (3) seeing that key evaluators and associates recognize and appreciate the essential value added by his or her presence and efforts. When these three conditions are met, people can trust their (self-interested) perceptions, confidently say what's on their minds, act as they see themselves being most effective, attend to the "right" priorities, and, in the process, put the organization ahead. This is our definition of empowerment, a term that is so readily misused in the former mentality.

Now it's time for us to specify the variables—the personal-competence elements that determine the specific course an individual's quest for empowerment takes. As we said, in the next chapter we're going to describe the method and techniques we use for comprehending an individual's distinctive strategy for maximizing these elements. But before you can conduct your investigation, you need a picture of what some of these elements are and the categories that everyone struggles to maximize, notwithstanding the fact that everyone has different issues and personal struggles in mind. Your ability to understand other people well enough to make your advice appropriate to their needs depends on your appreciating why they reason and see organization events as they do. The overarching schema is presented in Figure 6.1.

We start with the assumption that you are on track in concluding that the advice and feedback you have for other people are needed. However, as you surely know by now, we think that until you can view the other person's actions within the context of the mind-set that produced them, you can expect the important feedback you want to provide will not be heard, or heard but not understood,

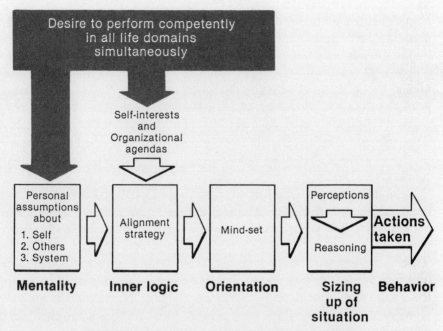

Figure 6.1. Schema for mind-set management.

or understood but not seen as on the mark, or seen as on the mark but not as compelling.

Variables in the personal equations that underlie an individual's mind-set

Throughout this book we've been alluding to a personal-effectiveness equation that gives rise to the mind-set that directs how an individual focuses his or her efforts at work as if such an equation actually existed. We've talked as if the variables in this equation combine to produce a strategy for thinking and valuing events that accounts for the distinctive, self-interested perceptions an individual has at work. And we've talked as if your advice will often be aimed at another individual reconciling discrepancies you see between what that person is attempting to do for him- or herself personally and what you see the organization requiring of that person. If this is the impression you've received, then you're on point with our thinking. Structurally, your advice is aimed at helping the individual to see either his or her own self-interests or the organization's requirements differently or rethinking the personal strategy he or she has devised for pursuing them both simultaneously.

Thus when giving advice you need to comprehend the variables in the personal equation that orients the individual; you also need to comprehend the strategy that person is using to pursue personal and organizational competency issues simultaneously and in maximizing and balancing variables that he or she sees as conflicting. For example, people with young children have to balance the performance of family responsibilities with the desire to work long hours to give the job what it seems to require and, they might rationalize, the financial security the family derives from high-quality performances at work. This was the dilemma that Ralph, the manager described in Chapter 3, faced with his summer schedule and the time required for his two boys.

Thinking about what an individual has to balance led us to the term "alignment" for characterizing the personal strategy an individual hits upon in maximizing his or her effectiveness at work. An individual attempts to "align" self and organization variables so that a single act serves multiple motives and few acts aimed at satisfying one motive set back progress on any other. Alignments, then, are the distinctive individualistic work orientations that result from people endeavoring to perform competently for themselves and their organization simultaneously. Mind-sets are specific applications deriving from them.

The construct "alignment" serves as a prompt for appreciating the interplay between what an individual does to be self-competent and what he or she does to be work-competent. While the alignment explanation places a variable into one of two different categories, we think it's rare for any variable to pertain to one category to the exclusion of the other. For instance, the first variable that we describe is the individual's desire to maximally utilize personal skills and self-resources in how he or she goes about performing work. Clearly the consequences of maximizing the use of personal skills and resources bear as much on living one's life in general as they do in performing effectively and competently on the job.

We identify nine specific variables, eight on the "self" side and one more globally stated variable on the "organization" side. (See Figure 6.2.) A discussion of each follows.

Self-competency variables

1. Utilize personal resources and skills. At work people systematically construe events to require what they see as their strengths and special skills. For example, people with strong verbal skills readily engage other people in free-form, give-and-take conversations. They like to call meetings, they enjoy making presentations,

Self-Competency	Organization-Competency
• Utilize personal resources and skills • Avoid nonskills • Pursue interests • Personal values • Personal commitments • Personality factors • Self-expression and personal style • Social programming	Produce what the company should be receiving from someone occupying this role and position

Figure 6.2. Alignment model of variables directing an individual's efforts at work.

and they will even precede written reports with a verbal introduction. In contrast, people with strong writing skills will churn out reports and memos and may even read from them when conducting a business conversation. On the other hand, people with strong quantitative skills will create more analytic assignments and make more use of numbers than people who lack math confidence. In short, people take particular stances when conceptualizing, when teaming up with others, and when attempting to be persuasive that emphasize personal qualities that they feel are their strong suits.

2. Avoid nonskills. At work, people construe events to avoid activities and functions that they, correctly or incorrectly, believe they lack the skills to perform competently. For example, people who have difficulty with conflict tend to avoid adversarial positions and may concede agreement rather than risk an argumentative moment. Likewise, people who don't feel comfortable selling, don't. They don't take jobs in sales. They may even resist selling their ideas inside the firm.

There are many reasons why an individual might avoid certain ways of proceeding, ranging from lack of training to lack of confidence or missing self-esteem, to inexperience. An individual may have the aptitude but not the skills. An individual may have the skills but not the confidence to use them. An individual may have had a bad experience that he or she wants to avoid having again. For our discussion here, it almost makes no difference. Tell us what an individual would like never to do, and we'll show you evidence of this aversion in the way that person formulates events and relates to them when construing what needs to be done and, in particular, what's required of him or her.

3. Pursue interests. At work people attempt to construe events in ways that make their jobs challenging and their daily activities interesting. For example, people who like to travel wind up spending more time on the road than people in the same jobs who don't like traveling. People who like computers find that their work requires more computer sophistication and enjoy developing those skills, while people who don't like computers pass up opportunities to learn more. Those people find legitimate reasons to delegate work that requires computer time.

4. Embody personal values. At work, people attempt to construe events consistently with their personal values. For example, people who value team play take more care in dealing with requests from other departments. People who value technical expertise treat the "experts" differently from those they consider merely to be "generalists." People who strongly feel minorities and people with a disability deserve a break consistently find ways to assist and to modify specifications. And people who are status conscious and materialistically inclined tend to value getting ahead and indulge themselves in utilizing perks and other benefits that rank achieves for them.

5. Fulfill personal life commitments. At work, people attempt to construe events to fit with the rest of their life commitments. For example, people with children, sick parents, or a troubled spouse arrange their work to free time for family responsibilities. Conversely, single and unattached people often pour more energy into their jobs. They attend more professional meetings and seminars, spend more time socializing with workmates, and derive more identity from their job than married people with family responsibilities.

Of course many people go to work actively thinking about professional development and career advancement. Their response to each daily event and interaction comes with a self-advancement spin. Their attention is focused on getting ahead, which means self-promotion and image making. They are out to develop the requisite social and technical proficiencies. They infuse assignments with dimensions that they perceive as career promoting and pay special attention to networking and forming relationships with people who might prove useful in pushing their careers ahead. And they avoid situations and actions that they fear are career threatening.

6. Personality. At work, features of an individual's personality, distinctive psychology, and even idiosyncrasies play a constant role in how events are construed. For example, people who like order put effort into structuring and prioritizing activities and may sometimes lack the flexibility to stop what they are doing to attend to a more pressing matter. At work, people who are emotional respond emotionally; people who like to be in control and dominate find that their managerial assignments require control and domination; people who were the first-born children from large families feel more pressure to give directions and be in charge; people who are big eaters schedule more lunch and dinner meetings; people who want to be noticed dress to be noticed; men who want to be taller are inclined to hire tall guys; people with whatever hang-ups and sensitivities find ways to legitimatize the expression of those hang-ups and sensitivities. In other words, people are always finding ways to express their total selves—good points and bad points—in the way they perform their job.

7. Function with self-expression and personal style. At work people have a knack of putting their preferred style into all their work involvements and to leave distinctive impressions. For example, some people like to convey high energy and aggressiveness; some people like to effect collaboration and to communicate sensitivity in their concern for the inputs of others; some like to constantly demonstrate that they are playing by the rules; others want to project independence. We could go on and on taking this tack, pushing the list out to infinity. The point is that people naturally put a great deal of energy into expressing themselves and putting their distinctive personal thumbprint on everything they do.

8. Social programming. At work people hold expectations that are far more a function of what they have been taught to value, expect, and do than what is actually required by the function they perform and what the company actually needs them to do to perform effectively. Some of this is cultural, macro to one's nationality and micro to one's family; some has to do with gender, despite recent trends in the blurring of sex-typed child-rearing practices; and some of this relates to factors that are idiosyncratic and vary by individual.

What people are programmed to expect impacts what they seek, what they notice, and what they miss. For example, some people are programmed to defer to authority, and this expectation accounts for their lack of open-mindedness to the ideas of juniors as well as their inability to scrutinize and independently evaluate thoughts that come down from those above. Actually, the negative effects of social programming is a huge topic that we engaged in depth during the consciousness-raising movement among minorities in the 1960s and early 1970s, and we concluded that consciousness of one's own social and corporate programming is essential to the individual's overcoming limitations that he or she brings to the job.[2]

Culture always plays a role in one's programming. In saying this we're thinking of many different types of culture. There's ethnic culture, immigration culture, era culture, feminism culture, age culture, geographical culture, family culture, singles culture, sexual orientation culture, special skills and profession culture, past-trauma culture, and "you-name-it" culture. For example, first-generation Americans are very clear about their differences from their immigrant parents and many second-generation Americans talk about their differences from their first-generation parents. For example, few people who grew up during the Depression participated in the expressiveness experiments that took place in the 1960s. For example, in large public accounting firms, contrasts are drawn between the conservative, look-for-what's-missing audit culture and the tax and consulting cultures that distinctively emphasize other qualities. For example, in contemporary business there is a TQM (total quality management) culture, there is the team culture, the strategic planning culture, and again we could push the list almost open-endedly. For example, there is an adult children of alcoholic parents culture, an abused child culture, a heart attack survivors culture, a parent with handicapped child culture, and the list goes on. Each contributes to how an individual frames his or her thinking in the workplace.

Organizational competency variable

At work, people attempt to perform the work that *they* believe the organization needs to receive from someone in their role and position. Doing so fulfills the contract that the individual makes with the organization in exchange for pay. It also fills one with a sense of service and accomplishment, and feelings of pride, teamworthiness, and self-esteem, which makes this an essential variable on the self-competency side of an individual's alignment equation as well. People may also perform work that the hierarchy insists they perform that they think is unnecessary, but this relates more to job politics and insecurity than to feelings of productivity, accomplishment, and self-esteem.

Giving the organization what one thinks it needs to receive is a crucial element in an individual's alignment. For example, at work people intentionally make what they know in advance will be unpopular statements, they work extra hours doing work that no one expects of them or thinks is necessary, they hold difficult conversations, they attend boring meetings—they do all sorts of things that few besides themselves would bother doing just because they think it's the "right" thing to do. Conversely, there are any number of tasks and activities that the hierarchy, oftentimes one's direct boss, insists that an individual perform but which that person intentionally skips, avoids, or neglects merely because he or she feels they are unnecessary, unimportant, and a waste of time.

Usually included in this work dimension are such givens as the organization vision, mission, strategy, and business plan. When, for example, that vision is understood and the individual sees it as valid and empowering, you can expect the individual to make it part of his or her alignment. When an individual sees it as irrelevant and personally compromising, then that person will attempt to distance him- or herself from it, even while taking the political steps that give lip-service acknowledgment to it. Nevertheless, what others think is also important and people pay attention to what others say and decide. This fact is clearly established by the Artifact of Mind insight and the theory of omnipresent organizational politics that's implied.

Alignments

Given the preceding discussion of variables, you can see that when you think about giving the same assignment to five people, there's only one prediction that you can make with any. certainty: Each of the five is going to perform that assignment differently. Why? Because each individual has unique skills, interests, values, quirks, and life situations to maximize and also has unique perceptions of what the organization needs to receive form someone in his or her role and position.

Alignments are the personal strategies that underlie how an individual is inclined to structure situations and see events in promoting what is personally important *and* empowering. They account for what an individual sees as an opportunity to demonstrate competence and what that person sees as a threat. They account for what an individual sees as important when evaluating someone else's efforts. They account for what an individual sees as his or her unit's mission and the actions that will lead to that mission being achieved.

Alignments are maximization strategies, not optimization strategies. An individual looks at the job and thinks about what is possible, realizing, of course, that, by its very nature, working in an organization involves compromise. Of course we all know this. We go to work for organizations because they provide opportunities for us to accomplish and develop personally what we could not do without accessing their resources. We do so knowing that trade-offs are inevitable. The ever-present challenge is to make sure that we know what we are compromising so that we don't give up something that has essential personal meaning, or is crucial to our self-esteem, integrity, and/or identity, and that we monitor whether we are getting good value in exchange for what we give up.

Alignments are orientation strategies developed by individuals attempting to maximize the output of the variables and constituent elements of their personal equations. They will change and shift as new skills are developed, fears are assuaged, job assignments change, life situations evolve, and so on. Alignments also change when an individual sees the possibility of shifting his or her orientation to maximize more self and organizational interests.

When you know an individual's alignment strategy and share that person's idea of what the organization requires, you as a prospective advice-giver have a valuable counseling service to provide. Nevertheless, an individual won't open up to your advice until that person believes that you view him or her with sufficient accuracy to not fear something essential to his or her total life well-being will be neglected by the alignment modification implied in your counsel. In any event, the individual is not about to change until that person sees the variables that need adjustment differently him- or herself.

Before an individual has fixed on an alignment, say early in that person's work at a company, or when he or she receives a new job assignment, you can expect that person to be ill at ease, as if he or she were in structure shock. Structure shock is similar to culture shock. In culture shock an individual first and foremost thinks, "How do they do it here?" even before thinking "How do I size things up and what do I think?" This keeps him or her off balance and transforms little decisions into major thought processes. For instance, an executive told us about how terribly inefficient and generally anxious he felt while conducting business in Indonesia. He was thrown off by the complexities of scheduling appointments in areas of Jakarta and outlying islands with unpredictable traffic tie-ups, plane schedules that changed without notice, and the formality of meeting with functionaries before seeing the person with whom he wanted to conduct business.

In structure shock, an individual lacks an orientation that tells him or her how to act when spontaneously faced with a new situation or being asked an unexpected question. Before making a response, this person has to run through a checklist of skills to utilize, nonskills to avoid, interests to be exploited, values to be embraced, needs of the organization to be met, and so on. Simple acts require tremendous self-deliberation.

But once an individual has been on the job for a while, he or she knows exactly how to respond. That person has evolved an alignment strategy that instantaneously signals opportunities and threats and instructs how to respond spontaneously to any circumstance in ways that are consistent with what he or she is trying to achieve both personally and organizationally. An alignment allows an individual to instantly spot subtle systems and subliminal issues that are involved when that person is asked, as you may have been, "Boss, I'm about to call our client to tell him our problem and ask how much delay he can tolerate." Immediately you know just what "spin" to tell that subordinate to put on that approach and framing of the question.

In most instances, alignments are experienced piece by piece until you get to the point where enough specifics come together that you feel you know enough about some individual's background and potential for empowerment to comprehend why that person orients the unique way he or she does and understand how he or she sees situations distinctively. Of course, there are special times when you get to experience someone's alignment holistically. This can happen when the two of you work long hours on a crash project together, when you act as someone's mentor, when you travel together on a difficult assignment, when you get involved in someone's personal problem such as alcoholism, a family death, or a marriage breakup. When people trust you, they open up and let you "inside" to see key personal factors in their alignment equation.

Some alignments are "effective," some "ineffective," some "successful," and some "empowered." An alignment is effective when an individual finds a strategy for orienting to work events that simultaneously maximizes what is self-meaningful and organizationally productive. For instance, at our school of management, a young research-oriented economist who enjoys his or her work usually has an effective alignment, whereas young professors in areas that are more applied and less academic, such as accounting, typically have a more difficult time. What our accounting colleagues do for self-meaning and what they feel they have to accomplish to fulfill their obligations to the institution are less often one and the same.

An alignment is ineffective when performing self-competently and taking care of personal needs comes at the expense of being organizationally productive. We call this type of organizationally ineffective behavior careerism, for the individual is, essentially, exploiting his or her situation for self-gain. An alignment is also ineffective when doing what the organization needs accomplished entails excessively long periods of self-sacrifice in which the individual neglects his or her self-needs for such things as self-competency, learning, personal meaning, and renewal. We call this type of personally ineffective behavior "overdedication," for the individual is allowing him- or herself to be exploited, which eventually leads to stress, complacency, burnout, or some other sort of self-induced pain. The individual is so organizationally focused that he or she overlooks opportunities to learn, develop, and grow.

We began this discussion by stating that there were three components to empowerment. The construct of an "effective alignment" covers the first two: (1) an individual utilizing his or her strengths and best abilities (2) in an effort that he or she perceives to be both personally and organizationally meaningful. But having an effective alignment is not sufficient for empowerment.

Empowerment requires the third component, the organization's valuing of the individual's alignment. We call this synthesis a "successful alignment." Of course, not all effective alignments are successful and some ineffective alignments are. Every company has its overlooked and misunderstood performers and every company has some self-indulgent or exploitative performers who are temporarily called successful. Nevertheless, we reserve the term empowered only for those people who both have an effective alignment and are considered by the people in the organization who matter to them most as essential value-added resources.

Recall that we've used the term organization politics to refer to the activities an individual engages in for purposes of developing the context for performing effectively and achieving public acknowledgment for his or her efforts toward those ends. That is, what people have to do to get others to see the value of what they are trying to accomplish and how they are going about it, gaining acceptance for their strategies, orientations, and alignments, is the *root basis* of organization politics. Thus there is a political dimension to empowerment.

Test your comprehension with a short exam

For a change of pace, allow us to review the alignment model of empowerment and its implications for advice-giving by administering a short exam. Here are the questions. We hope that running through them with us will provide you confidence that you've grasped our model.

Question 1

Are people with effective alignments (good for self, good for organization) always empowered and organizationally successful?

The answer is "No." Just because an individual has a strategy for operating competently, it doesn't mean that others won't resist. At work, personal competence does not equate with organizational success.

People who don't feel they have an effective alignment are easy to advise, particularly when you are aware of their key personal effectiveness variables. Your advice will bear on their alignment strategy and their finding a way to express what is personally important to them and what they see as organizationally productive in ways that allow others to recognize their organizational value.

However, when you attempt to give alignment advice to people who feel they have an effective alignment, your task is far more difficult. These people are looking for political pointers, not comments about what you think they ought to do to perform with greater competence. In their minds they already have the right formula for maximizing an enormously complex multivariate equation, and their problems relate to getting others to appreciate what they are doing. By not accepting that their solution is sufficient you are essentially asking them to back up two steps. Until they see that their thinking is off, their preoccupation will be on techniques and strategies for circumventing the obstacles created by you and others who are providing feedback that their actions are insufficiently effective.

Question 2

What determines whether others are inclined to value or oppose someone's contributions and positive efforts?

This should be an easy question to answer. It's the other person's alignment that determines what that other person is inclined to support or oppose. Everyone is interested in his or her own empowerment. It is the overriding agenda that decides one individual's attitude toward what a person with a different alignment does and asserts.

Your attempts to help another person overcome the self-interested resistance that emanates from a third party creates a play within a play. Essentially you are trying to help someone accomplish what you yourself are attempting to accomplish. You are trying to get deep enough inside your advice-recipient's skin to understand the meaning of the personal-effectiveness issues that your advice is addressing, while that person needs to do the same in taking a psychologically sensitive win-win-win approach in dealing with the resistance he or she has encountered.

Question 3

How do people with incompatible alignments conflict?

To answer this question you must understand that people with incompatible alignments actually see the same organizational events differently. People with incompatible alignments wil! argue over whose response is organizationally correct as if the option they are championing is independent of their own self-interested motives. Of course, what we realize is that each person comes with a built-in bias to favor the option that has the best chance of leading to his or her personal empowerment.

As we've indicated several times, rather than deal with the underlying issue of people with different alignments needing to frame reality for their own personal empowerment, people who conflict get sidetracked making rational arguments based on what they perceive as established organizational agreements. They debate alternatives, priorities, and values citing agreements that others cannot logically oppose. But we know these debates have a missing dimension, since each alternative, priority, and value links to indestructible personal-competence motives for which people hold an agenda-biased view.

In essence, people with incompatible alignments take any action that advances a self-empowering version of what is taking place and what is needed. This is why a three-minute decision requires a four-hour meeting with all kinds of positioning and posturing. Each person needs the situation defined slightly differently to stage the events for his or her possible empowerment. When a person can't be up front about his or her needs, that person is whittled down to quibbling details that can look picayune because, lacking the bigger picture, you have no way of appreciating their significance and meaning. But after you know the variables in the equation the other person is attempting to maximize, what was formerly a boring meeting that you endured out of courtesy or obligation is transformed into high-pitched action drama.

When giving advice, you need to remain mindful of the indestructibility of empowerment motives and the mutability of organization. Whereas most advice-givers argue on the basis of their advice-recipients' needing to conform to the corporate program, what you need to keep in mind is that getting someone who is not empowered to conform is no real service to that individual. What's more, you should also keep in mind that organization can be changed and, in fact, changing organization to liberate people to function intelligently with empowerment is the impetus behind every progressive new model.

To summarize, alignments are the personal-competence strategies that people adopt in interpreting and relating to all organizational events in an effort to function with empowerment. They, and the constituent variables they include, determine the distinctive mind-set organizations in which the people you advise conduct their personal and professional business. Techniques for reading alignments and ascertaining the mind-sets of specific people are the subject of the next chapter.

Notes

1. For more discussion, see S. A. Culbert and J. J. McDonough, *The Invisible War: Pursuing Self-Interests at Work* (New York: Wiley, 1980), and *Radical Management: Power, Politics and the Pursuit of Trust* (New York: Free Press, 1985).

2. See J. J. McDonough, "One Day in the Life of Ivan Denisovich: A Study of the Structural Requisites of Organization," *Human Relations,* 28(4): 295–328, 1975; S. A. Culbert, *The Organization Trap* (New York: Basic Books, 1974); and S. A. Culbert and J. M. Elden, "An Anatomy of Activism for Executives," *Harvard Business Review,* 1970, pp. 131–142.

7

Discerning Alignment Strategies and the Mind-Sets That Derive from Them

In Chapter 6 we discussed two of three essential research tools required for becoming a mind-set researcher: a theory that tells you how mind-sets operate in general and a model that specifies the personal-competency variables that give rise to a mind-set. What remains to be covered is the method and technique for reading an individual's mind-set and the prominence of specific variables. That's what this chapter takes up.

The method is asking "illuminating" questions and the technique is active listening.[1] Now that you know how people operate, and what information you need, asking illuminating questions readily follows. This chapter describes the questions we ask and how we go about interpreting the answers. However, because everyone operates with a different mind-set, somewhat different questions will occur to you. You'll find the answers to your questions to be every bit as informative as the answers we get to ours, because yours will be directed to filling knowledge gaps that are particularly relevant to your attempts to understand another individual using your particular mind-set. Of course even when you decide to begin with our questions, you'll be interpreting them your own inimitable way.

Coupling the theory that derives from the Artifact of Mind insight with the Alignment Model of Empowerment, you are equipped to conduct your mind-set research with enhanced psychological sensitivity. **You realize that the main objective of any question is to learn how people distinctively see their situations and how they reason in relation to what they see.** You know the nature of the variables that are likely to be prominent in an individual's desire to perform competently, but you don't know the specifics of their impact or whether other, more important variables are present. And you realize that no accounting of an individual's behavior can validly leave political forces out.

Now that you are primed to probe beneath someone's words for the importance of distinctive meanings, let's try a fifteen-second test. Let's say you are a mind-set researcher and someone comes up to you and says, "I just got a promotion." After you say "Congratulations, I wish you success," what's the next thing that you should do or say? Right. You should ask an "illuminating" question using whatever specific wording seems appropriate at the time. You want to ask something friendly like, "Tell me, what does this promotion mean to you?" Why this question? Because the Artifact of Mind insight has made it very clear: **In this life, no fact speaks for itself.** Without exception, you understand that the process of becoming mind-set–sensitive entails inquiring into the meanings an individual assigns to events.

We're just about at the point of listing the questions we ask when trying to comprehend an individual's alignment. However, before doing so, we want to tell you a story that reinforces the importance of getting "psychological" and asking illuminating questions when someone's actions fail to compute for you.

Case in point

The story began when we were called by the owner of an Italian-based company in the pricey, high-fashion women's apparel business. The owner asked for a lunch meeting to discuss what to do about Walter, the vice president in charge of his Los Angeles division. We were game, especially when he set the meeting place—a great-food restaurant with expense-account prices.

Accompanying the owner was his wife Gina, who, we quickly learned, plays a prominent role in selecting designers and deciding which fashions will be merchandised in California. While her husband jets back and forth between his headquarters in Rome and distribution and sales locations in London, Toronto, and Los Angeles, she currently resides in Los Angeles.

They took their time describing the entirety of the company's operations to set the context for our understanding the Los Angeles operation and the basis for their problems. As was explained to us on the phone, the problem was Walter. The owner wanted Walter fixed; Gina wanted Walter's head.

They told us about a thirteen-year acquaintanceship and an eighteen-month business relationship. We listened in amazement to a dramatic listing of blatant problems. We heard about a series of incidents in which Walter failed to support business ventures initiated by Gina. Gina was particularly critical of Walter's "not invented here" attitude. According to her, if someone else dreamed it up, Walter was guaranteed not to be behind it. In particular we heard an account of a recent dinner meeting convened to introduce her husband and Walter to the principal partner of a company that she wanted to enter a joint venture with. We heard how, during the dinner, Walter sat sullenly, seldom speaking, and going out of his way to display no interest whatsoever. This unprofessional expression hit a crescendo the next day when they awoke to find a four-page letter that Walter had faxed at three in the morning. Gina handed us the letter saying "Read this. You've got to agree. It's the work of a madman."

Insisting that we read it on the spot, she wanted corroboration that it was the product of a sick mind. Of course, providing such corroboration was not what we were about to do. We yielded to scanning its contents briefly, just to get the gist. Not revealing the entirety of our opinion, we gave serious consideration to the possibility that Gina was right. The logic was agitated and convoluted, and the content jumped from topic to topic.

Our response was a serious look followed by our asking, "What do you plan to do, how are you going to handle this?" The owner answered, "I'd like you to talk with him." We responded, "That's not our business. We don't see ourselves as hired guns who fix people to meet the interests and concerns of others. If you'd like us to sit in on a meeting that you or the two of you have with Walter, we'd be willing. You know there's another side to every story." Frankly, after reading the letter, we had an additional reason for not wanting to talk with Walter alone. We couldn't conceive of any account that would convince us that the letter was written by someone operating with all his marbles.

The owner was insistent. He turned up his charm and charisma to full volume, imploring us to meet with Walter. We yielded saying, "OK, if you can get him to call us we'll meet with him for purposes of management consultation. But, you realize, once we meet with him we can't then reveal what we learn. Right now we're acting as your consultants advising you how to handle a difficult management problem. Based on what you have told us, we're wondering why you are consulting with us instead of calling in your lawyer to work out the termination deal."

Over the years we've found that asking people their reasons for not doing the obvious is an effective practice. There had to be a reason why these people were going to great lengths to avoid firing Walter, and we wanted to know what it was. Nobody likes to fire anyone, but we wanted to know the special hold and appeal.

We were told that the two of them had met Walter years ago when the owner and Walter were older students working on their MBA degrees. We heard about bonds of loyalty and even some affection. Their attachment to Walter seemed to emphasize Walter's extraordinary intelligence, and we found this noteworthy because the two of them struck us as extremely bright themselves. They said that this was probably the best job that Walter ever had and they saw his alternative prospects as bleak.

Three days later Walter called requesting a consultation. We offered to come by since that's our standard practice. Besides, we wanted to see first hand if the office was as disorganized and screwed up as the owner and his wife had depicted it. Walter declined, saying that he did a lot of business on our side of town and besides he liked being at the university.

It took two meetings for us to comprehend the reasoning that could account for his sullen conduct at the joint venture principals' dinner and the circumstances that produced the "madman" letter. At the first meeting he told us his version of the dinner story and the letter and his history in the fashion business. He emphasized his admiration and deep respect for the owner and the difficulties of having to constantly backstop and compensate for the miscues of the owner's wife. He also talked about the importance of his job and how, for the first time, he feels the opportunity to express his creativity in a field and set of business operations that are inherently interesting to him. Then, at the second meeting, he really let down his hair.

That's when he volunteered his personal life history. For ninety minutes we sat captivated, listening to an extraordinarily told biography. Walter portrayed himself as a person who at a young age was identified as "gifted" and who spent the entirety of his schooling and his career succeeding at everything he tried but never, up until now, finding his natural niche. He also talked candidly about living a childhood with parents who were self-centered, "social-drinking" alcoholics, and his feelings of being isolated and having to fend for himself. He told us that his father was constitutionally sensitive to alcohol and that it took very little to get him high.

In response to our asking about his own drinking, he said that he too is constitutionally sensitive and that one, or at the most two glasses of wine at dinner or a glass of beer before going to bed is enough for him to let down and get distance from the stresses of the day. He also told us that he's aware of sometimes rubbing his employers the wrong way, and to earn compensatory points he works long hours to demonstrate his diligence and good will. While he didn't say, and we didn't initially ask, the long hours also seemed to compensate for a relatively isolated personal life.

He told us how, as a child, he planned his days to minimize contact with his parents. He kept a full schedule of extracurricular activities, frequently arranged to stay overnight at the homes of friends, and when it came time for college, chose a West Coast school to put distance between himself and his East Coast parents. From his accounts we could see that intelligence, thorough planning, and sidestepping of conflict were his key survival and coping skills.

On the other hand, Walter lacked a capacity for engaging differences in opinion forthrightly. By no means did this mean that he didn't have differences. It meant that he was a person who was often surprised by the intensity of his feelings and his attachment to opinions he had not expressed, who in the face of conflict would withhold stating his views and beliefs, and who came with a knee-jerk reflex for avoiding other people's control of him. When encountering a conflict, he was reluctant to put his cards on the table—to state the problem and let the other person help with the solution. His style was to absorb the problem, use his formidable intellect to figure out a solution, and then to take unilateral action to put the solution in place.

With this understanding, it was easy to see how Walter might appear controlling, cunning, and devious to people who didn't know what we had just learned. Of course, this wasn't Walter's intention, and we were developing a very sympathetic disposition to him. He was applying the very skills that had enabled him to survive his alcoholic home life to situations in which other people were well intentioned and willing to pitch in and help.

At this point we reflected on that dinner meeting and the early-morning fax. We could see how the planets were juxtaposed to produce the "madman" results. Walter had spent eighteen months absorbing and circumventing differences and that evening had been boxed into a meeting aimed at creating a venture he opposed. When we asked him, he had scintillating business arguments for his opposition. But he felt compression not knowing how to forthrightly engage the other two with his "facts." This, coupled with the fatigue of working long hours and his having accepted a second glass of wine, set the stage for his letter.

Rereading the letter in the light of what we had learned, we could now decipher its theme and coherence. It was a poorly timed attempt to take up eighteen months of accumulated problems and frustrations. The convolution and content jumping was actually an attempt to disclose a pattern of Gina's mishandling of business situations and Walter's behind-the-scenes rescuing of them. The three o'clock faxing represented a personal need to release from the buildup of pressures and the overload the dinner meeting had created, which, at the time, had caused his demeanor to appear sullen.

The immediate, practical question was, could he change? To change, Walter needed the basic model for engaging and negotiating differences, and people he could trust to practice it on. He needed to develop the confidence to try it and the skill to do so competently. If he developed these skills, the opportunities for practicing them were omnipresent, in social domains as well as at work. In addition, as our young-adult children would say it, Walter needed to "get a life." The good news was that we weren't dealing with any mere mortal; we were dealing with an individual possessing enormous capacities and, we thought, good will.

As management consultants and advice-givers, we counsel but don't give therapy. Providing therapy requires people with stable schedules whose focus is on the individual's self-unfolding and personal development. Ours is on the development of organizations and work teams. Thus we told Walter what we thought, gave him some phone numbers of therapists, and told him that when he was ready we'd help facilitate a team discussion to help him tell his employer and teammate Gina what he wanted them to know. We told Walter that we thought time was running out and that as soon as he could, he needed to strike some agreements about how the three of them might communicate more effectively.

The first attempt at an air-clearing meeting took place in our office three weeks later. Walter had asked if he could bring the other two by for an extended meeting, which actually took six hours over two consecutive days. We watched in awe at the first meeting as Gina grabbed the opportunity for catharsis and to vent her frustrations at working with Walter. At that meeting Walter was relatively quiet. Then we caucused with Walter, described what he might say if he were proceeding forthrightly, and the next day watched as he attempted to set the two of them straight. Once he got going, in every instance they accepted his corrections of the facts and his even-handed descriptions of the circumstances that had prompted his actions. Then we scheduled follow-up meetings directed at facilitating an interactive exchange aimed at allowing Walter to modify his relationship with the two of them and to become more proficient in putting his points of view out for open-minded discussion.

The purpose behind telling you this story is not to send you out in quest of a psychologist's degree. It is to provide you with a compelling motive for searching beneath the surface to understand the basis of people's work performances, particularly when you see someone taking action that you think no rational thinking individual would ever take. It is to convince you to commit yourself to researching an individual's mind-set prior to embarking on any course of giving personal-effectiveness advice—and certainly before taking any "corrective" action.

Questions we use for reading alignment strategies and learning about mind-sets

In Chapter 6 we provided a list of competency concerns—the variables that make up an individual's alignment. Now we want to provide you with a list of the questions you might ask in familiarizing yourself with someone's alignment and the mind-sets that derive from them. Asking any of these questions depends on your relationship with the other person and what motive that person imputes to your inquiry. Whether that person thinks you are getting "the goods *on* him," to gain a competitive advantage, or "the goods *for* him," so that you can better understand and assist, will determine the reception you get. And always, of key importance is the "bedside" manner you use when eliciting an individual's response.

The questions we're going to list are ones that we use in a workshop where the objective is to show participants how to get behind an individual's perceptions to read the alignment and mind-set that generate them. In the workshop, our goal is to assist participants in developing their skills in eliciting and understanding another person's alignment, and to accomplish this we have them practice on one another. Of course the secondary, and in many instances the primary, benefit is that in the process each participant finds out how one or more others experience his or her alignment and understand his or her distinct style and orientation to organizational events.

In workshops, people are provided questions to ask in sequence and instructed not to interrupt their focus on another person by providing their own reciprocal answer to the questions they raise. They're told the goal is to get into someone else's shoes and to stay there as much as possible throughout the entire alignment-probing interview. Experience has taught us that people lose clarity when they interpose their experiences and beliefs with other people's thoughts. Besides, we want people "to experience" the efficiency in which information critical to understanding another person's alignment can be acquired and the relationship bonding that takes place when they give someone focus and concentrate on what they hear.

The workshop format contrasts with how you appropriately conduct yourself in a normal work setting where reciprocity and conversational *inter*action make concentrating your focus on another person's mind-set and alignment strategy much more difficult to achieve and sustain. Conversations in which you ask a series of questions can lead another person to feel you are placing him or her under a microscope, particularly when the person does not feel your empathy and concern. Nevertheless, in natural settings there often comes a point where the person to whom you are listening achieves a level of momentum that allows you to relax and listen at length.

Our reason for displaying our workshop questions is not for you to use them verbatim. It's to illustrate the types of questions that can help you comprehend another individual's alignment and the thinking behind it. Keep in mind that an alignment is not something that an individual can explain directly to you. To comprehend it, you must learn the personal competence issues and concerns that lie behind how that person is inclined to construe events and the personal background factors that account for inner assumptions and personal issues of importance.

In our instructions to workshop leaders we caution "Don't take participants by surprise." We urge them to allot time for people to preview questions and to self-reflect on their complete answers prior to being asked to divulge them to someone else. We instruct leaders to explain that participants are only to say what they feel comfortable revealing based on the face-to-face rapport they feel with their workshop partner(s). We explain the importance of structuring workshops with guidelines aimed at lowering the risk of people being hurt by making themselves too transparent. Accordingly, people are paired with partners who work at different companies with instructions that all disclosures are to be kept confidential. In fact, whether people see their partner(s) again is wholly up to them.

While the questions we raise are guided by the list of variables in the Alignment Model of Empowerment, they do not follow a linear logic per se. Our objective in asking specifics is to get the gestalt behind someone's perceptions, sensitivities, and distinctive reasoning, and to make the disclosure process efficient. In normal, everyday settings, there are issues of social protocol, confidentiality, trust concerns, organizational agendas, and other complex issues to consider. There the classic personal disclosure maxim rings true:

"Openness begets openness." There maintaining focus on the other person is far more an ideal than what's practical.

We have already discussed the political skepticisms you will encounter when trying to become mind-set informed once another person senses problems and fears the use to which you will put the personal perspectives you acquire. Once there is a problem, suspicions about your motives will seriously impact the quality and character of any information you get. When you are in a natural, real-life setting, you need to station yourself as an advocate for an individual's well-being prior to soliciting the alignment information required for giving advice.

With this introduction, we're ready to present our alignment-discerning questions along with our reasoning for each and what you might learn from the answers you get.

1. Bum rap

Think of a "bum rap" or stereotype that someone has used in characterizing you and your limitations. State what is left out by this way of portraying you, or what is unfair, and explain why the criticisms implied in this portrayal are too simplistic or categorical. State whether you have taken any action to counteract this exaggerated representation of you. If you have, what did you do? If not, why haven't you challenged this characterization?

People who have the need to gain power and control over others can do so quite easily. All they have to do is focus on a "deficiency" and label that person as if that deficiency were present all the time, rather than evoked in certain situations or with certain types of people. They call that person "a compulsive _____ (fill in the blank)_____," or "too _____," or "has a problem with _____," and so on. Often the individual who is being negatively stereotyped, typecast, and labeled will admit to the validity of the accusation, even while being deeply troubled by it. That person is likely to feel "bum rapped" due to finding the characterization excessive, all-inclusive, out of proportion, overly simplistic, and/or too reductionistic.

People are seldom one way all the time, and, even when someone is generally one way or another, a categorically negative characterization will usually fail to portray the positive intentions that accompany what's being alluded to that predictably goes amok. Whenever an individual is negatively typecast, that person knows that the people doing it are intentionally putting out effort aimed at diminishing or overlooking their essence and net value to the corporation. Hence the term "bum rap."

Bum raps are frequently the result of an overused or misapplied strength that serves the individual well under some circumstances, but not all, or relates more to what was necessary for coping with a circumstance of the past. For example, an individual who is conceptual and highly articulate can be "bum rapped" by calling him or her overly intellectual, long-winded, and verbose. He or she may in fact often be too wordy, but no doubt there are times when that capacity for articulation serves as a major asset. There may even be current moments when that person's verbal skills benefit the corporation.

While the bum-rap question works well in a workshop, it's generally not a good way to begin learning about someone's alignment in a natural setting. Before you begin asking about "problems," you need to build rapport, which can be much better accomplished by inquiring about strong suits, special skills, work successes, and personal strengths. The educational structure of the workshop allows participants to be more direct.

Nevertheless, in natural work settings, the concept "bum rap" can provide just the inroad you need for advice-giving. The term is a cordial way of telling an individual that you value him or her despite the fact that you realize other people exaggerate his or her faults, and that you empathize with the pain such exaggeration can cause. The term bum rap allows you to declare your interest and desire to help with a problem that others claim is a core deficiency. It allows you to acknowledge a pattern of ineffective behavior without implying it's a fatal flaw.

2. *Intention*

What are you trying to prove or demonstrate to others and/ or to yourself? Explain why proving this is so important. Then, if possible, describe an incident that illustrates how what you are trying to prove is reflected in your behavior.

This is a "forest for the trees" question. It is aimed at identifying the more deeply rooted personal themes that are embedded in the thoughts, perceptions, and actions of another person. This is the basic question that needs answering in appreciating someone's alignment. Until it is, observers lack a valid means for appreciating the significance a situation holds, the "stakes," "threats," and "opportunities" that are symbolized by its occurrence, and/or the "category" of meaning in which an individual places it and/or the spin he or she seems intent in putting on all situations in this category.

The answer to the "What are you trying to prove?" question allows you to appreciate the larger, ubiquitous project the individual is pursuing whenever you observe him or her acting in a manner that is particularly noticeable because it is something that you would never do. To appreciate the meaning of that person's actions, you need to know what is fundamentally important. Then you request a tangible example as a means for checking your understanding.

In some ways this question represents a continuation of the "bum-rap" query. But while the "bum-rap" question inquires about surface behavior gone awry, and is pursued first in the workshop because it has a rapport-setting dimension, the "What are you trying to prove?" question is a more direct inquiry into deeper level intentions, including "I'll show you" reactive reasoning. Participants are instructed, "As you listen to someone's answer, see if you can identify self-ideals and doubts, probably planted in that person's mind during childhood, that produce a need for that individual to repetitively demonstrate some personal quality and the personal competency issues entailed."

Perhaps no other question that you ask will put you more squarely in the realm of an individual's personal psychology. But here your job is not to offer deep insights and psychoanalytic interpretations. Your assignment is more client-centered. You need to act like Carl Rogers, not Sigmund Freud. Your Rogerian assignment is to be no more than what you are: a naive inquirer who empathetically asks for reasons to explain that which you don't understand. When you confine your role to asking questions, you need to take care not to be insistent or to expect lightning bolt insight and instant change. Any change that takes place will result from the other person's self-reflection later on and, in all likelihood, will not be directly discussed with you.

When you are a prospective advice-giver functioning outside the workshop setting, knowing what an individual feels he or she needs to prove, and why, allows you to comprehend what that person is actually doing when all you have to go on are his or her words and behavior. Until you understand the life themes and personal-competency issues that underlie words and actions, you are vulnerable to getting yourself stuck trying to change someone's surface behavior, which is generated by a deeper issue than the forces that you see (mis)directing that individual.

How you obtain this information under everyday circumstances requires a little ingenuity. Often the answer is obtainable by asking an individual "What was your life like at home growing up? What was your family role? What accomplishments were you known for? What was the work ethic?" Taking this approach won't get you directly to the "What are you trying to prove?" question, but it will place you in the general neighborhood. In other words what you learn from asking these conversational questions will get you in the proximity of what you need to know, and you can take the conversation on from there.

3. *Work success*

Describe a work assignment that you take particular pride in having performed as well as you did (perhaps one from a former job or position). What was the personal significance of this accomplishment? What strengths or capacities were demonstrated? How were you challenged? Were any self-doubts involved? What does this accomplishment illustrate about your upbringing and what you had to overcome as an adult?

This question is aimed at identifying what the other person thinks are mainstay strengths. However, when people are asked directly about their strengths, there's an inclination to become self-conscious and overly abstract. Thus we ask about tangible successes and, in order to understand the significance, we ask about background factors, challenges involved, and self-doubts that were overcome. Of course it's entirely likely that some key strengths go unmentioned in a description of a specific work event and that you might feel the need to consider asking about additional success situations to provide the other person an opportunity to tell you about these as well.

Often the value an individual attaches to an accomplishment is generated by what that individual had to conquer. In terms of understanding that person's alignment, it's important to identify personal limitations surmounted and situational obstacles overcome. Comprehending them will greatly enhance your appreciation of the meaning an individual attaches to what he or she is doing and the distinctiveness of that person's strivings.

In natural settings people usually have little difficulty citing their accomplishments and often will even volunteer them. However, more important to you as a mind-set researcher are the meanings an individual attaches to his or her accomplishments. That's why you are interested in life struggles and what the individual feels he or she has had to accomplish. Instead of asking the person what he or she is good at, you merely ask what work accomplishment was the most rewarding. Then you probe for context and background by asking, "What made it so rewarding?" Phrasing it like this paves the way for you to inquire about meaning. This goes back to our earlier quiz where we advised you not to take success or even a financial reward as "stand-alone" concepts. We advised: seize them as opportunities for deeper inquiry.

4. Self-disappointment

Now let's examine the other side of the coin. Describe a work assignment (current or from a former job or position) in which you failed to live up to expectations (your own or someone else's). How did you fail to perform? What was the disappointment? How do you explain why your performance failed to accomplish what you wanted to demonstrate or achieve?

This question seeks to understand another dimension of the "What are you trying to prove?" question, number 2. But this time, the issue is addressed in terms of feelings of disappointment and failure, which are very delicate issues to probe. Blame and feelings of guilt are often involved, as are self-limitations and frustrated ambitions. Hearing out these feelings and issues challenges people's abilities to carry off the role of open-minded listener. In particular, it will challenge one's capacities to actually be, not just appear, nonjudgmental. Thus, when asking this type of question we instruct "Keep in mind that the object is to comprehend how the other person sees life and the situations and people who were sources of disappointment, not to judge whether this person is correct in his or her attributions of responsibility."

At work, "a disappointment" is a failed performance only in relation to what an individual was expected to accomplish, either by him- or herself or someone else. That is, only if a person is expected to produce 1,000 widgets, or be a Level B in the hierarchy while currently only at Level C, can that person be seen as failing for producing only 850 widgets or not attaining Level B. Accordingly, when you listen to an individual's disappointments, be sure to focus on understanding who set the expectation and why that individual had reason to believe the expectation would be realized. Keep in mind that embedded in feelings of disappointment are essential ingredients of an individual's self-concept. And just as we counseled before, be sure to ask for a concrete illustration.

In the daily course of work events, listening to someone speak candidly about one or more personal disappointments is more than just a window into the mind-set that person is using. It is also a staging activity for you to exert influence and offer assistance. But now a word of caution. When you get to this point and the other person decides to level with you, you'll find that your relationship is on the line as never before.

The "maker" or "breaker" will be whether your discussion of disappointing results is referenced in terms of *that person's* frustrations, and what he or she finds important, or in the context of your frustrations regarding how that individual is operating and failing to produce what the company needs. Maintaining a relationship in which you are seen as out for the other person's well-being depends on your ability to frame your response and advice in the context of what that person wants to accomplish most. Only then can you talk about what the company needs and be heard.

5. Review

State what another person might expect to learn about you from hearing your answers to questions 1, 2, 3, and 4.

In the workshop setting, this question provides a valuable checkpoint to make sure participants are accurately tracking what the other person is telling them from the standpoint of what that person feels is most important and revealing. As people perfect their skills they'll increasingly find this to be a "vanilla" question that reveals that there was very little they missed or failed to understand. But we caution workshop participants not to get competitive by thinking, "I knew that" or "Is that all?" Even when participants think they heard much more than what the other person now covers, we urge them to listen attentively, nod their heads, and remain interested. We tell them that repeating the obvious helps an individual cement important perspectives in consciousness.

Participants are instructed to speak up when they hear their partners saying things that are at variance with what they thought they heard previously. We suggest saying something nonconfrontational and tactful such as, "I missed hearing you say ___(fill in)___ " and then we urge them to remain silent, listening to the other person's comments without further questions.

Outside a workshop setting, this can be a strange question to ask, but raising it may be a good idea anyway. That is, after you've spent some time probing to understand how another person distinctively sees the world, it's useful for you to pause to ask what impressions that person thinks you are drawing. You might merely say, "I sure hope I'm getting an accurate picture of what's important to you and your concerns. Are you feeling OK about what you are telling me? Is there anything you fear I may not be getting straight?" When the other person starts responding, don't interrupt and don't set him or her straight on the details. Take notes. If, after you have heard the other person out, you still feel the need to come back to specific points, you can always do so. Once again, your main objective is to listen for mind-set sensitivities and priorities.

6. Organizational needs

Currently, what does your organization *actually* need most from you and your job? To what extent are you able to provide it? How does providing this match with your personal needs for meaning? How so?

This question invites an individual to reflect on his or her alignment, especially from the standpoint of deciding whether the organization receives that which it needs from someone in that person's role and position. Asking what the organization needs provides an opportunity for the individual to reflect on how he or she juggles needs for personal-effectiveness and meaning with what he or she perceives are the organization's priorities.

This question provides an opportunity for participants to think about the degree to which another person feels like a "square peg" in an organization slot that's made for "round" people and the extent to which this individual is willing to shave off his or her "sharp corners" to better fit in, and the associated costs. Are major adjustments involved? What are the obstacles to this person's correcting his or her misfit? And as always, we recommend that you ask for examples.

This question trades on the fact that, by its very nature, life in an organization always entails compromise. But precisely what's involved in any trade-off, and whether the individual sees him- or herself getting good value in exchange for what is being sacrificed, won't be visible until you accurately comprehend the personal stakes entailed. And of course the only way to comprehend what the individual has at stake is to inquire.

Outside the workshop setting, this question strikes at a very basic issue: how that individual balances personal needs with organizational responsibilities. Before attempting to influence and give advice, you want to hear what the individual sees as the variables that are key in an effective matchup. You want to listen carefully for disparities. Until you have an accurate picture of what the individual thinks, your "friendly" attempts to exert influence and give advice are likely to be seen as "aggressive" attempts to control.

7. *Image*

At work, how do you want to be seen? What image do you want to project? Are you aware of discrepancies between the image you want to project and how others actually see you? What are they? What are the chances that projecting your preferred image will be seen and valued by the people with whom you work, and that you'll be rewarded in your organization for possessing it? What needs to be accomplished for you to achieve that image?

At work, everyone wants to be seen as valuable. People want to be seen fulfilling an essential organizational role and performing it competently with their unique brand of competence respected as value added. Nevertheless, there are always disparities between the image an individual wants to project and how he or she is actually seen. How an individual sees and feels about these disparities is critical to discerning his or her strategies for reconciling gaps.

Taken together, the answers received to this question and the preceding one, on what the organization needs, will shape participants' opinions about the level of appreciation another individual receives from his or her current company role and whether it represents good value when reflected against what is being traded off. Sometimes participants will conclude that an individual is giving up too much and would be happier in a different role, a different job, or even in a different company.

When it appears that this individual is not getting sufficient value for what he or she is giving up, we instruct, "Search for missing factors. That person hasn't quit. Take his or her staying as a clue that there is more than meets your eye. Even if it's 'irrational,' see if you can identify the irrationality and its basis." Participants are told that it's OK to ask follow-up questions aimed at gleaning deeper-level understanding. We suggest lines like, "I hear you portraying your job as one that requires excessive compromise without offsetting advantages. Perhaps you are getting some benefits that you haven't yet mentioned." Then participants are advised to stop and listen to what they get in response. They are cautioned that they have just issued a very serious challenge; it's the work equivalent of "Why do you stay with your spouse anyway?" Our advice is to ask this question in

a way that communicates that there must be more than meets the
eye, and that, to have a whole picture, they need to know what that
more might be.

At this point most participants are silently at work formulating
hypotheses about what has caused another individual to stick with a
situation that is being portrayed as so unsatisfactory. They are urged
to keep these private until they have finished their research. Workshop leaders repeat, the time to share impressions is after the entire
investigation is completed.

At work, someone's image is both stereotype and opportunity.
It determines how others represent that individual, and perceive the
usefulness of his or her contributions, and the expectations they hold
for performance. Thus, when you inquire how an individual sees his
or her organizational image, you are asking how that individual thinks
he or she comes across to others. This should account for some of
the spin an individual puts on his or her actions. You'll find many
individuals who put a great deal of energy into changing their image,
believing that doing so is essential to staging events for their successful participation in them.

8. Work rewards

**At work, what do you get that you want, and how do you
ensure that you receive it? What do you get that you don't
want, and what needs to happen for you to be more successful avoiding it? What do you *not* get that you *do* want and
what needs to happen for you to get it?**

By the time participants get to question 8, they may be sensing re-
dundancy, as if they are nearing the point of diminishing returns.
Nevertheless, in a workshop setting, the time it takes to listen to
the answers for all sixteen questions is about two hours, give or
take a half hour. Moreover, in a workshop setting, participants are
developing and practicing mind-set research skills, and little is lost
by allowing them to practice longer than a more time-efficient inquiry
might take.

The "Work Rewards" question continues the inquiry into trade-
offs and compromises established by the preceding two questions,
even for people who feel on relatively solid terms with themselves
and their jobs. The twist here is the focus on how an individual sees
others participating or blocking his or her attempts to be effective.
Listening to that person's answers may trigger additional insight
about what this other person is willing or not willing to put up with.

In a non-workshop advice-giving situation, this question is a friendly way to ask an individual how he or she is doing, and specifically what that person would like to see going better. It's a particularly good way of approaching someone who might see him- or herself needing more hierarchical power to be effective or in comprehending that person's ideas about the roles others can play in bringing about a more desirable state of affairs.

9. Role models

List the people you use as role models. For each one, state what qualities and/or skills you seek to emulate. Next name the people who have been antimodels for you, and their qualities or ways of operating that have provided you with reasons to operate differently.

People pride themselves on being individuals with unique resources and capabilities and in being the builders of their own style. Nevertheless, people require models. That is, the architectural principles that underlie their self-constructions are selectively copied from characteristics of other people, adapted to their own value systems, abilities, and life situations. And, in the main, people are conscious of what they have identified as "borrowable," and from whom.

Another person's list of role models and admired qualities offers a means of understanding specifically what that person is trying to express in the conduct of his or her personal and organizational activities. At root, you get their value system. Likewise, identifying antimodels opens an additional window for viewing someone's value system. While antimodels provide a picture of what the individual is diligently trying not to become, oftentimes the reason a specific antimodel comes to mind is because, at some level, the person suspects that he or she is predisposed that way too. Accordingly, an individual's answer often turns out to be the life equivalent of saying, *"Officer, I don't think I was going too fast and, by the way, there's no need to look in the trunk."* For this reason, everyone's parents are basic departure points for understanding both models and antimodels, along with others whom you would never suspect, unless you ask this question.

There's not much more that needs to be said about models other than to state that this question is one of the most direct ways of understanding which qualities an individual seeks to emulate and how he or she attempts to impact others. Outside a workshop setting you may have limited access to an individual and only be able to pose one or two questions. For instance you might be at a "question and answer" session for your CEO, or find yourself next to an important person at a reception, a meal, or on a plane. Asking that person about role models can evoke in-depth insight into that person's character while remaining situationally appropriate.

10. World view

What do you believe is special and distinctive about how you see the world and interact with others? Give an example of how you view events distinctively. How does holding this world view help you capitalize on your strengths and distinctive resources?

This question invites a person to state what's distinctive about his or her world view and resulting modes of operating. It's aimed at revealing an individual's existential thumbprint. No one thinks of him- or herself as the standard company employee, which is ironic given how often everyone sees others that way. Thus this question is based on the premise that no one sees him- or herself as the "standard thinker and performer," and given this, what sets this person apart? The individual knows; he or she is confronted with uniqueness issues every day. Your job here is to stage the context for that person to tell you directly.

We tell workshop participants that this innocuous-appearing question can inform them about several dimensions of an individual's organizational experience: how well he or she fits in; how the person sees working at the company as either an opportunity or detriment to career progress; what are her longer term aspirations; and, by inference, the categories that person uses in factionalizing others in the company and stereotypes of the people in those factions.

When raising this question in a natural work setting, you need to remember that for most people, today's job is the next step to getting where they want to be tomorrow, and tomorrow's position is merely another step on a longer road. Asking "what's distinctive?" is an easy way to learn where the individual is heading and to see the spin and nuances he or she feels compelled to include in actions that you may have previously found confusing.

11. Background and personal considerations

Tell something about your early upbringing and growing up that continues to play a strong role in determining how you function at work and what you seek.

Background information provides a valuable context for appreciating the meaning behind someone's public behavior. Most people have one or more stories to tell about their past and how they acquired patterns of thinking and behaving. Often these stories relate to trauma and survival. In any event, it's difficult to accept individuals' aberrant reactions until you hear their "stories." After you hear them, you will read much more than "aberrant" into their response, you will also see what is positive and compensatory in how they cope.

In everyday settings, your attempts to influence and give advice benefit enormously from knowing an individual's "story." After you know the real meanings an individual attributes to certain events, then, whether or not what they are doing is bothersome to you, you will come to accept what you are dealing with as an indisputable given. You may not like it, but your actions will automatically change from fighting the other person to making practical adaptations in your dealings with that individual.

For example, an executive once told us, "To appreciate Nancy, and her apparent shyness and initial indifference to teamwork, you need to understand what she went through as a child, communicating for her deaf parents. It's not that she isn't open or that she doesn't trust people; it's that she has seen people be thoughtless and cruel and learned the importance of taking a moment to size up a situation before taking assertive action. She is extremely bright and is often aware of much more than meets the average person's eye. After she works with you a bit, she's an entirely different person. You just have to give her some time to warm to the situation. On the other hand, you should have seen her five years ago. Trust me when I say she's come a long, long way."

Knowing critical background details allows you to accept imperfections and to spend your primary emotional energy making, and helping others to make, constructive adaptations to them. When trying to influence people, for instance, like Nancy, you can say, "This meeting is one of those situations in which you need to push yourself to be more outgoing. Keep an eye on me. When in doubt, try to follow my lead." While Nancy will be able to use your instruction to override her internal program, that program will probably continue to operate—perhaps with less force—when she faces the next new situation.

12. *Where are you headed?*

What's ahead for you? Where are you heading personally, professionally, and familially? What does your vision of "tomorrow" entail? Be specific in describing your objectives. Do you need to make a change to attain them? If so, what changes will you need to make? In short, what do you need to start doing and to stop doing in order to realize your long-term objectives and life goals?

Two people in the same job are seldom heading for the same place. And even when they are, the next steps they take and the route each has in mind will no doubt be different. Only after workshop participants know where an individual intends to go can they appreciate the distinctive spin that person gives to events. Thus the clearer participants are about where their partners are heading and how they expect to get there, the more context they have for comprehending the rationale for an action.

Occasionally we encounter people who can't quite line up today's activities with where they say they are headed. This results from financial and style of life needs that appear beyond reach when doing what they would like to be doing most. This is that person's version of the starving-artist-as-waiter syndrome. Sometimes it's shortsightedness developed by background conditioning that blinds individuals to finding alternative ways to pursue their desires within today's organizational assignment. Sometimes it's because the person just can't quite get his or her head together and is operating at odds with his or her inner needs. Sometimes it's a problem in prioritizing and a need to place one foot in front of the other to take one step forward at a time. However viewed, in the workshop we advise participants to continue exercising restraint and to withhold their advice about what they see as impractical and unrealistic until they've finished asking the remaining questions.

Whether it's inside the workshop or outside in a work setting, we know of no topic more likely to evoke the inclination to counsel than an individual telling you where he or she is headed and how he or she plans to get there. Of course the reason is that you have the outsider's perspective and can readily see alternatives that escaped the insider's notice. People need help in breaking out of the logic that constrains them from seeing the same alternatives that appear clear to you. In any event, we advise caution in giving advice prior to understanding what blocks the individual from coming up with that same logical-enough advice on his or her own.

13. *After you're gone*

How do you want to be remembered by the people with whom you work most closely? How do you want to be re-

membered by your immediate family and your intimate
friends? What unifying inscription would you like to have
on your tombstone?

By the time workshop participants reach this question they usually
have a good idea about what the other individual's response will be.
Again we suggest resisting the temptation to demonstrate their
mind-set "sensitivity" by saying what they think, just to beat the
other person to the punch. Once again, we advise them merely to
listen—there's a fair chance they'll be surprised. Often something
fresh emerges that no one would have reason to expect.

Separating this question into work and personal life invites the
disclosing individual to distinguish between the two. Surprisingly,
some people don't make a distinction. What constitutes the hallmark
of their professional life overlaps the personal. If you don't hear the
differences, mention this fact and see whether some gentle prodding
can prompt the other person to distinguish between them.

Knowing what someone wants to achieve in his or her personal
life is essential to seeing the whole person. Instinctively, this is why
people ask one another about after-work and family activities. Most
of the time, in everyday settings, people get very little back other
than small talk and filler. People can ask 2,000 questions and still not
discover what they need to know in the way of themes and personal
life objectives.

Outside the workshop you can't just ask someone what they
want written on their tombstone, but you might find your way to
learning about someone's life motive once they know you are interested in them. What often works for us is a technique that deviates
90 degrees from what we just advised workshop participants. (It's
not 180 degrees; that would be talking about your own answer to the
same question.) It's to frame your tentative answer to the other person's life-motive question based on the impressions you've received.
Essentially you say, "I'm getting the impression that what's really important to you is (fill in the blank) . Then listen. You'll find that people are almost always willing to set you straight, especially when your
initial formulation is sensitively stated and in the ballpark of accuracy.

14. *What's left out?*

Name a personal quality or strength that frequently is omitted or compromised in your present assignment. Provide an
example of where this omission occurs.

By the time this question in broached, the other person has, no
doubt, become quite introspective. With such an intense inner focus,

he or she may be able to identify a personal quality that typically goes unexpressed at work that he or she especially values. Articulating this personal attribute, particularly with a concrete example, may reveal a problem that person has in realizing a more rewarding work alignment.

In a natural setting, this question is one that's easily raised, for it signals a belief in the other person's potential. And learning the answer before offering advice may present you some distinctive opportunities for exerting positive influence. What's more, finding out about a situation where a strength and "company resource" was not used may provide you with a bridge to comment on image and participation style.

15. Lessons learned

What was the last significant lesson you learned that changed the way you operate at work and/or how you relate with others? Why did it take as long as it did for you to learn? What's the next life or work lesson that you need to learn and internalize well enough to actually change and transform your actions? Explain why this has been a difficult lesson for you to get straight.

The answers you get to these questions can be extremely revealing. Your relationship will play a big role in determining the other person's candor. This is why, in the workshop setting, we suggest that participants wait almost to the end to ask them. We're counting on the fact that an intensive period of sensitive listening has created rapport and their partner's desire to put "the rest" out on the table for reaction and suggestions.

Each of the "Lessons learned" questions is more than just self-revealing; they are self-critiques. Even the first question, which asks for a lesson that has been learned, is a sugar-coated request for self-critique, since it implies that an individual spent months and years living with problems without gleaning critical insights from his or her experience with them. The sequence progresses to the person's current inability to accomplish that which he or she self-admittedly needs to do differently.

In the workshop, participants are reminded that their assignment is still to listen and empathize and not yet to engage in problem-solving or prescriptive advice. Caution is indicated because listening to lessons-learned-but-not-always-practiced naturally provokes a desire to tell the other person what he or she *now* needs to know. On the other hand, because of all the information and perspective received to this point, the situation is ripe for participants to relate to the mind-set in which the other person actually reasons. If it turns out at this point that a participant can't hold his or her advice back much longer, we recommend that person ask one more question before starting in.

The question we suggest is one that we think is important for any situation in which you want to exert helpful influence and give advice. It's a technique that also builds trust. Prior to jumping in with a specific piece of advice, ask the person you are about to help, "Tell me why you haven't _____ (fill in with the action you will be prescribing)_____." Given this information, you are set to begin.

16. Orienting others

What advice would you give someone you were hiring to be your assistant about how to appreciate you, how to interact with you, and how to get your attention when you are becoming a problem?

This final question relates to the Vickers quote mentioned in Chapter 3. Recall that it states: "A trap is a trap only for the creature that cannot solve the problems that it sets. . . . The nature of the trap is a function of the nature of the trapped. To describe either is to imply the other." Thus this question invites disclosure of holistic and candid self-reflection. It invites a person to reflect on how his or her mind-set and alignment strategy are likely to affect and create problems for others. And by inquiring about the type of individual who is likely to do well, you are taking another subtle step in urging your advice recipient toward internalization of the new, Artifact of Mind–inspired, mentality.

Conclusion

When accessing alignment information it's crucial to keep in mind that the music is more important than the words. All face-to-face encounters are flavored with speech inflections, emotions, body language, and countless intangibles that influence the meanings you assign to the concepts and words. Then the total gestalt is even more important. There's no way you'd relate the same way to written accounts of the same information. This is why we often say that alignments must be experienced to truly be known. In fact, workshop participants frequently feel emotional bonds acquired in one or two days of confiding in one another that transcend what they have established over years with "close" friends. Likewise for people who learn enough about one another's mind-sets in real-life work settings; it's commonplace for them to bond.

Regardless of the setting, the object of conducting mind-set research is for you to learn enough about the other person's alignment strategy to understand the meanings behind the actions you observe and the thoughts you hear expressed. In your company, there will be many times when you feel that you have accumulated, in bits and pieces, all the knowledge you need for understanding what an individual is going through, yet that person resists giving your advice real consideration. Don't be discouraged, this is your signal that there is something else you need to learn. And if you listen carefully to "the resistance," you'll receive some clues about where to look in learning it.

When you are out to understand an individual and the specific variables and issues that determine his or her alignment, inevitably there will be times when some facet of the other person's competency equation becomes so vivid that you are 100 percent certain that you know enough to give good advice—yet that person resists. Then you persist, knowing you are correct and the resistance is mere defensiveness. We frequently feel this way and persist, hoping that our energy and goodwill can squeak through whatever crevice of openness remains. And some of the time we succeed. But there is even a better tactic to use than pitting goodwill head-to-head against resistance. The best approach to use is giving the advice-recipient the control. Just what's entailed in relinquishing control is the subject of the next chapter.

Note

1. See C. R. Rogers and F. J. Roethlisberger, "Barriers and Gateways to Communication," *Harvard Business Review, 30*(4), 1952.

8

Gaining Control by Relinquishing It

The "new mentality" theme put forth in this book can be expressed rather simply: get inside the other person's mind-set prior to deciding on the influence you want to exert and precisely how to exert it. But what happens when the mind-set in which the other person is viewing events and reasoning is the problem? Certainly this is going to be the case as an increasing number of managers attempt to operate new models using their former mentalities. More and more you are going to see managerial styles that, at critical moments, resist and even sabotage the intended direction of a new model. You'll see people involved in a self-defeating process of feeling out of control and trying to regain their grip on situations where the only possible way to get control is to relinquish it.

Getting the new models to work will present you with a twofold challenge. You'll need to operate in the new mentality yourself and you'll need to assist others, particularly those in key managerial positions, to operate that way as well. How are you going to proceed? Using the former mentality, getting someone to operate differently is relatively straightforward. You issue directives, guide and counsel, hold training sessions, and reassign and fire the people who repeatedly and blatantly do it wrong on the presumption that you can hire replacements who are going to do it right.

Obviously, this way of proceeding presents some problems. The deeper message emanating from how you actually operate cancels out the message you intend to send. You can't expect "educational" tactics aimed at getting an individual to conform to the new "program" to lead that person to become increasingly respectful of what is distinct in someone else's nature. Herein lies the play within the play. When you are out to change someone's orientation, to be more mind-set sensitive, you've got to take a mind-set management approach. You've got to engage distinct elements of that person's makeup and you've got to help that individual overcome personal attachments to orientations that are obstacles to the relinquishing of control. You've got to relate to the fact that each person is internally relating to an alignment that represents his or her best personal strategy for performing with competence in situations where others reason and see things differently.

Advising people with personal orientation problems is the theme pursued in this chapter as well as throughout the remainder of this book. Keep in mind that each individual has something distinctive to reason through and that each situation faced poses dilemmas that his or her existing orientation and mind-set reasoning automatically engage and handle. Thus something distinctive needs to be negotiated in getting any individual to change orientations, especially in adopting a more mind-set–sensitive, noncontrolling approach.

Now we'd like to tell you a story that portrays how we went about advising a top-level manager whose personal orientation and overdone expression of the former mentality bothered almost every person reporting to him. It's interesting to note how relatively little it took to help him make the transition from an overbearing and brutishly overcontrolling orientation to one that iteratively became exemplary in demonstrating mind-set sensitivity. In paradigmatic terms, this example illustrates what any manager who wants to make the transition to the new mentality has to face and reconcile in the context of his or her own organizational activities. This issue was readily framed and successfully negotiated using Artifact of Mind reasoning.

Case in point

A company president we had known for some time called asking us to fly to the company's Dallas office to "fix" the division head in charge. He told us, "The people reporting to Barry are intimidated, and turnover is increasingly high. At first I bought Barry's explanations that the personnel problems were due to a booming marketplace where our company's (progressive) total quality program requires a level of excellence that people working in our industry don't face when working elsewhere. He had me convinced that currently

Dallas is a unique job market where technical people who resign at five this evening can begin another job at eight tomorrow morning. Barry told me that the same is true for most of our suppliers. He contended that they can sell as much as they make, and when we give them a hard time by demanding error-free quality, can readily take their components back and immediately sell them down the street. But now our long-time employees are phoning in with complaints and I can see that much more is involved. The problem is that people are intimidated by Barry and increasingly are feeling compelled to hide their mistakes."

Our response to such a request is almost always the same. We want to know what the boss has done to fix his problems and why he's calling now. In response to these questions, the president said, "Things are deteriorating to the point that last month Barry decided to take his team off-site for a 'bonding' retreat. The plan was to have a little conversation and mostly just golf. After I received the third call from his staff, I invited myself along. Barry is always a pussycat when I ask him reasonably and while he was dying to say 'No,' he had to answer in the affirmative. After golf we held informal strategic discussions, and on the second afternoon the people tried to tell Barry what they really thought. But when Barry made the mistake of getting red in the face and raising his voice, you could watch them circle their wagons as the conversation closed down.

"Afterwards I told Barry that there were problems with his management style. I described them as his constantly wanting to tell people exactly what to do. I said 'Barry, it's as if you want each person to spend the first year allowing you to prescribe their response to each situation. Then, in the second year, you want the person to consult the book of responses they accumulated the previous year, turning to the page that describes the situation they now face for what you previously told them to do.' "

We called Barry to tell him about our assignment. He said the president had told him we were coming and asked him not to tell anyone else out of concern that some people might get the impression that Barry didn't want them leveling with us. Barry said that he was glad we were coming, indicating that we could help him get out from under a bum rap. He said, "Finally my boss is going to get a picture of the truth." We said, "That's not exactly what we have in mind; we're not coming to report on you, we're coming to see if we can help. We'll call him to straighten out his mistaken expectation."

We told Barry, "We're coming as your management-effectiveness advisers. Our goal is to help you be your best. How can you take us into your confidence if we're acting as management spies?" We told him that for us to be of real assistance, he needed to feel he could level with us and not be burned by the results. We told him, "Any report the president receives will be made by you. However, we would like to find a date when he can be present for a late afternoon meeting on our second day, so that we can be on hand to help if you need us."

The president faxed us a list of people with whom he thought we should speak. Our plan was to spend the better part of the morning talking with Barry and then to have three or four interviews that afternoon, some more the next morning, a break to organize our thoughts, then a two- to three-hour recap consultation with Barry and then a brief sit-in with Barry as he reported to his boss.

We began our consultation by showing Barry the list of people the president had given us. We asked him what he thought of our plan for approaching them. We were going to say, "We're here as management coaches to help Barry be even more effective than he already is. Your job is to tell us what we need to know to help us coach him. While we plan to use what we learn from speaking with you, we will take pains to make sure that what we share with Barry is not traceable back to you." In response, Barry said that was fine but urged that we change our list to include some of the new people whose perceptions weren't colored by the reputation he had acquired when he held the marketing job. Our response was, "Help yourself, make our list a 'valid' one."

As we think back on years of consultations, we can't remember one that turned out to be more efficient. From the beginning Barry was open and candid, and while every human being is defensive, we can't conceive of anyone being less defensive, particularly in the face of the challenges we progressively levied at him. His openness and robust style allowed us to be straightforward and time efficient. There were even a couple of points where we raised our voices for emphasis and camaraderie.

We began by asking Barry for his impressions on why the president had called us to help him. Barry replied, "I'm known as tough and also fair. While I can get worked up, no one has anything to fear. Since taking over two and a half years ago I've not fired a single person." Then he added, "However, several who weren't up to our standards had enough sense to quit." We asked, "Which of your strengths is making you appear tough?" Barry replied, "It's my follow-up system that forces people to keep their commitments. People don't want to be held accountable." In our minds, this was a major clue. We found ourselves listening very carefully, for we sensed we were on the verge of viewing Barry's mind-set.

Moving on we asked, "What's your follow-up system?" Barry

responded, "I write everything down. I carry a 'To Do' list, and my calendar is full of actions to check up on. For instance, I'm often in a position of asking one of our managers or one of our many suppliers 'When can we have this?' with the 'this' being the action or item that we just discussed. When that person says Friday, I write that commitment down. Then Friday I find out whether it's been done. If it hasn't, I don't say anything. On Monday I check again, still not saying anything. Then I check on Tuesday. If it's not yet done, I continue to keep quiet, but if it's not done by Wednesday, I start getting upset."

For us the word "upset" was a bell-ringer, for we were thinking about what the president had told us about the wagon-circling at the off-site team-building event. We asked, "What do you mean by 'upset'?" Barry responded, "It doesn't upset me that the other person doesn't write it down. It upsets me that he doesn't remember. I don't like it when, what is important to me hasn't been etched in that person's mind."

We commented, "Barry, knowing a little about your business, we think the concept of your checking up on people is reasonable. However, we'd bet that what's bothering people most is not your attention to commitments but your 'upset.'" Interrupting, Barry asked, "Is it bad to be emotional?" We said, "Yes, if the emotions generally are 'upset.' For you it appears that 'upset' is an angry emotion targeted at forcing people to keep their commitments. From what you've said, you've got a way of operating that consistently and repeatedly puts you in situations where people haven't performed responsibly, and you feel justified in being upset and meting out emotional punishment. To us this pattern seems self-contrived. You couldn't find a way to operate that was more tailored to putting an emotional whip in your hand. Do you think another person with a different personality would perform your role by handing out so much rope for people to hang themselves with?"

Responding, Barry said, "You know, when I get upset I don't harbor any carryover feelings. I tell the people that this is just like playing football. We go out on the field, butt heads, knock one another down, and when it's five o'clock and the game is over it's time to forget all that roughing up and to go out together to enjoy a beer." In response we asked rhetorically, "Barry, are you getting lots of cues that the other people think it's five o'clock when you do?"

Barry went to the bottom line, "OK, OK. How do you fix this?" We replied, "What do you want to fix, their reactions or your reasoning? Fixing your reasoning is probably the easiest. All it's going to require is brain surgery." Barry laughed.

To relieve his immediate pressure, we said, "The quick fix is to avoid getting yourself into situations where you get upset and begin punishing the people you are depending on to help you. For example, you might print up some carbon-copy, prescription-sized forms that more or less carry this message: 'Action Memo from Barry Mathews. As Division Manager it's my job to work through people. We're in an industry that puts us under pressure to get things done on time and to the best of our joint abilities. You and I have just agreed that you are going to help by __(indicate what you want done and the completion date)__ . Then at the bottom say, 'Thank you very much for helping us.' When you hand that person the sheet, ask him or her to review the action and the date."

We continued, "Then to get yourself a different relationship, give the duplicates to Andy (Barry's assistant) and let her do the legwork for you. She can call or drop by to inquire if what is listed has been accomplished, and if it hasn't she can say, 'Barry asked me to find out if there's anything he can do to help.' "

We figured that Barry took us literally when he followed our suggestion by asking, "If I do this, aren't the people inside the company going to think that this is the result of my distrusting them? Are they going to now think I'm keeping the book on their sins?"

We answered, "They might, unless you have a kickoff meeting to explain it to them as a group. How do you think they'd feel if you got them together and forthrightly said: 'I want to change my actions and my reputation. I don't want to be the "enforcer," I want to get into the role of helper.' Then tell them that you'd like to get into a pattern of Andy's checking with them and your pitching in when there's a delay. Explain that you are going to tear up all slips as actions are completed and that you have no desire to keep a book on their late performances. Tell them that your desire is just to get things done and, if they check the record, they can see that you were never out to fire anyone. In fact, you can tell them that you are out to change your harsh-appearing approach so that no one will even want to leave. If everyone already knows there is a problem, this shouldn't hurt your image in the least."

Then we backed up and shared our perspective on his job security. We said, "Barry, we haven't heard 'thought one' that your boss wants you fired. Right now the business is booming, and you are making a lot of money for the company. Were he to replace you, the new person would come with problems too. Then your boss would have those problems to fix and he'd be worrying about getting results that you already produce. On the other hand, keep in mind that you are in a cyclic business and there will be a point where the division is up against the wall waiting for the business environment to change.

At that point if the people issues aren't fixed, there are going to be two major areas of deficiency, without one to counteract the other. When that point comes, we don't think you'll have many reasons for feeling secure if your tactics haven't changed."

We told Barry that we thought people bring their whole selves to the job and that seeing how dysfunctional patterns at work play out in other aspects of their life is a potential source of insight in helping someone see what he needs to learn and how he needs to grow. So merely to get the lay of the land we inquired, "What's your wife like, how does she feel about the issues we've been discussing?" Barry surprised us by replying, "She's just like me, except even more driven and perfectionistic." Trying not to let him notice how quickly our jaws were dropping, we nonchalantly asked, "How do your kids like this?"

Barry said, "The kids are doing great, in fact we just came back from a conference with our eight-year-old's teacher, who told us that Ty is an excellent student who is always out to be the first to finish while at the same time working extremely hard to get every answer correct." We asked, "What did your wife think about that?" Barry responded, "We haven't had time to talk about it, but I assume she thinks the same as I do. Ty is a terrific kid at home for that matter too. He's a total perfectionist. At eight years old he keeps his room cleaner than we keep our house. Sometimes he won't let other kids in to play there because he doesn't want them messing things up."

Talk about your blind spots; this bright guy Barry apparently had no idea what he was saying to us about Ty. On the other hand, we thought Ty might be the leverage point. So we asked him, "Are you sure you got the real message the teacher was trying to communicate to you? Are you sure she was saying that this behavior is a positive and not a negative?" Barry looked astonished. We suggested, "It's time for us to get going on our interviews. While you're thinking about it, why don't you give her a call? Tell her that you were reflecting on what she told you and that you wanted to be sure you had her message about Ty straight."

With the exception of the production manager, we found each of the people we interviewed candidly critical from the start. The production manager's problems were twofold. He had been mentored by Barry and seemed to be following Barry's "book." His difficulty in telling us steps that Barry could take "to be even more effective than he already is" resulted from his inability to see the limitations of his own style due to having Barry on a pedestal as the epitome of results and competence. And, of course, he was taking pains not to be disloyal. He wanted to disabuse us of any possibility that he even knew the problems and complaints of the suppliers with whom he dealt or the complaints of his organizational peers.

From the others we accumulated an almost endless list of the difficulties created by Barry's "sins." From them we relearned a valuable Artifact of Mind lesson. People who are made to feel incompetent and undervalued will see negatives leap out of every action taken by the person they see assailing them and their competence. While they are able to present significant and compelling personal experiences that document what they allege, ultimately the composite picture is a caricature, not a photograph, of the imperfections of the person they portray. We've been here many times before. And, until we caught on, we had a tendency to relate literally to their recitation of the facts as if those facts constituted sufficient documentation for drawing the only conclusion possible. In the present instance, the people who were harmed had total documentation for self-justifiably concluding what in the end Barry would need to reverse.

The first person with whom we spoke seemed to have it correct when she said, "Everybody is going to tell you the same thing. With Barry there's always a lot of initial blaming and then it's 'management by intimidation.' " As we went through our list, we heard one story after another about Barry's insecurity, his distrust of people, and how, in public settings, he humiliates people by shouting at them for lack of on-time deliverance of that for which Barry had good reason to think they had "committed." We heard an inside joke about people looking out the window as he exited his car betting on whether the "Good Barry" or "Bad Barry" was coming into work today. We heard allegations about how Barry treats women differently from men, and how his assistant Andy goes unscathed because Barry is sedated by her attractiveness. People spoke about his parsimonious use of praise, saying "Barry is a student of the 'I don't think you should have to thank people for doing what they are paid to do' school of management." There were even allegations that Barry enjoys seeing people squirm. And, very importantly, rightly or wrongly people attributed all management-level turnover to Barry's emotionally aggressive, demoralizing management style.

When we asked people "What do you need to do to make your operations function more effectively?" we heard many wonderful-sounding ideas that were not implemented because people just couldn't find the time to discuss implementation with Barry. When we asked people what they wanted most from Barry, they answered "respect." When we asked one woman if she had told Barry this, she answered, "He asked us at the retreat and no one said a thing.

How are you going to tell him in front of his boss, 'Gosh darn Barry, you gotta stop screaming at us.' "

It's gotten to the point that whenever we hear about an intimidating or abusive manager we always suspect childhood trauma. Then we remembered a couple of facts that stood out the only other time we had spoken with Barry. That was two years earlier, shortly after he had been promoted from marketing executive to division manager and vice president. At that time we had been advising the president on his management style and Barry was among the subordinates we were interviewing. We remember Barry bragging about being a "people person" and "tough enough" to take what the president dished out, whatever level of performance and results he required, no matter how ambitious the financial goals. In explaining his moral fiber, Barry cited a father who was the high-standards principal of the school he attended, a mother who worked, and an older brother who beat him up each day when, he said, "I was dumb enough to show up at home after school prior to my parents' getting there." At the time it struck us as odd that Barry couldn't get his parents to protect him.

We were impressed with the quality and dedication of the people with whom we spoke although, for obvious reasons, we found them a relatively underpotentiated group. They were excellent observers who were providing us "the book" to use on Barry. If our purpose was to intimidate, we now had ample data to use on him. But you don't cure an intimidator with intimidation. What's more, intimidation is never the way to get people to lower their guard in reexamining mind-sets for the roots of their ineffective behavior. And, as we said earlier, while we believed everything that the people said and felt, we knew that beneath the surface another dynamic was working. We feared that hammering Barry with the experiences people were telling us about would merely evoke a resolve to exercise more self-discipline. We thought the real opportunity lay in influencing how Barry reasoned.

We began our second conversation by asking Barry if he had been able to talk with Ty's teacher, and what his wife had to say about their conference. He told us, "I didn't have to call his teacher, I knew you were right. Of course there's something unhealthy about his need to stay on the good side of his mother and myself." We asked Barry what lessons Ty's situation had for how he operates at work and he replied, "I know I've got to let people make their own mistakes and learn from them. But in the management culture of this company there is no room for mistakes. My boss (the president) wants us to be in the top five in all industry categories and starts micromanaging when we drop to a six. With this attitude you can't allow people to grow in their positions by making mistakes." We countered, "There is a way to let people grow in their positions without making mistakes; it's just that you don't know it."

Extrapolating from the Artifact of Mind insight, we explained the three mind-set steps to problem solving: (1) sizing up the situation; (2) framing the problem; and (3) solving the problem. We told Barry that we thought other people saw him performing only steps 1 and 3, and then unilaterally without consulting them. We said, "Their not being involved in steps 1 and 3 and their not even seeing the second, costs you tremendously. When people complain that you don't respect them, the bottom line is that they don't experience you having a relationship with them. When you jump from how you see a situation to your solution you leave out the discussions that are most important to them. You put them at a total problem-solving disadvantage. Do you see why?"

Barry did not immediately engage our line of reasoning. Instead he got very emotional. Red in the face, raising his voice, he almost shouted: "Let me tell you something! When I came back from a week and a half's vacation Andy came in and said she was glad I was back because no one seems to be able to make a decision without me." Climbing into the ring and going toe-to-toe with Barry, we also used raised voices, and deliberately chose an expression that people had told us was "vintage Barry." We said, "That's the dumbest thing we ever heard of!" and then cracked a wry smile, which caused Barry to break up laughing. He said, "I agree, these wimps. . . ." We interrupted, "No Barry, you are the 'wimp!' You don't get it! It's not their behavior that we're referencing, it's yours. You are entirely missing the connection between your treatment of people and their response." Then we smiled supportively. Now that we had his attention, we could begin to explain.

We explained that between sizing up a situation and working on the solution resides the critical "problem-framing" step. We explained that problem solutions make sense only in terms of the problems that they are formulated to address. We gave a short Artifact of Mind explanation emphasizing that people frame problems according to their distinctive competencies. We explained that Barry has a highly developed and distinctive style of almost instantaneously moving from his experience of a situation to a solution and that this style negates the possibility of others framing situations for their competent performance in them. We told him, "This is why you face so many situations in which people break their commitments. They aren't breaking *their* commitments, they are breaking commitments that *you* have made for them."

Continuing, we said, "This is where you lose relationships. Your style puts people in the position of working on solutions to problems that they would never frame and package for solution the way you have. Best case, their actions can only follow your script. Worse case, they are floundering on a course that doesn't follow from their way of reasoning and seeing the situation, nor does it allow them to utilize their distinctive competencies."

Taking pains to be equal to the lesson we were trying to promote, we asked Barry whether our problem framing was a clarification. He indicated that he thought it was, but that it made him wonder why he has been doing it so differently and whether we thought he was totally ineffective. These were precisely the questions we were waiting for him to raise.

We said that we thought his style of team problem solving was "totally off," and that we could see good reasons for how it came about. We told him, "We were moved the first time we met you when you spoke about your family. Even though you didn't seem to realize it, we thought you were an abused child." In response to his stunned look we said, "You were abused by your brother's fists, and you were abused by your parents' failure to protect you. Certainly you must have complained to them, yet apparently they still left you to your own devices. Is it possible that this is when you learned to leap quickly from your perceptions of a situation to an action?" He replied emotionally, "Maybe. Probably. Yes!" Then we listened as he reflected on his childhood experiences of being told to come directly home after school and having his protestations ignored. For about ten minutes our job was to quietly listen and empathetically nod.

The intensity was tremendous and made us realize why God had created the need to go to the john. When we returned, Barry brought us back to the topic by asking, "You said before there is a way to let people learn without making mistakes." We thought, "Is this guy ever good! With clients like this, even Wayne and Garth could be great consultants."

We told him, "There's a fabulous technology for letting people solve problems without making mistakes. It simply entails asking them how they see the situation, what they see as the problem, and how they are inclined to solve it. It's a combination of 'problem posing' and 'active listening.' You simply ask people what they see, what they know, and what they are inclined to do. Listen carefully to be sure you understand why they frame the problem the way they do and what personal skills and competencies they are able to mobilize by seeing it that way. Be sure you understand what they gain from framing the problem that way. Then, if you still think it's necessary, tell them precisely how you see things differently. But keep in mind that you've got an iceberg here. Beneath the surface are personal competency issues that they don't think they can safely reveal. These issues involve personal life considerations, insecurities, you name it. When their ideas of how to proceed don't seem to make any sense, then you may need to get to what is blocking the obvious. But normally it's enough to listen and then to share your impressions."

We were on a roll, Barry was attentive, so we continued. "In sharing your impressions, keep in mind that you are working in a distinctive mind-set. Your way of being effective is tailored to maximize your resources, your work agendas, and your style of life issues. Their ways of doing things are tailored to theirs. What you and the people working for you have in common is your abiding concerns for the effectiveness of the operation. If, through your inquiry, you show respect for the other person's way of proceeding, you will build the positive and robust relationships you've been seeking. If at times you emotionally 'lose it,' people will understand if they experience your problem-framing inquiries as actions aimed at promoting their personal competency and effectiveness." We added, "Don't forget, **managing is 'staging the conditions for others to be effective.'** "

Our discussion lasted another hour, with Barry exploring the implications for changing his actions based on his new insights and reasoning. Barry clearly saw the connection between negotiating problem frames and building relationships and we were delighted. We also covered "heat of battle" situations in which one doesn't have the time to interact and reach agreement on the problem statement. We told Barry that when he needs people to click their heels and just do it his way, he can get there quickly by saying what he's up to, if he is willing to accept the responsibility for requiring people to act in ways that are not tailored to their strengths by offering some level of support and indemnification.

We were highly conscious of trying to conduct our consultation and advice-giving by engaging in "mind-set" management. To do so meant getting on track with Barry's reasoning before attempting to move it along. On track, we didn't need to draw attention to the specifics people told us. While we referenced some categories of situations such as our beliefs that people aren't leveling with him, we never needed to say a word about a specific situation.

There was nothing noteworthy about the concluding interaction with Barry's boss other than the president's utter amazement. Barry straightforwardly told the boss what he had learned, including a good deal about the personal variables that underlay his former management style and participation. Barry was sufficiently candid that we were instantly released from our vows of confidentiality. There were no secrets left for us to divulge. Of course the president was appreciative; he later claimed that he had witnessed "mental alchemy."

We saw follow-up as an essential dimension of this consultation. The Artifact of Mind insight instructs that Barry's seeing and doing things differently is insufficient for the people interacting with him to recognize that they are in a new situation. With their old filters they are inclined to see him acting the old way even when he is reasoning and acting quite differently. Needed are transition events. Especially after what they'd been through, the people working with Barry required a new road map and sufficient catharsis to free up the motivation to see him differently. Pent-up feelings can pollute an updating of expectations to the point where people can't act on what they have been told and think they now know.

We proposed two types of transition event. The first would be a group session in which Barry announced his insights more or less as we had proposed when discussing the prescription pad idea. Second would be follow-up, one-on-one conversations with each of the people who attended the group meeting. The plan for follow-up discussions would be announced at the group meeting so that individuals who wanted to blow off steam wouldn't be placed in a situation where they inadvertently humiliated Barry as he used to humiliate them. Both events would be staged to provide people the opportunity to experience Barry in the context of his new aspirations, to build a relationship through personal discussions, and to undergo the catharsis required to see Barry in a new light. We suggested that Barry take us along to a couple of meetings to observe and coach.

But coaching in Barry's office turned out to be an even better way of applying the insights that were cascading down on Barry. Right off the bat we encountered a bellwether opportunity when Barry told us how he had responded to one of his two sales managers when, the day before, the sales manager, Steve, had requested permission to fire two nonperformers who Barry thought were pretty good.

Barry said, "I heard him talking about the wrong solution and, being 'mind-set *in*sensitive,' I didn't want to reverse him on the spot. I realized that he needed to find his way to seeing the situation differently. So I told him to think about it overnight and to come in today to see whether that was really the best thing for the company to do. But what if he says he still does?"

We suggested, "If Steve says he still wants to fire them and has the documentation, draw out his reasoning as far as you can. Then, tell him he overlooked a factor that you need him to take into account before taking dismissal action. Tell him you need him to find out how those people view the situation and why they have been performing the way they have. Tell him after he knows their logics well enough to coherently repeat them to you, he then can do whatever seems right to him."

Barry followed our direction, apparently in spirit as well as with words, and the next week called to tell us he was thrilled with his results. He said in response he now has his supervisor's gratitude for not allowing him to precipitate an action that would have been unfair. Barry told us, "Steve learned that it was their reaction to what he was doing that was causing them to malfunction."

There is one postscript. Barry got the lessons so well that he's taken a stronger position in advocating for his division at headquarters. Instead of clicking his heels, he now converts requests for instant action into problem-framing discussions. The result is that finally he has a way of averting the spur-of-the-moment information-seeking and "fire drill" requests from corporate chiefs that interrupt daily routine and workflow. He says, "This results in fewer follow-up activities for me to police that are difficult for my people to wrap their minds around because they don't apply to our division." From our vantage point, it seems that Barry's changed style is forcing the president to conduct his conversations differently, with the result that headquarters is now being perceived as possessing a new degree of open-mindedness.

Case reflection

We hope that you see the difference here between mind-set management and actions taken merely to correct substandard behavior. To make our point, we chose a dramatically successful situation. Nevertheless, this result is not atypical of what people achieve once they internalize the insight that "organization is an artifact of the mind that views it." Then they understand that each person is out to maximize something distinctly different and they actively think about the conditions for each person to perform effectively his or her distinctive way. Yes, we are skilled and practiced exponents of this insight and can sometimes accomplish in two days what might take a complete novice eight. But if you are thinking that you are a novice, we would argue that you've probably already logged six days' worth of data collection and already know the downsides of the personal competency thrusts that underlie the reasoning of the person you'd like to help. Furthermore, we think that once you start operating with the new mentality, the next time will take you four days and then three and then two.

Implicitly covered in this example were three important issues: the advice-giver's supportive relationship with the performer, the advice-giver's mentality and ability to be perceived as taking an "objective observer's" mind-set, and the advice-giver's appreciation of the line of reasoning and personal competencies that the person who he or she is attempting to influence uses. Our example covered all three. Suffice it to say that these three issues are interrelated.

When someone you would like to assist does not trust you enough to open-mindedly consider your advice, it might be because that person is compulsively competitive and misperceives your motivation or because you are missing something in yourself that makes it difficult for that person to trust you, or because you haven't made a strong enough connection with the logic the other person is using. When you feel you're not getting through to someone, you might try the latter two avenues rather than getting fixed on the first. Merely ask something like, "I don't feel I'm getting through to you, is there something I'm missing in your thinking?" or "Perhaps there is something you don't trust in my motivations? Am I doing something wrong?" Of course after you ask a question, you have to provide the other person a sufficient period of silence to allow him or her to decide on the level of candor he or she is willing to expose. You'd be surprised at how many people ask great questions and then, in response to the briefest silence, begin talking and thus cut off the opportunity that their question just created.

In our encounter with Barry, we were newcomers sent by his boss and needed to take pains to structure events to assure him that leveling with us could not hurt him externally. Apparently he did not harbor extensive fears that we might hurt him internally.

We were delighted when Barry sought to influence the list of people with whom we were going to talk to include people whom he saw providing support for his preexisting self-concept. The Artifact of Mind insight tells us that there is no such thing as objectivity in work situations, and that people's experiences of objectivity are primarily matters of their seeing you in their corners. We framed ourselves as management coaches out to help Barry be even more effective than he already was. Sticking to that frame allowed Barry to stay in dialogue with us and enabled us to get others to candidly tell us what we needed to know.

There were points along the way when we thought that Barry

was quite defensive and not telling us the entire truth. And here is where we thought our experience really helped. We know that people can't tell us more of the truth than they can risk admitting to themselves, and we know that shaded truths spoken in one moment may be reconsidered and portrayed more candidly later. Noteworthy was Barry's initial denial of his son's problems and his collusion with his wife and her denial of them, we guessed to keep family peace. But he later told us that he didn't need to call the teacher and, on reflection, he said he knew what she was saying all along. Similarly, we thought he knew about the real nature of his management style problems. In fact several times he indicated that they were a function of "What else can I do?" reasoning, such as when Andy told him his direct reports wouldn't make decisions while he was out. This is what prompted us early on to suggest a prescription pad. Whether he took us literally or figuratively, he was at a point in the realization process where he had to know that there was something tangible that could be done. Without this assurance we could expect more resistance and defensiveness, for he might reasonably fear that we would paint him into a corner where he didn't know how to perform.

A possible theme from this story is that mind-set management requires a good deal of psychology and psychological training. It does, but not at the level of psychotherapist or deep theory. It's a level at which you are already functioning every day of your life. You think about people's behavior and their motivation for operating so differently from you and what you think is in their best interests, and you wonder how to get them to change.

Once Barry understood the importance of problem framing and mind-set management, he knew just how to help Steve. For Barry, the possibility of having two salespeople fired, given the morale morass that everyone including the president was attributing to his management style, created enormous anxiety. Given this raised anxiety level, his handling of Steve's request was exemplary.

The control-relinquishing issue

We introduced this case stating that we saw the specific "control-relinquishing" lesson Barry needed to learn as having paradigmatic importance. At the time we engaged Barry it leaped out as a natural derivative of the Artifact of Mind insight. People see each situation differently. What they see is driven by their motivations to perform with personal competence and self-esteem. "Problems" are statements about what the organization needs to have accomplished that are, in nuance and structure, based on people attempting to frame events for their successful performance in them. What people think to do in relation to a "problem" is a function of what they find personally empowering. When a situation is framed by one person based on assumptions that do not compute in someone else's reasoning, and/ or requires actions that someone lacks confidence that he or she can perform competently or conflicts with other dimensions of one's life situation, then that individual's success depends on fighting off the "disempowering frame." That person feels the need to substitute one that is better attuned to his or her personal competency motives and ways of performing effectively.

At one point, using the former mentality, Barry's boss advised him to delegate more and to leave people alone. Of course he did this without releasing Barry from his commitment to produce results. For someone with Barry's profit responsibilities and personal inclinations, such advice had to be Orwellian torture. Our coaching took a different track. It led to Barry seeing the value of using a listening approach where, successively, he inquired into how the other person saw the situation, what that person saw as the problem and opportunity, and the course of action that person's framing of the problem was leading that person to take. This way Barry learned what he could influence and what was beyond his control.

The way to gain control by relinquishing it is to learn how people see events and reason and then, if it's sufficient, to leave them alone to produce results. Needless to say, this does not release you from your obligation to track results. And when the results that you and the other person are expecting are not realized, you are positioned to take up that problem inside the framework in which the other person is reasoning and acting. This is where you can really have a dramatic impact. This is where Barry realized his greatest success in allowing Steve to figure out that firing two salespeople would only be another example of "blaming the victim" management.

Thus relinquishing control became a process of discussing and engaging such mind-set manifestations as what the situation is, how the problem will be framed, and what types of actions will allow the individual to pursue an organizational course that's both personally and organizationally effective. We never asked Barry to leave his opinion out. We merely asked him to refrain from expressing it prior to hearing the reasoning of the person whose actions he was attempting to influence and who was going to be held accountable for the results. That's what mind-set management is all about.

On the other hand, the only way to relinquish control and to also sleep nights is to know enough about the other person's reasoning to have confidence that he or she will approach the situation competently. This is why we advised Barry to do more than just give Steve a night to think it over. We told him to insist that Steve know his salespeople's views well enough to repeat in detail to him. Getting Steve to practice mind-set sensitivity provided him the mental confidence to relinquish behavioral control.

Whether or not any two or more individuals can find a sufficient matchup of their self-interested viewings of a situation and the problems, opportunities, and courses of actions that derive from their viewings is always an open issue. However, until such issues are faced directly, with self-competency motives a given, there is no possibility of reconciling them. When these issues are dealt with aboveboard and forthrightly, the outcomes can be relationship building. And the search itself, rooted in your understanding that everyone functions with different perceptions, motivations, personal resources, and different life situations, leads to a process that produces trust.

When there is a problem and you are operating in the former system, it's fairly easy to get people to pay attention to your "advice." In fact, under such conditions the boundaries between the categories "feedback," "advice," "influence," "instruction," and "directive" are blurred. But when you operate a new model, using the new mentality, it's not so easy to get people who are operating in the former, control-oriented mentality to pay attention, especially when they hear your advice removing elements of their control and they see you operating without the authority to enforce compliance with what you are suggesting. Getting people interested in the advice you have to give is the topic taken up in Chapter 9, the concluding chapter in Part II, "What You Need to Know Prior to Giving Advice."

9

Getting People Interested in the Feedback You Have to Give

If people thought the advice you wanted to give would empower them, they would seek it from you constantly, all the time! Getting people interested in your ideas and using what you say to function with more empowerment is the topic addressed in this chapter.

No doubt you've already had many frustrating advice- and feedback-giving experiences when you were not even able to get the attention of someone you wanted to influence. We have them all the time, and not only when we are trying to tell our teenagers that they might learn more by doing their homework with the television turned off. In fact, just last week we had a frustrating conversation with a high-ranking executive.

Case in point

The conversation took place when the executive invited us into his office after he had given a slide-show briefing on his operation and we all had a half hour to kill waiting for the next briefing to begin. This executive had nine managers reporting to him, one of whom drifted into his office with us.

Casually we asked the executive how he managed so many complex subordinate operations. He answered, "*We* do very well. But *I* make out very badly. I'm constantly under pressure and seldom have a moment to myself." Then turning to look at his subordinate he said, "If all my managers were like Fred here, my job would be a breeze. But they're an uneven group and there's one, Jim, whose very presence unnerves me." Then he launched into ten minutes on the negatives of Jim's style and the problems in his "straightforward" communications with Jim.

Partially to interrupt what was evolving into mere character assassination, and partially to give him feedback, we ventured, "Is there anything that you can say that is positive about Jim and what he contributes to your operation?" Quickly relating to the opportunity our question created, Fred rushed to Jim's rescue. Not giving his boss time to respond, Fred interjected, "Jim's a really good guy who produces excellent work. What you need to know is . . ." but then he was, in turn, interrupted by the executive, who launched into another three or four minutes of invective. In all this time we didn't spot a single positive adjective, let alone an endorsing statement and, although one can never be completely sure, this executive did not appear to receive the feedback that was implied by our question or his subordinate's efforts in attempting to vouch for Jim.

Obviously this executive did not perceive our feedback as prods to his consciousness, let alone hear it as empowering. From his reaction, we can't be sure he heard our words, or that he perceived us and his subordinate manager as attempting to give him advice. And there we were mentally congratulating ourselves for framing a simple question that held the potential to communicate so much. In our minds, asking the boss to say something positive was sheer cleverness. Not only were we telling him that his attitude might be contributing to his subordinate's malfunctioning, but we were advising him how he might go about repairing a troublesome relationship. In our minds we were trying to empower him. Apparently he was too caught up trying, in his mind, to remain in "control."

Under other circumstances we might have been more direct and forceful, but that didn't seem an appropriate role for us to take here. This manager wasn't asking questions. He didn't seem interested in learning something new. Of course we were picking up one cue after another from his subordinate Fred that everyone's interests would be served by our pressing this point. But given the drop-in circumstances and our lack of mandate for legitimately saying more, we didn't see how we could appropriately engage this executive more assertively.

To us this manager appeared primarily interested in catharsis and receiving support for his point of view. But in our minds catharsis was self-indulgent and disorienting, and neither we nor Fred wanted to provide him support. Substantively and emotionally it was a stalemate.

In retrospect, this seems to be the type of feedback-giving opportunity that, in structure, we've witnessed thousands of times before. We were facing an individual who appeared to be oblivious to the impact of his thinking on others, who did not appear to be in a feedback-receptive mode, and who we were confident would benefit from the advice we were giving if only we could get him to pay attention to the message we were trying to get across. And we knew about the intractability of his lack of interest because on another day, or even in the next moment, this individual could have been one of us. The question, of course, is "How do you get people into a feedback-receptive mode when their needs are to get or maintain control?" The answer is counterintuitive. You give them the control.

What's needed to get people to open up to your influence?

The alignment model tells us that people are motivated to scrutinize your message for feedback and advice when they see your actions aimed at helping them to feel self-competent, organizationally productive, and externally valued—the three requisite conditions for their empowerment. They need to see both you and your message as helpful. Consequently, we see two issues that you need to consider in cultivating feedback receptiveness: the recipient's interests in the issue you are questioning and his or her relationship with you. The latter is particularly important in your recipient hearing your message accurately and in trusting your judgment and advice.

We have already described some of the essential attributes of the relationship required for an individual to trust a feedback-sender. You must be perceived as bridging to the mind-set in which the recipient is reasoning and you must *not* be perceived as having a sub-rosa personal agenda that competes with the recipient's self-interests. But what about the recipient's interest in the issue you want to address and the substantive message you want to send? What produces an individual's interest in the substance of the feedback you have to give?

The advent of the new management models has produced a rash of micromanagement practices by managers who are feeling out of control. Apparently, operating in the progressive new management systems with only their former mentality to draw on has thrown them for a loop. The result is that managers who used to know better are now inclined to nitpick and get into too much detail using personal paradigms that don't match up sufficiently with the personal-competence interests that drive the actions of the people they attempt to influence.

The negative effects can vividly be seen in group meetings where far-reaching topics are taken up as if the discussion will not cease until every individual in the room has had his or her concerns satisfied. This produces long, inefficient meetings and laborious consensus-seeking, turf-protective group discussions of the type we've come to abhor.

Recently we figured out a way to restructure group discussions so that people can exert influence and give advice without paradigm-incompatible micromanaging. This is a format for introducing the new mentality and changing the influence dynamics so that those who need to be influenced can feel sufficiently secure about the boundaries of their retained authority to have an open mind, while those who seek to influence them feel sufficiently assured that they will have an adequate opportunity.

Case in point

An early application of this format came in response to a situation we encountered when we were called by the newly appointed CEO of a large medical center who wanted either "a presentation or a short workshop to help me deal with a proliferation of 'trust problems' I've inherited among my top administrators."

The CEO told us, "Like so many health care institutions, our medical center has been caught in a changing marketplace with an operating model that suddenly is no longer profitable. We're a specialists' hospital relying on indemnity revenues in a marketplace that has turned to emphasize primary and managed care." He continued, "My predecessor's first instinct was to take the cost-cutting route and he did me a favor by being the bad guy who cut people and services. Nevertheless, this is not the type of action that's going to replace declining revenues." He told us that new relationships with insurers, physicians, and even patients were required. A task force of industry and financial experts had been enlisted to provide a new model. Then he said, "Our internal processes need help too and that's why I'm calling you."

Apparently there had been discussion about inefficiencies in the functioning of OceanView Medical Center's Administrative Council, and the hypothesis had been advanced that increasing trust would cause members to function more effectively as a team. His idea was for us to meet with "Ad Council" members to give a talk on trust and what might be done to raise the "trust quotient" of the team.

As is typical in our response to such a request, we asked to talk with two or three members of "the team" to hear a bit more about the medical center, their roles in managing it, and their thinking about what was needed for the medical center to operate more effectively and profitably. We got an early reading on the group's trust quotient when, in response to our request, we found ourselves scheduled for private meetings with each and every one of the eleven Ad Council members. At this point we negotiated a change in venue. We said we'd take on the list if, after we were finished, we would be allowed to come back to give the group our "feedback." The director was happy to oblige. He didn't need to feel defensive, because the problems had been there when he arrived.

From our interviews we learned that there was wide-scale unhappiness about the excessive time required for Ad Council meetings. Typically the Ad Council meets several times a week, with full agendas, and it was commonplace for a two-hour meeting to stretch into four. Agendas included all matters that concerned more than one department, with the purpose ranging from information sharing to decision making. We learned that all felt their work together was burdensome but that no one saw a reasonable alternative. After all, managers explained, "We need a voice in all medical center decisions that affect the running of our individual departments."

When we asked managers their opinions about the effectiveness of the other Ad Council members and the operations reporting to those members, everyone had criticisms and specific ideas about how others might function more effectively. However, we learned that group members lacked the means for helping one another face up to alleged deficiencies.

Apparently managers were vigilant in protecting themselves from criticisms and convoluted in telling one another what they thought should be fixed in that other person's departmental functioning. We heard that outside the meeting room the situation was worse. Any attempt to discuss or make suggestions was reacted to as an invasion of the recipient's territory. No wonder the members felt the need to attend all meetings. They had to micromanage the "news" as well as one another's actions.

While we were in the process of preparing our feedback we attended a physicians' meeting. The topic was improvement of outpatient services and the enhancements that might lead to improved services and augmentations of revenue. Also attending this meeting was

Mel, the Ad Council manager whose administrative assignment included outpatient services. The discussion was impressive. We listened to several medical directors with well-thought-out ideas for what would immediately make outpatient services more "user friendly" both for the patients and the physicians referring them.

To us, just about every one of the suggestions sounded practical and readily implementable and each seemed to involve far more in the way of common sense than extra costs. With their list on the board, the physicians turned to Mel to seek his concurrence and the hospital's commitment to implement. Mel's response was enlightening.

Instead of responding to the proposals on the board, Mel flipped on the transparency projector to show the steps he proposed to follow in performing a thorough systems analysis. These steps included months of interviews and a process for deciding on a systems redesign that would take a year to begin implementing. In response, one of the medical directors inquired, "Mel, can't we do both?" and then went on to explain. Respectfully she acknowledged the strategic validity of the process Mel had proposed and agreed that the physicians' ideas were, primarily, tactical and pragmatic. She said, "I don't see anything we're proposing that can't be undone when you come forth with the definitive system. Frankly I think delaying on implementing our ideas is strategically incorrect."

Mel was dumbfounded. Inarticulate and faltering, he claimed that immediate, short-term changes weren't possible, using a fragmented rationale that no one saw making logical sense. Afterwards, one of the physicians took us aside and told us, "That double-talk is typical of what we always get from administrators, and Mel is one of the good guys."

From our interviews we knew precisely why Mel had been so reluctant to commit. He had been caught between the proverbial rock and hard place. He couldn't agree to any action, however correct, without first consulting his Ad Council colleagues. He couldn't even publicly agree that the physicians' proposals were valid for fear of having his opinion reversed in Ad Council discussion. Furthermore, agreeing to any course without Ad Council concurrence would break the "teamwork" bond and engender group distrust. On the other hand, there was no way he could directly decline the physicians' proposals without looking unreasonable and appearing to confirm the physician-held idea that the people who managed the hospital were "blundering idiots." Later on, in the privacy of his office, Mel admitted to us, "The physicians' ideas make total common sense, but my hands are completely tied."

Combining what we learned in our interviews with what we learned watching Mel verbally disassociate, we were ready to give our "trust" report. We had a clear picture of the changes required for Ad Council members to operate more effectively as a group. We wrote a two-and-a-half-page report, which we painstakingly labeled "Confidential *Draft* Report and Discussion Document for the Eyes of Ad Council Managers Only." It was a review of how these managers saw their situations, followed by our recommendations for changing the group's discussion format and removing obstacles to individual members acting sensibly. We distributed it in advance of our scheduled face-to-face discussion with the twelve-member group.

The report and our presentation cast trust problems as the by-product of the Ad Council's inefficient decision-making format, not the cause. We were forthright in admitting to our going-in bias that a twelve-person committee should not engage in group decision making, especially on matters pertaining to the core operations of one of its members. The report explained our belief that such a large consensus-seeking forum drags decisions down to their lowest common denominator, builds compromise into all ideas and actions, usurps control, and makes individual accountability nonexistent. To cover ourselves, we acknowledged that there were topics, such as strategic planning, where twelve-person discussions leading to a consensus opinion, but not decision, was important. Then we added another note of caution about the dangers of relying on consensus opinion even when engaged in strategic planning.

We explained that the group's role should be to empower its members to make effective decisions in areas of their individual expertise and authority. We explained that this could be accomplished by using Ad Council meetings as consciousness-advancing and advice-giving forums but not for group decision making. We proposed a process whereby individual managers would present "rough-cut proposals" of actions they were inclined to take, or statements of problems that needed solving, for purposes of engaging one another's viewpoints and learning from the discussion.

We contrasted what we were proposing with the current group process where individuals state and defend their positions and then turn passive as others criticize and argue for modifications of detail. We explained that open-minded listening is possible only when the individual whose plan is being discussed retains the authority to act as he or she subsequently determines is best.

We asserted our belief that after a group discussion each presenter should retain the authority to decide. Whether and precisely how that person includes other people's thinking and recommendations in the course he or she decides to take should be subject to that individual's personal reasoning. We advised that, after a decision is made, the decision maker should briefly report it to the group along with the logic that he or she ultimately found compelling.

We told them that after a decision is made there is nothing more for people to debate. At this point, the purpose in reraising a topic is "update," not further discussion. The decision maker has exercised his or her responsibility and now must stand accountable for the results. When a person decides differently than how someone else advises, that person has to bear the responsibility for overlooking a position that might eventually turn out to be more correct. Of course, over time, decisions can be reversed, revised, or superseded as experience in living with them produces further data.

We told advocates and advice-givers to be prudent in their use of group time. We told them, "If in reacting to a 'preliminary roughcut proposal' you don't feel the proposer has truly grasped your point of view or seen its value, make a lunch date, write a memo, go over to that person's house on the weekend and don't stop communicating until that person knows how you think and comprehends why you believe as you do." To advice-recipients, we added, "When you think the action you are about to take goes against the advice of someone who has gone the extra mile to persuade you, be sure to communicate as much as you can about the considerations and assumptions that directed your thinking. This way the advice-giver can stay in dialogue with you and watch subsequent events for evidence that might eventually move either or both of your beliefs ahead."

We told the group that "empowering" members, not micromanaging and controlling them, was the concept that would lead to time-efficient meetings and effective, influential discussion. We said, "This is the only sure-fire way we know for promoting your need to know what others think." We explained that empowering another person entails first affirming that person's decision-making authority and then placing the burden to be correct squarely on that person's shoulders. That way advice-recipients will feel the need to hear you out and make sure that all advice is scrutinized for potential wisdom. The onus is on them to listen and to make more considered and progressively smarter decisions. Hypothetically they have little to lose by becoming open-minded listeners. They can open themselves to persuasion with full knowledge that they can toss off what doesn't fit with their way of seeing things and being effective.

While Ad Council members said they bought our proposal "in concept," they said the idea of actually following it presented problems "in action." They raised the issue of individual member weaknesses and the fact that "incorrect" decisions not only affect other departments but cause the Ad Council, as a group, to look bad. They told us that our proposal would be much easier to follow if everyone in the group were a strong performer.

We responded by noting that their CEO still performs the safety valve role of hiring and firing and has the responsibility to coach, support, and advise individual members. We reminded them that everyone in the group does in fact operate with delegated authority. We said, "Authorizing individual managers to make decisions in the domains of their authority does not relieve your CEO of his responsibility for ensuring that the people to whom he has delegated decision-making authority use sufficiently sound logic." We explained that there were methods that group members could use in exchanging personal-effectiveness feedback to assist one another to see perceived deficiencies and to exchange advice aimed at helping one another to operate more effectively.

To illustrate these methods we gave three examples of feedback-exchange methodologies used in other management groups, including the one we had used in helping the advertising executives, described in Chapter 5. The managers were willing to give it a try and asked us to convene a two-day off-site event preceded by a feedback survey and data exchange.

The peer feedback exchange, this time without the CEO, was the beginning step in Ad Council members' authorizing one another to assume responsibility for their individual departments and activities. Additional steps were necessary, but we are not taking those up here. It's sufficient to say that all of these focused on assisting Ad Council managers to release from a history of group decision making and micromanaging by peers.

Switching courses helped the managers to further appreciate the inappropriateness of the overly controlling processes they had been using. They could get away with these only as long as OceanView operated in the black. Years of working in this mode obscured everyone's noticing dynamics that reminded us of what is commonly labeled "co-dependency." These managers appeared to be feeding off of one another's weaknesses and insecurities. New members were apparently socialized with such rapidity that no one broke the pattern. But the system went "tilt" when the pressures of staff reductions, cost curtailments, and the need to develop revenue-enhancing programs hit all at once. Paradoxically, attempting to control one another put each of the Ad Council members out of control.

Giving people the control and then holding them responsible for the results are the conditions for their needing your feedback

It's a fundamental principle that people reject feedback that they perceive subtracting from their ability to be in control. It's the same for grownups in organizations as it is for children who, sensing that asking permission will get their request turned down, just take the extra cookie and hope no one will notice. Our suggestion for restructuring the process was to put OceanView managers in a situation where they would receive decision-making authority and then stand accountable for the results. In the former mode, either the group made the decision, in which case no one had to stand nakedly accountable, or the group discussion process dragged on to the point where, in effect, decision making was pushed up to the executive in charge.

This example illustrates how people drift into routines for disempowering others when their needs for control become primary. Attending long Ad Council meetings consumed the time and energy directors needed for managing staff and creating positive proposals in domains of their authority. Of course the main reason for attending meetings was to keep an eye on the other guy, lest he or she be inclined to take actions that infringed on their authority, not that anyone had the opportunity to exercise much of that authority within the time-consuming process that was being used.

At OceanView we made the assumption that having to stand accountable for results would be sufficient impetus for creating "a need to know" what knowledgeable others think. Certainly this condition was lacking in the story we told at the beginning of this chapter about the high-level executive who appeared not to even hear our feedback. That boss behaved as if he never had to stand accountable for his part in being unable to create a positive and empowering relationship with a "problematic" subordinate who had such a crucial role to play in his unit's functioning.

Other considerations for getting people interested in the feedback and advice you want to give

There are other important considerations to take into account when attempting to engender a need to know with the people you want to advise. Your feedback- and advice-giving attempts will benefit from considering these as well. As implied in the OceanView example, distrust is a barrier to openness and feedback receiving. Elsewhere[1] we have taken up this issue in depth. We asserted our belief that no more effective management tool exists than a trusting relationship. We asserted that, with trust, flawed plans and imperfect systems can be made to work, and that without trust, the best conceived plans and most enlightened management systems will not.

Likewise for developing receptivity for the advice and feedback you have to give. A trusting relationship is an essential ingredient. Without one, the other person either has to be on the ropes staring disaster in the eyes, or you've got to have that person in such a stranglehold that he or she has no recourse but to listen. It's far easier to get openness when others see you as out for their interests, intelligently reflecting on their work situations, operating without a competitive agenda, and, as we've been mentioning, with sufficient knowledge of the variables in the personal equation and the orientation they're using to maximize personal and organizational output.

Another critical consideration in engaging an individual's openness to advice is that person's psychological state. Occasionally you'll meet people who are up against the wall in terms of temperament, situation, or time. That is, don't expect someone who is on bad terms with him- or herself to have the capacity to open-mindedly take your advice and feedback as more than gun-to-the-head input. Don't expect someone whose child is having an operation or who has just been called for an IRS audit to be that interested in hearing what's bothering you about his or her behavior. And don't expect someone who is overcommitted to be interested in advice that improves quality while his or her main concerns are focused on finding the time to cover everything he or she is charged with doing.

Another critical consideration is slightly different in kind. It has to do with the difference between the level of the feedback and advice you want to give and the level of the feedback and advice that the individual you are attempting to advise is open to and seeking. We've alluded to this issue several times. It was illustrated in the example of Ralph, the manager who had problems planning a summer month with his boys, described in Chapter 3. While we were delighted when Ralph took our advice and was able to reposition himself to meet family and work commitments responsibly and self-meaningfully, we were disappointed that he didn't pick up on the deeper mind-set issue that, unrecognized, we fear will get him into more hot water in the future. That was our chance to really be of help. But we never got the feeling that Ralph extrapolated to get the general point relating to his overly responsible, heroic orientation. With his immediate problem "solved," we were unable to interest him in the deeper-level understanding that might prevent new problems of a similar ilk. We'll have much more to say about advice and feedback levels in Part III.

Each of the aforementioned considerations focuses on the importance of determining your advice recipients' interests in knowing and learning prior to initiating feedback and advice. Failure to cultivate open-mindedness and a need to know carries the downside risk of strained and broken relationships and unrealized opportunity, not to mention precious time expended without results. This is why it's so important that you begin advice- and feedback-giving by investigating your target person's desire to receive advice in the domain in which you seek to give it; that you conduct advance research to learn the key variables in that person's personal-effectiveness equation; and that you comprehend the mind-set paradigm in which that person thinks and the orientation in which he or she acts upon when framing your comments for consideration.

Work overtime to embed the Artifact insight in your company's culture

After reading this you might be thinking, "OK, I surrender! Thanks for the ride, but this is much too much. This advice-giving thing has become far too complicated. I'm just going to honestly tell people what I think and leave it to them. If they're able to use what I have to say and to change, that's great. If not, it's their life to live and they have to accept the consequences. The toll for my helping others has become too extreme!"

If you think this way, we can appreciate your feelings. Fortunately, we can offer a bit more help. The help comes directly from the Artifact of Mind insight, which, hypothetically, is a constant reminder of the fact that everyone sees and configures the same organizational events differently. When the person you want to advise has this insight internalized, and is aware that personal competency motives interact with perceptions, that person comes hard-wired with the need to know. Thus open-mindedness to feedback- and advice-giving may be the most compelling reason yet for working overtime to get the Artifact insight embedded in your company's culture.

The Artifact of Mind insight stipulates that everyone sees the same organizational situations differently with implications that one's perceptions are not only strengths but limitations. It tells people that, by definition, there will be features of every situation that escape their perception and that others will always view the same events differently and conclude differently than they conclude. Compensating for this limitation requires that people solicit other viewpoints and, in particular, open themselves to how you and others react to their production and conduct.

Likewise, people should understand that your perceptions and beliefs regarding their actions and the orientations they should be taking are not objective or necessarily more realistic than their own, or maybe that your beliefs are a bit more realistic but just don't fit with all the variables in their personal-effectiveness equation.

When someone has the Artifact of Mind insight internalized, other people's advocacies and attempts to influence should not make him or her feel excessively out of control. That person can afford to open-mindedly listen and now hold you off merely by saying "I understand what you are saying, I can say it back to you. But I'm not sure that it fits with the situation I'm facing. Obviously there are either some factors that you are weighing differently or some dimensions I haven't fully articulated. I need some time to think it through further and I'll tell you how I come out." That's what our proposal for changing the process used by the Ad Council managers attempted to accomplish. We intended to create open-minded thinking by structuring assurances that alternative viewpoints would not put people out of control. This required that decision-making jurisdictions be observed.

Thus when you feel an individual is not open-mindedly *considering* your advice (note, we're not saying "following" your advice, we're merely saying "considering"), first and foremost you need to inquire into the root cause of that person's resistance. That's easily begun merely by asking, "What am I missing, what's wrong with what I'm proposing?" Then use what you learn to direct your approach. It may be time to attempt some personal consciousness-raising, such as what Ralph would require to break a pattern of heroics and overcommitment to the point where these characteristics became his fatal flaws. It may be time to work on the structure and process of group relationships, such as what was required for Ad Council managers to seriously consider one another's opinions and viewpoints and not have the quality of their conclusions dragged down by the process. It may be time to work on the group culture, such as what was required at the "please-your-boss" bus company described in Chapter 4. Or it may be time to work on your relationship with the person resisting you, such as what was needed by the managers who were trying to get Ken to release from his "at CDX" expressions described in Chapter 5. These managers never seriously inquired what Ken didn't trust about them. They merely set out to "help" him.

The bottom line is that we're back to where we began this

chapter, but with some essential added dimensions. You've got to get the other person feeling enough responsibility for being correct and feeling enough control to pick, choose, and reject elements of any piece of advice according to its ability to move his or her personal equation ahead. That is, only when an individual feels sufficient control to open-mindedly consider and then to reject influence and advice can he or she open up to your advice. And here the Artifact of Mind insight makes an invaluable contribution. In explaining that everyone, including those who would like to exert influence and give advice, sees the same situations differently, an individual is provided a rationale that adds to his or her feelings of control. As paradoxical as it might sound, we find that until the person you are trying to influence has a no-fault scheme for rejecting your advice, it's entirely likely that person will be unable to experience your advice as even mildly helpful in spite of your certainty that it will be empowering.

This concludes our Part II discussion of "what you need to know prior to giving advice." Now we're ready to get into the actual process of giving advice and "matching advice with the need and the capacity to receive it." That's the topic of Part III.

Note

1. See S. A. Culbert and J. J. McDonough, *Radical Management* (New York: Free Press, 1985), and "Trusting Relationships, Empowerment, and the Conditions That Produce Truth Telling," in F. Massarik (ed.), *Advances in Organization Development* (Norwood, N.J.: Ablex Publishing, 1993), Vol. 2, pp. 154–170.

III

Matching Advice with the Need and the Capacity to Receive It

10

Mismatches in Levels of Feedback Sent and Received

Even when people pay attention to the feedback you send, they're not necessarily going to get your point. In fact, based on our experience, we'd have to say that their missing your point is likely to be more the norm than the exception.

Very often the reason they miss your point is because you are sending feedback at one level and they are receiving it at another. For example, perhaps you are talking specifics to a new employee who mistakenly thinks that you are making a generalizable point and is looking to come up with a formula for success. Or perhaps you're talking to someone whose behavior you've observed for some time, trying to address the thinking behind an entire class of misdirected behavior, illustrating with a specific, and that person thinks it's the specific that's important and, in the process, misses the bigger point. Understanding that there are different levels of advice and feedback, recognizing mismatches between the levels at which influence is being given and sought, and learning how and when you can bridge levels are the subjects of this and the next two chapters.

To familiarize you with mismatches and the approaches you can use to bridge them we begin this chapter with an intriguing story. It's a situation that vividly illustrates the executive-level havoc that gets created when a leader functions in the former mentality, not engaging the mind-sets of the people with whom he interacts. It's an illustration that ordinarily we wouldn't include because it's still in the works and, while we're optimistic, we can't be sure how it's going to turn out. On the other hand, because it's not concluded, it presents us with many of the same dilemmas you will encounter when the feedback and advice you give is received at a different level than you intend it.

Case in point

The story is about a company president named Byron who realized that he needed to change the character of his leadership style. Although he didn't say it at the time, we think, at a subconscious level, he recognized that this meant changing his mind-set and making the transition to what we've been calling "the new mentality."

At our initial meeting Byron told us, "Since taking over two years ago I've focused primarily on streamlining. I've cut back on product line and consolidated organizational units. Both of these activities play to my analytic strengths. Now it's time to turn my attention to improving teamwork and communications, which I like to do but, admittedly, these have not been my strong suits. That's why I'm asking for your help." He said, "I'd like *you* to start by building rapport among people on my management team. However, I think *you* need to begin with two executives who, my friends tell me, are making 'sniping' comments about me." We replied, "We'll be glad to speak with them, but then we'd like to help by coaching *you* to build your team."

Byron then went on to tell us about one of these executives, Gordon, who had, the week before, "casually" told him, "I want you to know I'm not happy" while they were sitting together during a short plane ride. Attempting to coach, we responded, "Did you ask him why he wasn't happy?" Byron shook his head "No." When we asked him what he guessed, Byron answered, "I assume it has to do with territory. While some gained in the streamlining, he's among those who lost units and people." Nodding our heads we asked, "What do your 'friends' say?" Byron told us, "I haven't asked them." Then Byron added, "Oh yes, I do remember hearing that Gordon was a candidate for my job, but in no way could he have been seen as a serious contender." At this point we were wondering whether Byron was telling us more about what he would be thinking if he were in Gordon's situation than he was telling us about Gordon. We had never met Gordon, so we had no idea either.

We responded, "In our experience there is seldom anything casual about a subordinate telling the big boss he's unhappy. Is it possible for you to straight-out ask him why? Apparently he needs you to listen." Byron said he would. We thought just his inquiring would be a relationship-booster, and the discussion might lead to Byron's finding out about a potentially missing dimension in his approach to people.

Two weeks later we were back in San Francisco meeting again with Byron. After pleasantries he began, "Today I'd like you to spend some of your time with Jeff, whom I'm thinking about bringing in to run this year's strategic planning." Interrupting his flow, we inquired, "Before we start with Jeff, tell us what you learned from Gordon." Byron responded he hadn't asked him yet, despite the fact that they had, in the interim, been at the same out-of-town meeting together. Byron looked so guilty and so earnest in declaring that he would hold that discussion soon that we readily acquiesced to discussing Jeff.

In response to our asking, "What's up with Jeff?" Byron replied, "He's an interesting study. Jeff's an exceptionally bright guy whose operation was folded into other activities during our consolidation. I've kept him on because he's knowledgeable about our business and has so many of the intellectual qualities we need. I thought I'd let him take a whack at leading this year's strategic planning. The guy who did it the last six years is using a tired formula that produces documents to which no one pays much attention. This year's planning is very important, I need to get my thumbprint on it and don't want people once again taking it lightly." We responded, "In terms of getting your thumbprint on it, shouldn't this year's be *your* strategic plan?" Byron emphatically agreed, saying that's what he was intending.

We asked, "What do you have in mind for our conversation with Jeff?" He replied, "Jeff has communication problems, and I wonder whether I'm making the right choice." We responded, "We're happy to coach him, but you've got to make the decision yourself. We'll be glad to help you and the people on your 'team' any way we can, but it's up to you to decide who is on the team." Byron responded, "Oh, I guess I didn't state it correctly. I gave Jeff the assignment, it's just that it hasn't been announced. Now I merely need him to overcome his communications difficulties and be successful." Privately, we reflected, "Byron also has some communications difficulties, and his appear to stem from how he thinks about people."

Byron took us down to Jeff's office where, coincidentally, we met "unhappy" Gordon. Byron explained the purpose of our visit and, after a few minutes, he and Gordon left. This is when we learned that Jeff reports to Gordon. Silently we worried, "Uh oh. For his cohort, Byron selects someone who reports to an alleged sniper."

Alone with Jeff, listening to him talk about his last assignment, we quickly saw what we surmised must be his communication "problem." Jeff appeared to be one of those engineering types who, when he thinks he has his facts and conclusions correct, states his viewpoint clearly and with the confidence of Moses atop Mount Sinai, tablets in hand. There was nothing garbled about his communications. But if you were one of the people he was talking to and you saw situations differently than he saw them and weren't prepared to roll over and go along with his version of "the truth," you'd probably find his statements excessively opinionated, strident, and harsh. Otherwise, Jeff struck us as a highly articulate, clear-thinking expert and a well-intentioned, intelligent communicator.

Our meeting with Jeff took just over an hour. In it we developed a perspective on his new assignment that, given his communication style, caused us to think we had useful advice for him. We told Jeff, "We hear you talking as if you think this is going to be *your* strategic plan or perhaps the company's strategic plan. However, we think Byron sees it quite differently."

Continuing we said, "Of course you'll want to check this further, but we think your assignment is to work on 'Byron's strategic plan,' which means that your role is to help him create it. Of course it's about the company and its strategic directions, you've certainly got that part straight. But we got the impression that Byron feels his leadership is on the line and having his mark on the strategic plan is going to be a way of asserting it. As we see it, this is going to be a situation where you lose each time you hold out for your version of 'the truth.'

"The way we see it, this situation provides you an excellent opportunity to advance to a mind-set that allows you to counteract what others have referred to as your 'communications *difficulties.*' In this assignment, your role is to draw people out and get their input, and to portray it for Byron's consideration. When you feel that the someone is, from your way of seeing things, out in left field, your job is merely to ask that person, 'How would you respond to a contrasting view that says. . . ?' That way you don't have to take anyone's opposing viewpoint personally."

Next, we asked, "What about Gordon's role in directing and influencing you? He's your boss isn't he? How can you essentially be doing staff work for Byron while reporting through Gordon? Isn't he going to feel obligated to be a value-added?" Jeff replied, "You just hit the nail on the head. We're already getting into a routine of irritating one another and bickering about hypotheticals. Gordon's got a lot to suggest that may not be what Byron wants to see in the plan.

I'm feeling like a man caught in the middle." We said "Of course—you are!"

Then we asked how Don, the person who had performed the strategic planning for the last six years, felt about Jeff's taking over his function. Jeff responded that he didn't think Don had been told. He said Don was in eastern Europe conducting business negotiations and wouldn't be back for a week.

We asked what Don's assignment looked like without strategic planning, and Jeff said he didn't know. He said that, to the best of his knowledge, strategic and business planning had occupied most of Don's time for the last few years. But Jeff couldn't be sure because of his former location in an operational department. We had heard enough to feel alarmed. It was time to clarify in a conversation with Byron.

Asking Jeff to accompany us, we went and knocked on Byron's door. We said, "We'd like an hour with you and Jeff and then, if you can swing it, another half hour to finish up the business we were working on in your office yesterday."

In the three-party conversation we took pains to frame the issue not to betray any critique that we would reserve for Byron or Jeff individually. Role clarifying for Byron, we said, "Jeff, you need to know that Byron sees this year's strategic planning as crucial to asserting his leadership and building a spirit of teamwork. While he wants the plan to address some short-term financial parameters, he also intends it as a guide for people up and down the ranks to use in making their daily decisions more strategic." Byron played off our framing and, for the first time, explained his plan in depth to Jeff.

Turning to Byron, we said, "Yesterday you asked us to coach Jeff on communication problems, which, you had told him as well as us, have been a source of negative feedback you've received that's becoming a liability to his career in the company. We did some coaching, and there are two issues you should know about. First is Jeff's communication style and how you can help; we'll get to that shortly. Second, there are some political exigencies associated with the current way you have this assignment framed that could cause Jeff to have problems that exacerbate his imperfections."

Getting specific, we said, "If it's your plan, why do you have him reporting to Gordon? Won't this lead Gordon to believe that he is supposed to play a value-added role in the planning, as he has done the last four years with Don reporting to him? Likewise, what are you and Gordon going to tell Don, who even in eastern Europe is likely to hear the 'jungle drums,' when he returns terror-stricken realizing that his primary assignment has been given away?"

If Byron felt uncomfortable about the spot we had put him in, his face never showed it. Quickly he said he agreed, the only sensible arrangement was to have Jeff report directly to him. We knew that this was a matter about which we'd need to speak with him later, in light of his untested belief about the cause of Gordon's unhappiness. Then we asked Byron what Don was going to think and feel. He didn't need us to say more. He got the gist and said he would take care of this as well. In response, Jeff made a point of overtly breathing a sigh of relief.

Then we took up Jeff's alleged communications problems from the standpoint of emphasizing Jeff's strengths. We said that we found Jeff to be a very articulate and clear-thinking individual who had an excellent capacity to starkly express that which he believed was true. We thought these capacities could be well utilized in writing a strategic planning document and that his forthrightness would be a valuable resource in providing Byron with the give-and-take discussions that would be useful both in drawing him out and challenging his going-in ideas. We also took up the advice we had given Jeff about how to conduct his conversations and then discussed the guidance Byron could give Jeff in helping evolve an open-minded communications style.

We offered some additional process advice for the strategic planning, which, on one hand, reflected our apprehensions regarding group decision making (discussed in Chapter 9), and, on the other, embodied the new mentality lesson. We emphasized the importance of engaging each individual's mind-set—the lesson that from the beginning we had been trying to get across to Byron. We advised Jeff and Byron to produce a "discussion document" early in the process in which they state their going-in assumptions and initial proposals as a departure point for drawing out other people's viewpoints and hearing their differing and contrasting priorities. We recommended that Jeff use the document as a sounding board that evokes alternatives and that he urge people to explain their views to the point where he could clearly grasp the logic and reasoning behind an advocacy.

Then we suggested a follow-up stage where, after the conclusions were publicly announced, a concerted effort would be made to contact people whose advocacies were at odds with the directions specified in the resulting plan. Again, to emphasize the importance of engaging another person's mind-set, we said, "You don't want contributors feeling that their advocacies are votes, or that not having the conclusion come out as they want is a defeat that requires them to spend significant energy trying to prove themselves correct." We continued, "Just as everyone needs sufficient engagement on the front end to know that their reasoning was accurately received and considered, they also need sufficient engagement on the back end to understand why the resulting plan concluded differently than they had advocated."

When Jeff left, we asked Byron what he was going to do about Gordon and Don. Byron began with Don. And he was quick in coming up with solid "in the best interests of the company" logic as well as compelling verbiage aimed at convincing Don how he's going to be better off in the new role he planned for him. We cautioned, "Byron, you are a well-intentioned guy but we fear that you are crossing yourself up by repeatedly making the same mistake."

Then, as if to emphasize our point, Byron matter-of-factly asked, "What is that mistake?" We answered, "We think there's a common thread in most of the issues we've taken up with you thus far. We think you need to spend more time inquiring into people's thinking, and listening to how they actually see the situations they are in. This has been the core of most of the advice we've offered. You proceed based on your idea of someone's situation as if that's sufficient understanding. In our experience, it almost never is. In fact, we don't think there is a man alive who thinks about his situation like you think about yours or about his. Certainly it would have been better for you to have asked Don how he felt about having someone else do strategic planning prior to giving the job to Jeff. If you think the substitute functions you plan for him are career advancing, then the advisable thing would have been for you to have discussed them first and allowed him to go through the pros and cons for himself. You didn't, but perhaps the next time you will. In fact the next time is staring you in the face right now: it's coming up with Gordon. In changing Jeff's reporting relationship to you, you just removed something else from his territory, strategic planning. If your hypothesis is correct, this is going to make him even more unhappy."

In response, Byron went right to the fundamental control issue. He asked, "Why would you ask anyone a question when you know the answer you are going to receive is one you don't want to hear?" Obviously he had Don on his mind as well as Gordon, and we appreciated that. It's at this point that we became confident that there was no way we would be able to call this project a success until we helped Byron change his orientation from functioning in the former mentality to functioning in the new. Clearly this was the cause of many teamwork glitches.

We answered, "When you ask people a question, there are always several possibilities. First, their answers can influence your perspective, and second, you still have another shot at affecting their reasoning. As boss, you can always exert influence and determine the outcome. You can say, 'What you're saying makes total sense, but it also poses certain problems for me, and this time I can't go along.' Then you can engage the substance of that person's reasoning and explain the logic you find more compelling. In the process you ought to be learning a great deal about the person you are talking to. Win, lose, or draw, your relationship ought to improve."

Continuing, we said, "For example, with Don, you might begin with an apology and then sensitively inquire into his concerns, which are likely to include concerns for career progress, how an assignment with so much travel will affect his family's life, his view of how others in the company are going to interpret your withdrawing a high-profile strategic planning assignment from him, and issues that the two of us speculating in your office will never guess. Ask him to think about what he would like to do next, either in the company or elsewhere, and tell him that you and Gordon would like to help him find his way. Tell him you have some ideas but you'd prefer to listen to his thinking prior to disclosing yours, for what he says might further advance your thinking. If that makes him too anxious, then go ahead and state your thinking and the points he can influence." Byron thanked us and said that's what he would do.

In this interaction, Byron showed himself to be a well-intentioned executive who was eagerly seeking suggestions for how to help and manage people more effectively. But we hadn't gotten through with the deeper lesson about how his use of what we call the "former mentality" causes him to practice management as a manipulative art. Byron had shown himself to be a fast-take learner on specifics. He gets the point—he gets the same point each and every time! But he hasn't internalized the value of eliciting and engaging the mind-set that the other person actually lives. Byron acts as if engaging viewpoints that appear to be at odds with where he thinks he wants to come out threatens his control—as if he ever possessed that level of control. Until the new mentality clicks in, the core technology of his management style is going to be schmoozing, manipulating, and outsmarting other people.

Two weeks later we were back up in San Francisco, working at the company again. Byron filled us in. He told us that the strategic planning was rolling along nicely and that he had held a reassuring conversation with Don, who was back in the country. He said travel and vacation schedules prevented a face-to-face meeting and he had to settle for an "in-depth" hour-long phone conversation last Sunday afternoon. Don had assured him he was comfortable with what "the company" had planned for him and would spend the next month revving up the eastern European business. However, Byron also mentioned that another executive spoke with Don yesterday and may have mistakenly come away thinking Don was having problems. We asked, "What makes you so sure he's not?" Byron said he would double-check with Gordon since Don was off for a short vacation.

We got to Gordon first and what we learned was an eye-opener. If he was feeding us an inauthentic line, we went for it totally. We came away believing Gordon was a very able, well-intentioned executive whose alleged "sniping" might have been the result of lobbying another executive, who was known to have Byron's ear, to give Byron almost precisely the same personal feedback that we were trying to get across. We also learned his version of Don's conversation with Byron, which seemed plausible both in light of their friendship and years of working together as well as our experiences with Byron. According to Gordon, Byron told Don that giving the assignment to Jeff was necessitated by a temporary need to find something useful for Jeff, intimating that he could have strategic planning back next year if he wanted it. Then he tried to convince Don that an as yet unspecified new business development assignment would be even better for his career progress. Gordon said that to maintain image, Don was pretending that he was OK with the arrangement but was making himself scarce to prevent Byron's seeing him in a dour mood.

We asked Gordon, "What do you intend to tell Byron?" He replied, "These are the types of situations I dislike most. If I tell him the 'facts,' it's a small betrayal of Don's confidence. If I shine him on, I'm working against myself. I think I'll merely tell him that this situation bears watching and that I'm sure it will end well if we take care of Don." We reflected, this is where even the best of the good guys get done in by the former mentality. Circumstances had made it impossible for Don and now Gordon to give Byron the type of feedback that could send him self-reflecting.

Case reflection

We began seeing the problems with Byron's reasoning and his need to develop mind-set sensitivity when he first told us he had not asked Gordon why he was unhappy. At that moment we thought, either he knows already or, despite extroverted appearances, he's an introverted problem solver who works primarily off internal data. We became more aware of his need to see people differently when we witnessed the disparities between his stated desire for teamwork and improved communications and his behavior, which, at key moments, seeks to control and direct other people's mind-sets.

All of the specifics we took up with Byron, from asking him the cause of Gordon's unhappiness, to cuing him to the reporting squeeze he was creating for Jeff with Gordon, to alerting him to problems he had created for Don, to recommending a process for engaging people who, in the strategic planning process, publicly commit themselves to viewpoints that are at odds with the final plan, were aimed at getting Byron to see people as *subjects* to be "listened to" rather than *objects* to be "directed." In each specific instance, Byron got the point. But he didn't catch on that the "problem" was not specific situations, but the general case of how he views people.

Where we are today

After this much effort you might reasonably think that the mentality issue should be self-evident. But it is not, and we don't yet know what's causing the block. We sense insecurity but we do not see the source and we cannot confidently rule out the effects of socialization and a deep-rooted attachment to the mentality that got Byron to the exalted corporate position he now holds. People are never eager to abandon the formula they rode to "success." In any event, we need to find a way of challenging Byron to confront himself.

Getting more data

Initially we plan to proceed by getting more data out on the table to see what Byron thinks. In the interest of team building and improving communications we will sequentially repeat the pattern that we began with Jeff. First we will talk with Byron to get his picture of another person and the opportunities for that person to improve his or her effectiveness and contributions to the corporate team. Then we will talk with that person to hear his or her personal-effectiveness concerns, alert to any role that Byron might play in them. Then we plan to bring the two of them together to discuss issues the subordinate authorizes, framed in a neutral way. We'll hope that the process of creating mind-set engagements will produce a database that Byron eventually finds sufficiently compelling to provoke a reevaluation of how he deals with people. Then we'll talk with him about the view of people that leads him to behave as he does.

Alignment sensitivity

Proceeding this way will afford repeated opportunities to meet with Byron to develop a personal relationship. Progressively we'll accumulate a fuller picture of what's important to Byron and the variables

that are important to the way he stages situations for his empowerment. We'll be looking out to learn more about his background,
especially his leadership role models and, specifically, what qualities
he seeks to emulate.* With some people it takes a sledgehammer to
the forehead to interrupt years of self-sealing reasoning that preclude
an essential lesson being learned. We certainly hope Byron won't be
one of these.

Pattern recognition

When the time seems right we're poised to again ask, "Byron, do
you see a pattern here? Is it a pattern you're going to continually
repeat?" Then, depending on Byron's response, we'll either challenge him further or go ahead and meet the next person and see how
Byron engages that individual and the effectiveness issues that are
raised by that individual.

Depending on his reactions, we could either continue asking Byron if he sees a pattern or, alternatively, bring out the confrontation
sledgehammer. The sledgehammer might be saying something like,
"We now can give you eighteen examples of how the assumptions
you make about yourself and other people make life difficult for others and negatively impact their productivity. And probably we can
get you to agree with fourteen of them. How long are you going to
hold out?" Then, for sure, we'd keep quiet and listen.

Feelings and relationships are key

By the third time we met with Byron, all talk of specifics was intended to inform him about a flaw in his "orientation" that, un-
changed, could result in a steady stream of new problems and specifics. Byron didn't have a mentoring boss and we thought that,
subconsciously, that might be what he was getting from us. Our job
was to help him get a handle on what he was doing that worked
against his own effectiveness. He was counting on us to help him
change a pattern of thinking and acting he had spent a lifetime per-
fecting.

In looking out for Byron's interests we wanted to be kind, firm,
and increasingly demanding, but not cruel. Certainly Byron's reactions would, to a great extent, determine how we worded things and
conducted ourselves. Of course merely writing the words makes this

*The question raised is a specific application to question 9 on our Alignment
Questionnaire described in Chapter 7.

type of challenge sound quite straightforward and reasonable. But our relationship with Byron and his feelings about us are involved, and that adds responsibility. Feelings and relationships are the catalytic agents that decide the meaning and value of any communication and determine what gets across. The Artifact of Mind insight tells us that no thoughts or feelings make it through someone's filters without significant disparities between what's intended and what's received.

We'd try not to make the challenge personal

Whenever the issue is orientation and mentality, eventually the other person acts out the same dynamics with you. After all, if it's something that is ingrained in that individual, why shouldn't he or she also behave the same way with you? With Byron it's already started with us. He's changed scheduled dates on short notice without apparent concern for what we have to go through to reschedule two days out of town to meet with him, which includes our changing appointments with others in his company as well. We merely get a call from his secretary asking for next available dates.

But as advice-givers our job is to maintain a relationship with Byron and not to add stress to the communications. A long time ago we commented that *"succeeding in an organization is like trying to score at pocket billiards. The smart players always have two objectives. One is to put the ball in the pocket, and the other is to leave the cue ball in a position to successively put more balls in the pocket.*[1]*"* Of course, in this analogy, the cue ball is our relationship with Byron, the person we are advising. Making it a personal confrontation lessens the control we have on where the relationship will wind up after the moment of impact.

Making an advice-giving encounter a personal confrontation is always a last-ditch effort for getting your message through the other person's filters. Afterwards the relationship and trust level would be forever different. In Byron's mind we'd be transformed from "objective outsider" to "agenda-biased outsider" with a point of view that constantly requires scrutinizing for competing agendas.

At some point we think people are entitled to hear the "truth" as straight and as directly as we think we know it. And if we were to be so blunt as to use a confronting scenario like we fantasized earlier, we wouldn't be so naive as to think that it would produce breakthrough insight. We'd do it to make an indelible point for Byron's future reflection. If we're on target, then our words will serve as hypotheses for Byron to consider when he watches himself act and think in other situations and relationships. Perhaps when encountering some subsequent "people problems" he'll make the connection.

The problem with sledgehammers is that they sometimes work

Many advice-givers, either in desperation or through loss of patience, impulsively pull out a sledgehammer to break through someone's resistance. The problem with the sledgehammer approach is that it works just often enough to allow people to think it's viable. This is when you self-justifiably lose your temper, blame people, or worse. What we've found "worse" is when an advice-giver makes a sweeping characterological statement that imputes "always" to whatever he or she is criticizing, or is encountering as a class of situations, or finds troublesome. Saying that someone *never* cares about people, or is *always* a bully, or *doesn't* have a sense of humor, or unconditionally *is* an anything is worse because it puts the other person on the defensive, thinking not about the incidents that create the "rule" but about the exceptions that can be used to invalidate such a negative characterization and threat to self-esteem.

Use the other person's words

Whenever you need a way of referencing a patterned dimension in someone's behavior, the smartest thing you can do, from a technique standpoint, is to ask the individual for his or her terminology. Ask the person, "What do you call what you are doing? Why are you doing that? What does it feel like inside of you when you do that? Is there a certain type of situation that evokes that type of response?" and so on. Then, in your discussion, use the individual's own words when referring to that behavior and the needs and fears related to it.

Using the other person's terminology and concepts frees you from any baggage that person might attach to your words while providing tangible evidence that you are seeking to understand his or her experience. It puts you in that person's corner, looking at dilemmas, problematic outcomes, and behaviors that appear self-defeating. In our initial meeting Byron dropped a clue, and now it's time to use it. When we get a chance, we're going to go back to the term "teamwork," and go long and strong asking him what he thinks produces it.

People intending to give "orientational" advice don't necessarily provide all the help that's required to "get it"

We call the level of advice that we needed to get across to Byron "orientational." We see him needing to change much more than his behavior; he needs to change his orientation toward people. If we can help Byron to see people differently, then he's going to start acting differently in a host of situations we can never anticipate.

Pressing an individual for orientational change, of the kind we are after with Byron, demands a great deal. It entails taking a situation that another person has framed in one system and transforming it into a different situation requiring a different set of thought processes and actions. However, often overlooked in the reframing is the fact the other person's allegedly mistaken framing fits with that person's needs to construe situations to require skills and interaction patterns that he or she is confident of executing.

Herein lies the structural rub. While you are trying to get another person to change how he or she is thinking, reasoning, and orienting, so that this person can function with greater personal and organizational effectiveness, that person is thinking how to be effective in the situation at hand using skills he or she can execute self-confidently. Practical considerations are salient in his or her mind. That person does not want to undergo a complete mental restructuring; he or she would like to get by with a skill adjustment or perhaps a sensitive rewording. It's as if your advice-recipient is wondering, "If I start reasoning as advised and begin seeing events differently, do I possess the skills to act competently in situations I haven't anticipated?"

We've seen Byron use the interaction skills required to retrieve data he lacks; we don't think that's the problem here. Perhaps he needs some reinforcement and reassurance. The skills we think he needs to acquire have more to do with the skills for learning about another individual's actual mind-set and for seeing the amount of influence one gets from that knowledge. And we think the psychological key is to discover how he ever got the idea that he could get along without this type of information and without the relationship bonding that the exchange of such information can produce.

On the other hand, many would-be advice-givers inadvertently add to an advice-recipient's problems by focusing on specifics when attempting to give advice that moves beyond specifics to orientation. They do so attempting to develop clarity about what's wrong with the other person's orientation. This results in feedback-recipients thinking that finite behavioral changes and/or the exercise of more self-discipline will produce greater work effectiveness in instances where nothing short of a change in orientation will. It leaves feedback- and advice-senders thinking the real meaning of their message was missed while recipients believe they have performed as advised.

While Byron may believe that he has performed as advised, we not only are clear that he has not, as you can see from the preceding discussion, but we guarantee this is not where we are going to stop. But many advice-givers fail to discriminate between levels of advice and believe the recipient understands the orientation principle when that person makes statements of "finally getting it" based on advise on how to handle specific situations. Such mismatches and circumstances can produce results that are horrendous.

By means of illustration, consider the difficulties faced by a savvy program development manager whose boss told us "I'm at my wit's end trying to get Bill to change." While the specifics of Bill's predicament are distinctive, we find his situation prototypical of one we bet you've encountered several times yourself. The feedback clearly told Bill his orientation was off but no one was framing the message to be sufficiently clear at the proper level. As you read this account, think about what you might have done when faced with giving feedback and advice in a similar situation where you work. There are many people who would have acted more or less' the same as the well-intentioned people whose feedback proved meaningless to Bill.

Case in point

When we asked Bill the "What's the last important lesson you learned?" question, Bill hesitated a long time before answering. He seemed to be searching to find precisely the correct phrasing. Finally, he replied, "I've learned to fit in and to do a much better job of watching out for my priorities by avoiding fights that unnecessarily jeopardize my projects." He said this in an optimistic tone, as if his impending success were a fait accompli. However, when we compared what Bill said to his boss's account of Bill's difficulties we could see a communications mismatch and elements of a disaster in the brewing. Consider the specifics.

Bill had gone to work as a fixed-salary employee in a division that was about the size of a company in a different industry that he had entrepreneurially built from scratch and profitably run. He took his permanent-status position after serving briefly as a consultant, which gave both him and his new employer an opportunity to get to know and value one another. Bill is the type of person who instantly gives the impression that he is extremely bright and that he won't rest nights while any essential task is undone. His competitive attitude communicates that his side is going all out to win, and if you know what's good for you, you won't get in his way.

Shortly after assuming regular employee status, Bill began creating problems. He displayed a penchant for showing corporate administrators and support staff what he saw as the inefficiencies and flaws in the administrative processes they were following and the ridiculous bureaucracy created by these practices. He vigilantly sought and exploited loopholes in the system, he said, "To make a bigger point." He displayed a personal style that others saw as overly familiar and was prone to shouting when those reporting to him "are acting in ways that cross me up." He negotiated deals with vendors that, while financially beneficial to his firm, deviated from the arm's-length relationship that fit with his firm's mainline image and reputation. And his interactions with executives in other departments were often seen as disrespectful. At first Bill ardently confronted and challenged each opinion and protocol with which he disagreed, and there were many. Later he learned to circumvent problems by ducking discussions that might yield answers he didn't want to hear. Eventually the people whose views were being circumvented caught on and began complaining.

It took almost no time for corporate directors to begin sending Bill's boss the word that Bill's behavior needed modifying. While his business results were appreciated, Bill's mode of operating was viewed as "degrading of administrative personnel" and "disrupting established corporate practices." Bill's boss patiently counseled him, emphasizing how every member of the "corporate team" wants to think well of him- or herself and have the feeling that he or she is a valued and essential contributor. Bill was asked not to withhold his point of view, just to be more respectful of others and more sensitive to the fact that his acts of highlighting pockets of corporate ineffectiveness and moments he termed "sheer stupidity" were being received as attacks on the people involved. Bill responded with concern saying that he never wanted to hurt others. His boss said, "Each time we talked Bill left me with the distinct impression that he would immediately improve his treatment of people and act more respectfully when engaging the systems they operated."

In Bill's mind he tried hard to adjust his behavior and to become what he called a "good corporate citizen." And because of this he became progressively frustrated, he said, almost to the point of impulsively quitting when his boss continued to bring new "situations" to his attention. Apparently each time Bill's boss took him aside, Bill would agree with the boss's analysis and ratchet up the self-discipline.

Then came a memorable meeting in which Bill was reviewing a project and its problems with a group of top corporate executives. Taking offense at some veiled criticisms, Bill stridently announced that he didn't like the way others were trying to make him the fall guy for a problematic situation he had not caused. He claimed that others in the room were far more to blame but too cowardly to admit their mistakes. Then he stormed out.

Those present tried to excuse his behavior on grounds that he had, in fact, been performing tirelessly overseeing a project with which he was highly identified and that a blowup of this intensity was aberrant even for Bill. But despite striking this incident from the record, it had been etched in the minds of witnessing "jurors." Afterwards Bill's boss counseled that Bill's job could be saved only by Bill's limiting his participation with top management to answering questions and providing information. Limits were put on his authority so that, from then on, his boss had to be included in any precedent-setting or problem-solving discussions in which a top-level executive was involved.

Ranking high on Bill's list of favorite work activities was foreign travel. His job required overseeing projects being carried out by the company's three European subsidiaries. However, corporate criticism peaked when word came back from Frankfurt that, at a business dinner, Bill drank too much and perhaps was indiscreet. He allegedly criticized corporate staff, spoke derogatorily about the company's "misguided" priorities, and offended a customer by, as the customer put it, "becoming too familiar with my girlfriend and giving the impression that he wanted to see her home."

The next morning the fax machine was burning up with competing eyewitness accounts of Bill's allegedly offensive behavior. Regardless of the accounts' accuracy, for Bill's boss's boss, Bill was down to his final last chance. He instructed Bill's boss to prepare a letter detailing fifteen months of Bill's disruptive and disrespectful behavior to formally advise Bill that the next time a problem occurred, he would be out. To cover his own situation, the boss decided to accompany Bill on his next European trip, figuring that this way he could protect against trouble while collecting the additional data that could be used to document Bill's misadventures to avert the possibility of a suit in the event of termination.

After the incident and letter, Bill was extraordinarily contrite. He openly admitted that he needed to change his style. He claimed that he was highly committed to his work and that he thought that the company, for all its faults, was first-rate. He said he really valued the opportunities his job gave him to contribute in an industry that he believed in, and in which he was now positioned to build his personal reputation and identity. This was about the time we asked our "last important lesson" question.

In embellishing the lesson, Bill said, "Finally I've got my priorities straight. I'm not going to risk messing up what I value most by making mistakes and pursuing ego needs that aren't, in the larger scope of things, all that important." Then he added, "I know I can't get away with the same things I could when I was running my own company. I know I must be less direct and more diplomatic and that it takes time to straighten out systems when other people's egos are on the line." All of this was said in a tone that left no doubt that Bill intended to give it his all. Clearly he intended to be more sensitive and to exercise yet greater self-discipline.

In response, we said, "We're not so sure you've got the right concept yet. In fact, we see your situation differently than you just portrayed it." But Bill had just "solved" his problem and was wedded to his latest new best-foot-forward approach. He said he was pressed for time collecting figures for an important overseas trip and that he would get back in touch just as soon as he returned. We got the message clearly, this was not the time to persist. We had to content ourselves with a little relationship building, awaiting the next crisis and resulting need to know. Unfortunately the next crisis came too soon, and we didn't get our chance to comment until Bill was phoning to ask our advice about how to portray this experience when interviewing for his next job. At that moment his sadness and disappointment were so great that we didn't have the heart to say more than just answer his questions.

Bill had problems, and he probably made significant progress given the way he saw situations and reasoned. But he never engaged the feedback and advice offered him at the level of intended impact. Bill continuously focused on the problems he had and the discipline that working in someone else's company required. But despite the fact that he kept grasping for the logic, he never seemed able to get to the level of reversing what about his underlying reasoning and orientation was at the root of his problems with the company.

The irony here is that, notwithstanding natural resistance, Bill was actually looking to specifics to tell him more about the underlying principles and to discover an orientation that would ensure his rubbing people the right way. But all he could hear from feedback sent was people's desire that he use greater self-discipline in respecting their territory even when they performed incompetently.

From our angle it appeared that Bill viewed every situation as an entrepreneurial owner would, which, in the back of his mind, meant that everybody should take direction from him and operate in a maximally cost-effective and function-driven way. He understood that robust, shoot-from-the-hip, speak-your-mind relationships are basically good for business and, mistakenly, he thought others would see the wisdom of proceeding as he did. It wasn't that he didn't care about people; it was that he was operating in a self-empowered mind-set, assuming that he could model the leadership posture that others would eventually assimilate. Nothing he said caused us to doubt the sincerity of his motivation to change or his caring about people and his desire to be kind.

It appeared that Bill's bosses and the people who were critical of his interactions with them never got their messages across. Paradoxically, each bit of progress and each exercise of self-discipline only further distanced Bill from the people who were trying to have an impact on him. They saw his positive steps forward as cosmetic solutions that temporarily obscured the basic problem. It was not a greater exercise of self-discipline that feedback senders were after. They were interested in changing his orientation from owner-boss to employee-teammate. We interpreted their complaints as the result of their being made to feel like bit players in a corporate production in which Bill saw himself having the only starring role.

We never thought the problems were all Bill's. The people who gave feedback and advice probably needed to be more clear—first with themselves and then with Bill—about the level of learning and the type of change they thought Bill required. We don't feel particularly critical of them because they were proceeding the way that most people proceed. They tell the other person what's wrong and count on that person to make it right and eventually to figure out the orientational flaw and change their thinking to reflect it. But in the fast-tempo course of organizational happenings, this is not how most recipients behave. They feel pressured to keep working "efficiently," preferring to make minor adjustments that don't throw them off the track they are on. They think that later on they'll find the time to get to the deeper issue that they see their feedback-givers urging them to consider. When we came along, implying that we had orientational advice to give, Bill didn't have the time, much as Ralph, the finance guy with the solved summer problem, didn't need any more help, and Byron, whose immediate management problems were being solved, didn't "get" the fact that he wasn't learning the key lesson.

Mismatches in levels of feedback sent and received

Both cases discussed in this chapter demonstrate the importance of feedback being directed at correcting the mind-set bias that causes a patterned way of operating that is both personally and organizationally ineffective. They capture two instances where solving the problem at hand left the apparent "real" problem uncorrected. In management circles this is referred to as "papering over the problem" and "solving the symptom." Of course the perspective taken in this book asserts that one can never be completely sure. There's always the possibility of a more potent life-competence issue being served by the nonoptimal approach you see someone taking at work.

People have a natural way of signaling that more is at stake than meets the eye. They get defensive and they resist correcting an action that they just agreed they were doing "wrong." Unfortunately people can act this way even when the value of the advice you are offering far outweighs the value of the personal priority they are struggling to address using the behavior and orientation that you are alleging is workplace ineffective. This is why getting them explicitly involved in the advice-giving and influence process is the only "best way" to proceed. The alternative is manipulation, with resentments and negative politics the predictable fallout.

The cases described in this chapter reflect two of four categories of feedback- and advice-giving and seeking matchups. Knowledge of these categories and a few more examples to use in staking out the other two categories will provide you with a means for testing your determinations of what the other person is actually looking for in the way of advice when he or she resists and acts defensively. Then you will know what you need to do. Explaining these categories and providing you a description of what you face when you go out to exert influence and give advice is the subject of the next chapter.

Note

1. S. A. Culbert and J. J. McDonough, *The Invisible War: Pursuing Self-Interests at Work* (New York: Wiley, 1980), p. 23.

11

Different Levels of Influence and Advice and the Categories of Interaction They Create

Case in point

An executive surprised us by requesting "either marriage or divorce counseling." He told us, "I don't know what to do about the problems I'm causing Ryma (his secretary and assistant). I'd like you to talk with her, then you make 'the call.' " He told us the reason was not incompatibility or lack of quality effort on her part. It was that working for him was taking an extraordinary toll. It was Wednesday; she had been out since Monday and was expected back tomorrow. She had told him it was "stress." And, he said, "Clearly I'm the cause."

We had met Ed during a management shootout in which the boss he eventually replaced had been working hard to get him fired. From the beginning we were impressed by the high-principled way he conducted himself during a power struggle that went on for months. Ed later shrugged off our insinuation that his conduct was extraordinary. He said that his adversary was in a tough spot and he felt compassion for him.

Ed told us that the most plausible solution to his problem with Ryma would be to have her swap jobs with his deputy's secretary. He said, "That job has fewer pressure points and Pete is far more easygoing than I am. But this certainly is not what I want, for Shirley is not nearly as skilled or speedy as Ryma. Besides, I just plain like Ryma a lot. We really help each other and we're good friends. Working with Shirley I'd have to supplement with 'temps,' which I would rather avoid. It sets a bad precedent, and they require additional supervision that I don't have time to give. In any event, I'd be drafting Ryma back whenever Shirley was out sick or on vacation."

Our talk with Ryma was very efficient; it took under thirty minutes. She made it clear that she likes working for Ed but fears for her health. She sees Ed as a high-quality, self-critical, perfectionistic performer who will rework a letter, a document, or report until he gets precisely what he wants. And in almost every instance she can see the last increment of added value. She also told us that Ed is an outstanding thinker and team player. She liked the fact that he is constantly being drafted for special task forces and consulted on matters of high-level corporate strategy. She told us that she likes working on important, high-status projects and feels obligated to work late when extra effort is needed. She said, "I can go days and weeks absorbing the stress, but sometimes I'm at the point where I know that the next straw, and that's all it ever is—a straw, will break this camel's back."

Ryma said, "It's impossible to plan my day because I can never tell when completed work will have to be revised to make something that is 'right enough' even better. I know it's wrong, but periodically I take all the pressures home. My husband and teenagers are good sports about my time, but I feel guilty when I come home over the edge after working late or when I have to come in on weekends to clean up loose ends." Then Ryma volunteered a piece of personal history that in our minds decided the advice we wanted to give. She told us, "My father was also a perfectionist and, in his case, I worked my entire childhood to please a man who couldn't be pleased."

To us, it was a clear instance of work chemistry being arranged by the "devil." We had two people who really liked each other, who valued one another's work, who wanted to continue working together, who periodically, because of their temperaments, caused the other anguish. In an ideal world, the solution was clear. Both Ryma and this high-principled executive would have to change their orientations. Ed would have to learn to lighten up on his compulsiveness and perfectionism to settle for "good enough." And Ryma would have to control her excessive need to please an authority she respected who, unlike her father, was paying off with acceptance and appreciation. We figured that if each were to go daily to psychoanalysis, they could individually accomplish what they needed to learn to change their chemistry in a mere three to four years.

Fixing the specifics and leaving
the orientations alone

But the world at work is not an ideal world. Feedback- and advice-giving aimed at the ideal, instead of the practical, are inefficient. Benefits are measured against costs. If either Ed or Ryma wants to work on personal evolution, that's grist for their own time. Thus this time we passed over the opportunity to give "orientational" feedback and advice and instead focused on giving advice that, "instrumentally," would fix the situation at hand.

We convened a brief meeting with Ryma and Ed. First we acknowledged what we thought were the underlying assumptions. We told them that we were working with the impression that deep down each was looking for a way to continue working with the other, and that staying together was contingent on finding a way to help Ryma manage her stress. We said, "Both of you need to know when you are nearing the point where the next 'straw' Ed puts on Ryma's desk will be experienced as weighing a pound."

We reviewed the devilish situation in which Ryma found herself with Ed. Then we proposed that she install a "personal-pressure barometer." We said, "You guys need some way of gauging the effects of the straws." With this, the executive turned to Ryma and said, "You do realize that whenever I think you are under pressure, I try to back off. But you keep up such a happy and willing front that I'm not always able to keep track of your workload and have no way of judging your pressure." She replied, "I know I do, and I don't want you worrying about me all the time."

In response to our barometer suggestion, they devised a three-sector circle with a center spinner. The sectors were colored green, yellow, and red. As corny as it sounds, Ryma has placed it in an inconspicuous spot on her desk and to this day, diligently keeps the spinner pointed on the right color. Just as diligently Ed monitors it as he zips through her office on the way in and out of his.

We include this story to extend the point that feedback and advice are given and sought at different levels and that finding the appropriate matchup between level of advice given and sought is what you should be aiming to achieve. Of course getting an open-minded reception for the matchup you seek also depends on each of the considerations we've mentioned. It depends on the person you are advising seeing that you are responsive to essential dimensions of the personal equation in which he or she is operating; believing that your personal agenda is not competitive with his or her best interests; hearing you communicate in a framework that closely resembles the one in which he or she is operating; and feeling that the two of you are in a basically goodwilled relationship.

We need to tell you one more story to finish mapping the spectrum of feedback- and advice-giving and seeking matchups and mismatches. We think you'll find this a familiar type of situation, and because you know it so well, we're going to omit details to keep the storytelling efficient. It's an account of a mismatch in levels of feedback given and sought that took place at the OceanView Medical Center, described in Chapter 9.

Case in point

Recall how, in our OceanView consultation, we recommended that Ad Council members be authorized to make decisions on their own, with team meetings devoted to people giving their opinions and advice in response to a responsible party's preliminary thinking. This was our recommendation for empowering a group of administrators that previously had been dragging one another down. Of course giving people the authority to act and giving them good advice is one thing, but getting them to think open-mindedly about the good advice they receive prior to using that authority is another. In this respect, OceanView turned out to be a terrific challenge.

The challenge of getting people with authority to think open-mindedly was highlighted by Carl, the new CEO, reiterating that the medical center's future business depended on the development and marketing of new specialty programs to contracting HMOs. He asserted that to this point the medical center wasn't capitalizing on major areas of physician expertise, such as heart and cancer. Several times he instructed his marketing manager, Laurie, to take the initiative to develop and market new programs but there was no action on her part that he could perceive.

Two months of talk and no apparent action led Carl to request a "showdown" discussion with Laurie. He called her to his office to ask what she had planned. She responded that she was busy with her existing marketing duties and waiting for the physicians to give her the details of the programs they had promised to develop. She said that she had met with several medical directors as well as the senior physicians in their departments to explain the medical center's business development interests. She said she would go out to market these programs just as soon as the physicians put them on line.

Carl told us, "When I heard Laurie's response, my blood pressure went through the roof. I was losing it completely so I pretended there was an important phone call I needed to make and asked for a half-hour recess. When we reconvened I calmly told her, 'You've got it all wrong.' I said, 'I'm afraid it's going to be a lost cause if you wait around for physicians who, for years, have been competing and fighting over patients and facilities to put something together on their own. It's time for you to take the lead in making sure new programs get conceptualized and made operational in a format that you can sell.' " He went on, "I told her, 'It's time for you to change your job. Your old marketing job was "publicity," your new one is "program development." ' I told her not to waste her time marketing existing programs that under no circumstances were going to impact our bottom line. I said, 'Unless we start marketing some new revenue-producing programs soon, we're all going to be out on the streets looking for our next jobs.' "

He said, "Laurie responded by saying, 'If that's what you want, count on me to get it done.' But her next breath was a request for me to instruct Mel (the administrator who oversees medical services) to support her efforts in taking an aggressive stance with the physicians in getting them focused on program development. I told her, 'Cajole him and if that doesn't work, tell him to just get out of your way. Explain this is not a jurisdictional dispute, this is our existence! If you are clear I don't think he'll need my instructions. But if he doesn't respond and you still want me to drag him in here and give him the facts of life, I'll be glad to.' In response, Laurie said, 'Mel's a good egg. Probably if I speak more emphatically he won't present any real opposition.' "

While Laurie got "the message," from Carl's account it appeared that she didn't understand it. She knew that to be on the square with Carl, she needed to be in the business of developing revenue-producing, market-worthy new programs. She clearly got the message about the actions and behavior that would allow her to be seen as functioning effectively doing what her boss wanted her to do. But Carl told us, "In the process I learned that Laurie is the type of person who requires clear directions. Now the question in my mind is how much progress she can achieve between the last direction I gave her and her need for the next."

We introduced this story saying it should sound familiar. Now we can add that if it does, it's probably from the standpoint of your seeing positively intentioned performers, functioning with dated or ineffective orientations, who seem unable to adjust their mind-set and relate to your advice in terms other than politically sensitive acquiescence. This was not a case of Laurie's being unwilling to give her boss what he wanted even if what he wanted was a different mind-set and orientation. Giving the boss what he wanted was totally consistent with Laurie's orientation, but figuring out the more appropriate orientation was not.

We're now at the point where we can be more systematic in explaining our model for feedback-sending and receiving matchups and the opportunities and consequences of each. The model is the result of forming a four-celled matrix composed of the interactions of the two basic types of advice and feedback that are being sent and sought. We call these instrumental and orientational. (See Figure 11.1.)

Categories of advice and feedback given and sought

INSTRUMENTAL ADVICE

We use the term *instrumental* to refer to advice that specifies what actions an individual should be taking to achieve the results he or she wants to effect. It does not deal with changing an individual's thought processes or the underlying assumptions that lead him or her to naturally construe events a certain way.

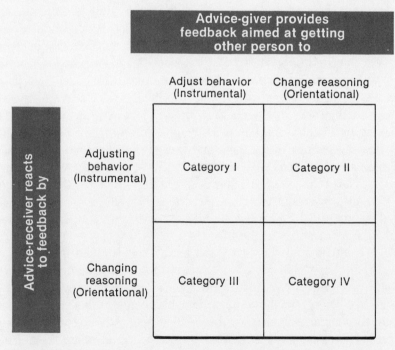

Figure 11.1. Categories of advice-giving and receiving matchups.

Instrumental advice proceeds on the assumption that an advice-giver is helping a recipient to accomplish what that person is trying to achieve by supplying information, regarding discipline, sensitivity, skills, technique, and discrete actions to be taken. It entails feedback that does not require recipients to construe events differently, although it is often aimed at helping them see elements of a situation that formerly escaped their attention and to see options for responding that they have been inclined to systematically overlook. In short, it is advice based on acceptance of an individual's perceptions and reasoning, and his or her objectives in the situation at hand.

In other words, instrumental advice is aimed at getting the recipient to make situationally appropriate behavioral adjustments while using the same basic mind-set that he or she has been using all along. Sometimes this advice is even solicited and then it's impossible to distinguish "advice" from "tell me how" instruction.

ORIENTATIONAL ADVICE

In contrast, *orientational* advice and feedback are aimed at changing an individual's mind-set to cause that person to see and frame situations differently than he or she previously has been construing them. The premise is that the recipient is involved in an interlocking set of effectiveness problems in which no appreciable, long-lasting improvement takes place without the individual changing how he or she frames events and/or attributes meaning to people's actions in them.

Orientationally, the feedback objective is to change the assumptions an individual makes when viewing events and thinking about how to focus his or her energies in them. Because the objective is to make an impact on someone's inner logic, that person's current goals are not necessarily considered givens. That is, personal goals are likely to change when an individual views a situation differently and reasons differently about what needs to be accomplished. Orientational feedback- and advice-giving assumes that people are out to perform competently and with empowerment but does not assume that a specific individual is unalterably set in his or her thinking about what ultimately is required to do so.

Comparing instrumental and orientational advice

Whereas instrumental advice is aimed at helping an individual to *perform* more effectively given the way he or she already thinks, orientational advice is aimed at helping an individual to *think* more effectively. While instrumental advice is situational and often limited to instructing someone how to carry out some action or how to effect a desired reaction in a specific person, orientational advice is aimed at changing how an individual reasons about a class of situations and/or a category of people or even people in general, and leads to a person rethinking objectives, goals, and even purposes.

Sometimes the line between instrumental and orientational advice and feedback is not easily drawn. In the earlier example, Laurie changed her orientation toward marketing, but not because she thought differently. She changed because her boss told her to change and following the directions of a boss she respects conforms to her long-existent reasoning mode of wanting to do what the job requires. Laurie redefined her orientation based on doing what was required to reach her goals, which is the core premise of instrumental reasoning. The issue for our discrimination was whether or not a change in underlying assumptions and mind-set was required. You'll find that your recognition of this difference will be assisted by remembering that orientational changes affect several different domains of an individual's life simultaneously.

It's usually a desire to be more effective in a specific situation that evokes an individual's interest in receiving or seeking advice, which by definition is a quest for the instrumental. That is, an individual wants to know what adjustment, modification, or change in behavior will allow him or her to overcome obstacles to achieving that which he or she set out to accomplish. This person is interested in knowing what behavior will be more effective in a specific situation and will have more appeal for the person or people he or she is attempting to favorably impress and influence. Feedback is sought because that individual believes others who face similar situations or relationships know techniques that enable them to operate more effectively. Sometimes an individual extracts a rule from what he or she learns in a specific situation and applies it to a class of situations or relationships. In either case, unless the individual's thought processes change, the motivation is to make a behavioral adjustment that accomplishes his or her goals using roughly the mind-set and orientation that person has, all along, been using.

Orientational advice is aimed at getting people to reassess the personal assumptions that underlie their daily reasoning and to make substantial adjustments in their thinking. This entails getting people to reassess some root assumption made about themselves and their underlying nature, or about the nature and desires of others, or about the nature of the organization and the organizational systems in which they are functioning.[1] Getting people to open themselves to such reassessments entails a level of commitment that usually takes

place only after an accumulation of problems and/or a serious disconfirmation. Up until that time, the rule of parsimony is operating. It
takes much less time and effort for an advice-receiver to be influenced instrumentally. But reassessing fundamental assumptions that
lead to life attitudes and patterns of relationships and goals for all
situations requires significantly more time and emotional energy.

Categories created by matches and mismatches of advice-giving and seeking

Now let's examine the types of interactions that take place between
advice-givers and seekers, depending on the level of advice given
and taken. Making this discrimination we're able to identify and label
four categories of advice giving and seeking interaction (see Figure
11.2): behavioral effectiveness, political accommodation, socialization, and breakthrough learning.

    As you can see, none of the interaction categories is solely de-
termined by what the advice-giver actually intends to send. They are
all determined by the level at which the advice-recipient reacts to it.
Of course the level the advice-giver intends plays a role; in fact, the

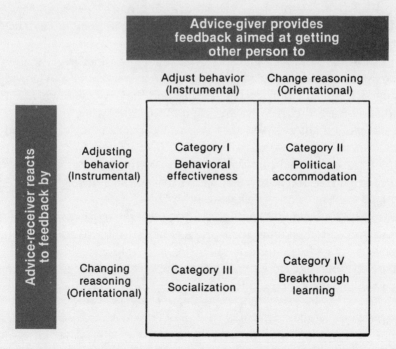

Figure 11.2. Categories of advice-giving and receiving matchups and
types of resulting interactions.

advice-giver will often take pains to communicate accurately and will read the recipient's reaction and subsequent behavior as feedback and use that feedback as an impetus for subsequent clarifications.

The Artifact of Mind insight provides valuable perspective in thinking about overlaps and disparities in levels of advice-giving and receiving interaction. It instructs that it's not what an individual does or intends that counts, it's how that individual's actions are self-interestedly seen.

Category I: Behavioral effectiveness

From the standpoint of efficiency and effectiveness, behavioral effectiveness is far and away the easiest category in which to send and receive advice and feedback. It's the category in which the advice-giver is not out to change the recipient's mind-set; he or she is merely out to give pointers on how this person can perform more effectively given current reasoning and perceptions. Reciprocally, it's the category in which the advice-recipient is looking for pointers on how to handle a specific situation and individual, or type of situation and class of people. This is the category in which you *instruct* someone who wants to dress for success to stop wearing white socks to work. If that person sees you as dressing more conventionally than Madonna or Weird Al, it's entirely likely that your advice will be creditable and receive serious consideration.

This is the advice-interaction category in which we engaged Ed and Ryma. We merely listened to their assumptions and goals, recapped their situation to check whether they thought we had their situation framed correctly, and then straightforwardly gave them our feedback and advice. And they reacted correspondingly. It's also the category of advice we gave Ralph, the finance manager in Chapter 3, when we presented him with our idea of the actions he might take to cope with a troublesome situation that we saw having the potential to bury him, at work as well as at home.

When giving instrumental advice to someone who solicits it from you, the communication process ought to be relatively straightforward. It's matter-of-fact, shoot-from-the-hip instruction time. You and the other person exchange perceptions of what needs to be improved, acquaint one another with your individual assumptions, and exchange views about what's needed for that person to move forward successfully. Whether or not an individual decides to follow your prescription, and precisely what twist or spin gets put on it, is an issue to be decided.

Category II: Political accommodation

In this category, the advice-giver is out to get another person to change how he or she perceives events and reasons, while that person is merely looking to take specific (instrumental) action that satisfies the immediate needs of the situation and the people in it. This results in a mismatch and conflict of intentions. The advice-giver is thinking, "Don't you get it? It's your way of seeing things and reasoning that's off and being more effective requires more than merely disciplining yourself to act differently," while the recipient is thinking, "Tell me what I need to know, what to do or how to appear, to get the reaction and the results I want. I want to satisfy the people who are counting on me so that they will give me support, or at least say I'm doing a good job." The advice-giver is groping to express, "The behavior you need to change is merely a representation of your mistaken way of thinking and interpreting situations and people's actions in them. If you merely change your behavior the problem you're having is not going to go away." Conversely, the recipient wants to proceed toward current goals, reasoning and seeing things more or less as he or she always has.

Resisting a change in orientation creates an advice-giving conflict that needs to be reconciled. There are three possible resolutions: (1) The advice-giver yields and switches to making his or her advice instrumental, which changes the interaction category from Category II to Category I. (2) The advice-recipient concedes by acknowledging an orientational problem and this moves the interaction from Category II to Category IV. (3) Neither party switches and they enter into a cat-and-mouse interaction in which the advice-recipient pretends that changes in behavior are actually changes in orientation, while the advice-giver acts as if *accommodations* in behavior represent progress in orientation. The third condition is actually Category II and that is why we label it **political accommodation.**

This is the category in which Laurie received Carl's feedback. Clearly Carl was asking Laurie to acquire a different mind-set and she understood that he wanted her to change her orientation. But her desire to give Carl the behavior he wanted far exceeded her interest, and perhaps her capacity, to sort through the personal assumptions she made to identify which ones Carl was contesting and whether she wanted to or could make a change. Carl wanted Laurie to reason and see events differently. He wanted her to proceed as if she were an OceanView owner, who would do what was necessary to get revenue-producing programs on line, and as if not having them would immediately bankrupt the company.

Laurie's response was unquestionably instrumental despite the fact that she probably thought she was giving Carl precisely what he wanted—a new orientation. We interpreted her actions as instrumental to being perceived as functioning correctly and doing her part to make OceanView profitable. She wanted to fulfill Carl's expectations of what it took for someone with her job to help the medical center become profitable. But Carl didn't see her changing any fundamental assumption. He was left feeling that Laurie would always be dependent on his telling her the next "right" way to proceed.

Whether or not Laurie's current orientation equips her to lead a physician-planning effort to come up with market-worthy new medical programs remains to be seen. Likewise for her exerting leadership in relationships with Ad Council peers. Of course Carl's goals for Laurie are more ambitious. But given the number and magnitude of management problems at OceanView, in the short run Laurie's response was good enough for Carl. In fact it may even have taught Carl to adjust his orientation to Laurie based on what he now sees her having the capacity to do. He might now be reasoning that if Laurie had a different capacity, she'd be working in a big-time advertising agency instead of at his regional medical center.

Category III: Socialization

In this category, the advice-giver sends messages aimed at getting another person to adjust specific behaviors, while that individual is looking to extrapolate from the advice to figure out an orientational formula for success. This reflects a mentality that many newcomers assume when joining a firm. They want to decode the company "program" so that they can feel secure and fit in. The objective is to discern which ways of reasoning and operating have good corporate currency, and adopt those orientations in order to give the company what it values. Lessons learned in specific situations are scrutinized for the formula that will allow them to be applied in a class of situations. In effect, people are looking to socialize themselves. They seek to internalize what is required externally and to live their lives as if it were personally correct.

Of course the trap in extrapolating a template for general practice from any message that's been sent to help an individual adjust his or her response to a specific situation is the possibility of people internalizing patterns of behavior that the advice-sender never meant to instill and would never advocate or endorse. The advice-recipient "psyches out the system," and in the process "psyches out him- or herself" as well.

From the standpoint of the Artifact of Mind insight, providing specific, instrumental advice to someone who is looking for a more effective way to reason and see organizational events reflects a mismatch and advice-giver insensitivity. It features an advice-giver providing instructions in a situation in which he or she is far better off asking questions. Structurally speaking, the advice is being treated as a behavioral formula, with the only variable being the behavior of the advice-recipient. A problem has been specified and all remedies have the same punch-line ending, "this is the right way to behave." The advice-recipient is being told to measure up to the requirements that the system had long before it ever heard of this recipient and his or her personal attributes.

This is the category in which we saw Bill operating. Recall Bill was the manager with the entrepreneurial orientation, described in Chapter 10, who said he wanted to become "a good corporate citizen." Bill knew something about his orientation was off and he wanted to fix it. Continually he searched through feedback he received relating to specific problems looking for the corporate DNA. But steeped in his freewheeling logic, he could never quite deduce the correct genetic code. His idea of teamwork was being smart enough to do what was "right." He seemed unable to comprehend the style of teamwork that others were looking to receive from him. The result was a series of adjustments, each one reflecting the thinking that this time he understood the formula for getting along.

While Bill's management, and for that matter almost everyone who gave Bill advice, wanted Bill's orientation to change, no one ever provided him with a clear statement of what was needed to get his behavior "genetically" correct. Bill heard people speaking and providing advice only about specifics that bothered them and he couldn't get the connections between those specifics and the misaligned assumptions that were driving his participation. If he could have, he might have dropped his entrepreneurial indulgences and begun seeing things in a way that truly allowed him to be "a good corporate citizen." But Bill was unable to extrapolate from the action-specific feedback provided him to figure out precisely the required orientation. Perhaps he should have been able to piece it together from the feedback he received, but, for whatever reason, he did not.

Category IV: Breakthrough learning

In this category, feedback is given and sought at the level of orientation and mind-set learning and change. While this is the most sought-after category, it's also the one in which, on demand, positive results are usually somewhere between difficult and impossible to achieve. This is the category in which psychotherapists and their clients conduct a large portion of their conversations but, without the catalysts of "severe adversity" and "devastating failure," make only sporadic progress. It is the territory where corporate team building and strategic planning meetings aim to produce "results," but seldom do these results emanate from changing people's underlying assumptions, which is required for long-lasting, fundamental mind-set change. It's the level you go to in contemplating your most perplexing performance-effectiveness problems, for it is here where an individual's, or a group's, true potential is best realized.

Most of the case studies we've described thus far entail advice-giving attempts to get through with orientational lessons aimed at producing breakthrough insights and learning. And even the dramatically successful instances, such as the outcomes achieved with "CDX" Ken in Chapter 3 and "Blaming" Barry in Chapter 8, were preceded by a series of Category IV influence and feedback attempts by people who couldn't get to first base. In every instance, the eventual breakthrough learner had gone years without grasping what advice-givers had vigorously advocated.

As you go about attempting to influence people and give them advice, you'll find that breakthrough learning is your most frequent goal. While most of our stories stop prior to people's attaining breakthrough results, please don't interpret this to mean that breakthroughs never take place. They simply hadn't taken place on the issues we were describing at the point we left off. Our intent is that by your reading about these people, and the actions that we and others took, your feedback- and advice-giving capacities will be increased.

While the turnaround lessons are those in Category IV, we assume that you also will find ways of giving helpful advice in the other three categories. On the other hand, there's an incredible amount of lost capacity due to not being able to achieve Category IV results. We could go on and on about what might have been achieved if only someone could have gotten through to Ralph, Laurie, Bill, and others. If only the conditions had been right for engaging these people in Category IV interactions with lessons that were obvious to the "outsiders" who knew them, their situations would be entirely different.

We've had plenty of opportunity to study Category IV advice-giving and seeking, since this is the category for which our assistance is most often solicited. People who are challenged and in a bind, sensing the opportunities and perils in front of them, eagerly, and sometimes desperately, reach out for "expert" help. They do so even though in the back of their minds they know that, if they are lucky, the most they're likely to get in response to their request for an emergency-room operation is a bit of infirmary first aid. Perhaps this understates what we can deliver. But it's our way of saying that facilitating breakthrough learning is not something that you, we, or anyone we know of, can deliver on demand.

This is not to say that people don't have breakthrough lessons or that mind-sets and orientations don't change. It is merely to say that there is no formula for producing this type of change, no matter how vivid and compelling the data and life situations you've got at hand. It doesn't mean that you shouldn't try. We think that your "failed" attempts will often make it a lot easier for the next set of advice-givers, in the next set of circumstances, to succeed. Specifically what's needed in the way of conditions for helping an individual to engage open-mindedly and open-emotionally in breakthrough learning leading to orientational change is the topic of the next chapter.

Note

1. These assumptions are discussed in detail in S. A. Culbert, *The Organization Trap* (New York: Basic Books, 1974).

12

Breakthrough Learning

For the last five years we've been keeping track of Category IV activities and, in particular, the conditions under which people achieve breakthrough results. We've observed people at work and analyzed their conversations. We've interviewed people who we heard had broken through self-limiting orientations that, for years, they had resisted changing. And we've conducted research in which we've asked people to anonymously fill out questionnaires in which we ask them to describe a "breakthrough lesson" and the circumstances that were present when it occurred in search of "milestone" conditions. Describing these milestone conditions required for breakthrough learning and specifying how you can mobilize them are the topics of this and the next three chapters.

Thus far we've identified three conditions that must be met prior to Category IV interactions producing what turns out to be actual breakthrough results. We call these conditions **set-breaking, conceptual clarification,** and **emotional bonding.** We've also identified a fourth condition, **anchoring the breakthrough lesson.** But this fourth condition doesn't become a consideration until after a breakthrough lesson is learned. When we place these conditions in sequential order they become a model that describes what most people go through when achieving breakthrough results.

We use this model when we're called upon to facilitate the interactions of people engaged in giving and receiving advice aimed at influencing orientations. We also apply it in our counseling efforts with individual students and managers. In the process we've learned a few application principles that we can quickly describe for you right now. We've discovered that the presence of two of these conditions without the third is insufficient. We've learned that while there are actions that an advice-giver can take in promoting each of these three conditions, set-breaking and conceptual clarity are the only two over which that person has any degree of control. We've learned that the third condition, emotional bonding, is one that defies logic and rational prescription and can defeat even the most heroic efforts. An unspecifiable chemistry, not just more effort, seems to be what's required.

In this chapter we're going to illustrate these breakthrough learning conditions in a story about an executive whose boss struggled long and hard to get him to change his orientation. But before we do, we need to mention one more important issue. Whether or not a breakthrough, mind-set, orientational lesson is learned can be determined only by scrutinizing what advice-recipients actually do, not by what they say they are doing. The expression today is "walk the talk," a slogan that arises from the frequency and ease with which people whose reasoning has not changed are able to temporarily convince themselves and others that they are actually different.

Now for the illustration. As you read it through, see if you can spot how we went about staging the conditions required for breakthrough learning. If you've read this far, no doubt you're seriously interested in influencing people at the orientational level, which means that periodically you attempt to do something similar.

Case in point

In reviewing the performance of his director of business affairs, John, the company's president, said, "There's no question about it, Mike is my 'star *problem* performer.' For months I've been after him. We've defined and redefined his department's mandate to maximize what we need from him most. He's got all the personal attributes, but I don't know how to get him to function effectively." John then went on to extol Mike's abilities and his loyalty and long history with the company. He made it clear that he felt close to Mike and wanted to keep him in the company.

John then told us about his attempts to get Mike to change his orientation. He said, "At first I tried being very supportive, but finally I had to resort to candid criticism. Then I made his entire peer group vice presidents, leaving Mike behind. But the message still didn't seem to get through. Desperately, six weeks ago I gave him this 'dire' performance appraisal." Then he handed us a copy. Borrowing it back for a moment, John emotionally read it aloud. Carefully John raised and lowered his voice to dramatize the precise words he had used in an effort to criticize Mike and put him on notice. However, we weren't sure that we could have detected the "dire" nature of his message without his accentuated vocal inflections.

Trying to be supportive, we responded, "Listening to what you wrote it's clear you were trying to be candid. However, when people don't want to face their predicament, and its serious potential consequences, we find they can easily slip past messages as intense and as critical as the one you just read."

John responded, "That's why I'm so upset. I'm not getting through to Mike, and I don't know how to make it more clear. We need more output, which means we either hire in a senior-level manager to direct him or bring in the staff required to get the work accomplished. And despite our tight budget, I'd hire more staff in a minute if I thought it would cause his operation to function correctly. I want your impression about whether we're ever going to get him to perform." Then he gave the details on the specifics of Mike's "deficiencies." This time he added that each of the new vice presidents, Mike's former peers, also complain about Mike's lack of production and unresponsiveness to their needs.

Next we met alone with Mike. We began by asking Mike if he knew about our work with the other managers and why he thought his boss had arranged this meeting. He said he had noticed us but had only a vague impression about the nature of our consultations. He said that, in making arrangements, John had merely told him that we were helpful in facilitating communications and that he hoped we could help him and Mike to better understand one other. He said John told him to be totally candid and to call him when we were finished so that he might join in the conversation.

If Mike understood the seriousness of John's concerns, he wasn't letting on. In an attempt to gain the appropriate focus, we took out our copy of his performance review. We said, "John told us he arranged this meeting because he sees you as a deficient performer whom he wants to see turn around." Shocked at our use of the word "deficient," Mike stiffened and said, "That's not at all how I understand John." Picking up our copy and scanning it he said, "John refers to performance deficiencies, and that could be said about anyone. But nowhere do I read 'deficient performer.'" Without debating this, we asked him for his views on the problems mentioned and on some of the situations John had told us about when explaining how Mike's mode of operating was insufficient.

Mike responded, "Before I get into addressing the problems, I need to tell you about the business affairs function and how it was conceived to perform the critical bridge between sales and marketing and the agreements we strike with our manufacturing partners and customers." Listening carefully we could not detect discrepancies between what he was saying and the objectives John had cited. But when Mike described the specific functions he performed and the activities he had devised for carrying them out, the problems John described came into focus. There wasn't anything illogical about what Mike was doing or failing to do, it was that the order with which he performed his activities seemed significantly at odds with John's priorities. He said his problems with John resulted from his always being just about to do exactly what John wanted him to do most but, because he hadn't done it yet, John could not see it was about to be accomplished.

In response to each of the problems John raised, Mike had a well-thought-out way of explaining how John held an incorrect impression. In his mind, John and he saw things differently, and his views were the "correct" ones. He had a great deal of respect for John and was convinced that, with time, he would eventually win John over to his way of interpreting events. In fact Mike was so articulate and convincing that we began to think the meeting with John would feature Mike taking up issues one-by-one in setting John's thinking straight.

Our understanding was appreciably advanced when we asked Mike if he thought he might similarly be able to squelch the vice presidents' concerns about him. Expressing puzzlement, he asked, "What makes you think the vice presidents are critical of me?" In response we asked, "Do you mean this is the first you have heard about their criticisms?" When he assured us it was, we said, "Well of course you'll have to ask those guys yourself. We can tell you that John specifically mentioned their unhappiness with your failure to convene biweekly contract review meetings. John believes that he has several times specifically 'ordered' you to hold them and that this is 'memorialized' in your recent performance review. He's told us that even though he sent you a written directive, you still aren't holding them regularly."

Mike responded, "Those meetings aren't a good use of anyone's time. By the time they're held, they don't accomplish anything that hasn't already been accomplished in my discussions with the specific people who need to be filled in. I honestly don't see one reason for holding them." In response, we asked, "Isn't their wanting to attend those meetings reason enough for you to hold them?" Then Mike surprised us by answering with an emphatic "No!" We asked,

"How about the organization politics? Don't politics dictate your holding these meetings? The vice presidents believe that they want them. John says he has ordered you to hold them. Yet you don't hold them because you don't think they are a good use of your time."

We continued, "Now you can see the pattern. There are differences in expectations. In your mind you are correct. But your allegedly 'correct' responses are getting you labeled 'deficient performer' by everyone above you in the company hierarchy." We said this carefully. We didn't want to be hurtful, but we needed to drive home the point that being "right" is not enough and that Mike's orientation was off because it allowed him to justify not engaging his evaluators in the context of the realities they lived. Mike then emphasized the key difference. He said, "Being in the company from the time it was small, I always hoped that we could avoid organization politics and dispense with activities that serve no other purpose than getting your ticket punched."

In response, we said, "This may be a crucial insight in your understanding how the orientation you've taken is getting you labeled deficient." Then, we counseled, "Incidentally, we view politics as a natural consequence of people with different responsibilities and different personal agendas requiring one another's support. Politics per se are not good or bad; they just are! People have stakes in what you do and how you go about doing it. If you think they are wrong, have it out with them. Do yourself a favor, don't leave them with the impression that you are ignoring them. Apparently you've got people upset to the point where they feel they have to damn your entire production in order to get your attention and exert some influence over you."

Mike's flushed face told us we were getting through. Then he asserted, "Well where, then, does John think I'm going to find the time to accomplish all that actually needs to be accomplished while spending more time with everyone who wants to have a say in how we negotiate deals?" We responded, "That sounds like an important issue to raise with him." Mike was getting angry. Heatedly he went through his list of frustrations, including the upset he experienced when the announcement of the vice presidential promotions was made. Hurtfully he found out the same way everyone else found out. He read a duplicated notice stuck in his company mailbox.

After two hours with Mike and a half-hour recess for him to digest the conversation, it was time for John to join in. Mike began by aggressively challenging John, saying, "The consultants have told me that I am a 'deficient performer.' Is that really the case?" Apparently that was too stark a beginning for John, who attempted to sidestep the "deficient performer" terminology by going through the same specifics that he previously had listed for us. Mike then interrupted, "Do you mean to tell me that if I answer more correspondence and double the number of customer contacts, even the ones that don't appear particularly strategic, then your needs will be satisfied?"

While we could appreciate Mike's logic in responding instrumentally to the specific problems John raised, we understood that John was working at a different level and Mike was not responding as John wanted him to. To help, we pitched in. "From our conversations with each of you, it appears that you agree on objectives, and miss one another on the topic of how to 'orient' to events to reasonably accomplish objectives. Experience has taught us that 'orientation' is a very difficult topic for people to discuss with clarity."

Seizing the cue, John tried a couple of clever approaches. First, he tried describing how he needs people with orientations that complement his own in contrast to Mike's, which tend to replicate his. To illustrate, he talked about bringing Mike along to a customer meeting and thinking how analytically skilled and verbally artful Mike's performance was. However, upon leaving the meeting John told of having second thoughts. He said, "Mike, I realized that I could have accomplished the same results on my own and that my real need is for you to set up these customer meetings and conduct them without me, which, despite my constant admonitions, is something you seldom do."

Then John tried a Shakespearian analogue. He compared the deliberating and lamentful Hamlet with Fortinbras, a man of action, who went out conquering before his opposition could get wind of his intentions and mount a resistance. John asserted that he needed Mike to be his Fortinbras, and that a man of action possessing Mike's analytic and verbal skills was assured of success. In an attempt to further drive this point home, John expressed his feeling that Mike would spend ten years beating the bushes for grouse, which, during the period of bush beatings, surely would have already flown away. Unfortunately, neither of these metaphors seemed to accomplish much in terms of getting Mike to change his orientation.

Mike then brought up the issue of the criticisms made by the vice presidents, his former peers. John was significantly more emphatic than we had been in pressing these criticisms. He confronted Mike on the matter of not convening contract review meetings. Mike responded more or less as he had with us. This time he added that John's heavy travel schedule prevented John from attending most of the meetings. Mike said it was ridiculous to hold them without John there to make decisions. He said that without John, the meetings regressed to redundant exchanges of information. John countered this belief by stating that he would fully support decisions arrived at in those meetings and in fact would now be willing to extend Mike's authority to include negotiating "parameters," price, and even signing contracts. John said he merely needed to ensure that Mike understood a few cost issues that would take only a few minutes to explain.

Viewing his new authority as progress, Mike raised the topic of politics. When John expressed dismay that Mike avoids exposing his self-alleged "correct" beliefs for discussion in contract review meetings, Mike countered "If I do, then I open the door to these guys making requests that are going to overwhelm us with legwork. Where do you think I'm going to find the time to accomplish all that detail work?" Then, rhetorically, he asked permission to hire a subordinate.

Finally John bit the bullet. He responded, "Mike, I'm at the point where I don't know whether to hire your boss or your subordinate." He went on, "Even as we speak, this is a live question for me. We're simply not getting the outreach we need and someone has to get it done." Mike appeared stunned. After a long, uncomfortable silence, he looked up at John and said, "Then these guys were right from the beginning, I am seen as a 'deficient performer.' " John closed his eyes and slowly nodded.

Believing that Mike and John had each stepped up to the line, we asked, "Mike, how about thinking of yourself as having two jobs. One is to be the boss directing you and your activities and the other is the actual performance of business affairs functions. In such a scenario, what would the boss's job entail?" Mike then described what he had formerly termed "the politicking side" of the directing job—meeting with customers, negotiating agreements, and convening meetings to bring others on board and get their commitments to the proper type of follow-through. John interrupted him saying, "There, you've got it. That's what I want you doing 95 percent of the time! While you call it politicking, I call it networking and directing." Mike's face flushed again. With a tone of disbelief he exclaimed, "You mean it's that simple?" John looked at him amazed.

We asked John whether he thought Mike sufficiently understood the change in orientation that he had been trying to get across. He nodded affirmatively. Smiling warmly he said, "Mike, if you think you've got it I'm willing to take another shot. Go ahead and hire the horsepower you need. I'll find the budget." Later on John said, "I've never seen Mike so emotional and, frankly, he's never seen me so worked up."

The milestone conditions required for breakthrough learning

We were very conscious of the milestones required for Category IV learning when we attempted to facilitate the Mike–John interaction. We were also clear about the progression to be followed: first **set-breaking** or **conceptual clarity,** then **the other,** and finally **emotional bonding.** But all the model provides is the specification of these milestones; it does not provide the route. Giving feedback and advice aimed at orientational change entails taking an unpredictable journey, oftentimes filled with hijinks, adventure, and almost always with demands for emotional involvement in areas that no one can predict.

In the beginning we didn't know whose reality was more "correct," although the real issue was whose reality would prevail. As facilitators, our job was not to decide who was correct. It was to get the different realities lined up and the participants engaged in discussing and negotiating them and moving ahead. However, once we embarked on this course it became apparent that Mike had not previously related to the performance-effectiveness messages that John had been taking pains to send.

We use the term **set-breaker** in referring to the events and moments that finally, and incontestably, signal someone that his or her orientation is off and requires changing. But despite all that John had been attempting, he had not successfully sent such a signal. Up until the point when we got involved, Mike had resisted thinking there was anything off in his orientation and set. Thus, in trying to help Mike and John to engage one another and progress, we needed to get Mike to receive what John was saying in an attempt to get his attention.

The first opportunity emerged when we held out the recent performance review and referenced the "dire" deficient-performer message Mike was avoiding. The second was when we made reference to all of the vice presidents finding fault with his performance, which Mike was refusing to take seriously because, in his mind, they were "wrong." The third was when Mike raised the topic of all his peers being promoted, which we heard him saying was his demotion. We could have more emphatically underscored this message; however, we didn't want to hurt his feelings any more than absolutely necessary. Besides it seemed to us that Mike already had been hurt, but without receiving the set-breaking message John had been attempting to get across.

As the situation unfolded, we thought that most of the potential set-breaking moments emerged in relatively rapid-fire succession.

But they didn't seem to make a difference until John bit the bullet by convincingly telling Mike that he was at the point of hiring someone to carry out the functions that he had been begging Mike to carry out. Later on John told us that he wished he had told this to Mike months ago when it was obvious that he wasn't getting through with his message. He said, "Nothing would have made me happier than to have had an additional vice president. Holding out on Mike has caused me considerable pain."

Once the set is broken, an individual needs to have a **sharp concept** or slogan that describes how he or she was formerly reasoning incorrectly or insufficiently. This is where the way in which you frame your advice can play a significant role. The concept emerges from what you state is the cause of the individual's problems. For example, once John established that he felt Mike was a redundant resource in customer meetings he clearly established what he wanted from Mike.

We think important groundwork for Mike's achieving this conceptual clarity came when we advised him to change his outlook and orientation in response to the needs and perceptions of key others and to attend to organization politics. We think it helped him to finally register John's expectation that he engage other people's opinions and realities and deal with them on-line, as he heard them. Conceptual clarity was cemented after Mike described the "political" job of someone who might be placed in the hierarchy above him and heard John convincingly declare that he could either have that job or the one he was currently performing. At that moment he had conceptual clarity. He could become the boss or the subordinate.

We think that **emotional bonding** with the new orientation began when John convincingly declared that he was only a hairline away from hiring Mike's overseer. We thought it was achieved in the moments following Mike describing the "boss's" job and finding out ". . . it's that simple." These were vividly emotional moments, for John as well as for Mike. Both appeared to be experiencing vulnerability by facing up to a situation that could possibly betray years of friendship and personal loyalty. These seemed to be the moments Mike switched commiting himself to address the goals and priorities that counted most to his evaluators. In short, this seemed to be where Mike "bought into" changing his orientation.

Anchoring the breakthrough lesson

It was a month before we got back to the company to see whether the progress we thought had been made was actually taking place.

We thought it an appropriate passage of time to see what ambivalence would shake out. First we met with John, then Mike.

John told us, "Frankly, I'm a bit suspicious and I can't decide whether my suspicions are well-founded. Clearly Mike is responding, but I don't know what he's going to do when he decides the crisis is over. I'm left with the nagging feeling that I'm asking him to play a role that requires a stomach he lacks. In order to be sure, I'm going to dictate a list of the activities and accomplishments I absolutely expect."

In meeting with Mike we took a light approach. Tongue in cheek we said, "We're here to give your final exam. We have three questions: (1) What did you learn? (2) What are you doing differently? and (3) What additional questions do you have?"

We were delighted to learn how straight and clear Mike had his situation formulated. In response to what had he learned, Mike said, "I've learned the importance of being proactive and the importance of getting people in the boat with me." He elaborated appropriately.

In response to what he was doing differently, Mike mentioned all the activities we thought John might put on the list he planned to dictate. However, we could detect a note of cynicism in Mike's voice and we reflected this back to him. Mike explained. He said that calling on small companies might be an extravagant squandering of an important limited resource—his time. He told us that he doesn't like "formula calls" and that his preferred approach is to "navigate" a bit more. This all sounded reasonable, but we felt that this was a bit of an exaggeration and an ego-bolstering caricature of what John was expecting, and we said so.

And as far as "further questions," Mike was anxious to engage us in a deep discussion of what he sensed was John's suspiciousness. He said, "I've written some memos to John as a means of tapping him on the shoulder to say, 'this has been done.' " We said that sounded like a good idea and then provided him our take on John's desire to see Mike succeed and his fear of possibly being taken in by his desire. We added, "Don't forget, you're the guy who wrote the job description you are following. When people have such latitude, they typically design the job to match their strengths and avoid their weak suits. How would John know whether you plan to assume roles he's previously seen you avoid and, one might logically argue, in which your performance is untested?"

Anchoring appeared to be accomplished when, as we were finishing our conversation with Mike, John dropped by to talk about his idea of an activities checklist to avoid the possibility of Mike's misinterpreting his expectations. He said he would work on a list over the weekend and take Mike through it the following week. In response Mike smiled and said, "There's no need to bother, I have one here in my desk that we can discuss any time you find convenient."

Case reflections

This case appropriately illustrates the imprecision of any "breakthrough learning," mind-set–change methodology. In significant and prototypical ways, Mike resisted and ignored John's attempt to get him to change his orientation. Then he fought it again with us. He resisted having his "set" broken and implied that attending to the political dimension of his job would be a corrupt sellout of what he valued most for the company. To a considerable extent, the conversations we had with him felt hit-and-miss.

On the other hand, this example shows the efficiency of focusing on deeper level lessons and struggling to produce them. In one long afternoon we accomplished what John and the vice presidents had been unable to achieve with Mike in over a year of discussion, confrontational action, and high-pitched emotionality. Even his peers' promotions had failed to drive home the right message.

In telling this "success" story we don't intend to imply that a simple switch in orientation is going to make all of Mike's problems go away. "Simple" is seldom an accurate description for what's required for anyone to switch orientations, and few breakthroughs lead to instant success. A change in orientation merely means that an individual exchanges problems of one type for problems of another. And the new problems are often the result of having to operate in unpracticed ways with skills that ultimately need further development. That is, once an individual switches orientations he or she finds that different skills are required.

For example, prior to changing his orientation, Mike never saw himself functioning as a "politician," which he now sees as a key added dimension to the new role he needs to assume. Will his idea of political functioning overlap what others are requiring of him? Does he, in fact, begin this skill at ground zero, or has he been "political" all along without realizing it? Will he ask for advice and coaching when he isn't sure how to respond to specific requests made of him, which is something he never did when he thought everyone else had the "wrong" picture of his situation and he was the only one who saw things correctly?

These are matters that need to be engaged along with others that are impossible to anticipate in advance of committing to a new orientation. Certainly it would be unrealistic for anyone to expect Mike to function perfectly or even to have a high batting average from the start. And will his critics cut him the needed slack? The Artifact of Mind insight leads us to expect that others will always view events in terms of their own needs to function effectively in them. Thus we can expect that Mike will continually be subject to people placing unrealizable expectations on him, backed up by the culturally sanctioned belief that their demands are "objectively" founded.

Notwithstanding all the complexities, there is a major benefit associated with changing and upgrading one's orientation, no matter how many new skills are required. Not only do immediate problems dissipate, but finally the individual has the opportunity to succeed. The latter is particularly important for people who, in seeking instrumental solutions to the effectiveness problems produced by their current orientations, find that their only achievable goal is to push back a collision course with failure one day at a time.

Now that you've been introduced to the steps required for converting Category IV interactions into breakthrough learning, we're ready to deepen your understanding. That's what the remaining three chapters in this part are aimed at accomplishing. We want to heighten your capacity for realizing the category in which you and another person are interacting and then in determining the potential of getting to Category IV. Once in Category IV, we want to heighten your capacity to accurately assess the probabilities of the other person converting your advice into a breakthrough lesson actually learned.

13

Assessing the Feasibility of Achieving Breakthrough-Learning Results

This chapter is aimed at deepening your understanding of the differences between the four advice-giving and receiving interactions (depicted in Figure 11.2) and what you need to know when, as an advice-giver, you find yourself interacting in one category but desire to interact successfully in a different one. In particular it further enumerates the milestone conditions that need to be covered when interacting in Category IV, attempting to achieve breakthrough-learning results.

Case in point

At the lunch break of a strategic planning retreat, a chief financial officer with a reputation for being a "people person" approached us with a classic problem based on a classic misconception. It's a problem that illustrates the importance of knowing the category of advice-giving interaction that you and the person you are trying to influence are in and making an accurate determination of whether you can get to Category IV and whether interacting there can produce results. The classic problem is how to "fix" a subordinate who is missing an essential ingredient. The classic misconception pertains to how, when it comes to thinking about orientational learning, the human mind tends to think in terms of lightning-bolt breakthroughs as if, suddenly, total illumination will replace darkness.

In this instance Erica asked, "What can I do to help Lydia (her accounting manager) get 'the ingredient' she's missing? Please don't get me wrong. Since I've gotten a sense that there's something off, I've been doing my utmost to help her improve. Last December, to get her attention, I gave her a lower percentage pay increase than I gave the rest of the department. Then, a few days later, I gave her a detailed performance review with examples of the problems I've been having. I thought I was being precise but her counters to each of the problems I mentioned made my complaints sound vague. I felt helpless watching her turn my words to mush. I was talking 'angle of approach' and 'way of reasoning' and she was talking 'effort' and 'precision of results.' The thing that really hurt was her inability to understand what she called my 'unfairness.' And since this review came immediately after a two-and-a-half-week period in which she had gone all out working sixty-five hours a week, it was impossible for me to get through to her.

"I replied by saying that what we really needed was a manager who gets 'the team' involved in her thinking, delegates, and clears her platter to have fewer obligations so that her lead role in assignments is teaching and the development of staff. I said I would try to help by holding weekly meetings to discuss her questions and activities. I told her, 'Let's use these sessions to review workflow and what you're doing to improve the thinking and performance of the people in your department.' Her initial response was to work a seventy-hour week creating detailed skill charts for each supervisor and lead person. These charts portrayed jobs as a set of discrete tasks, and this should have been my clue to the nature of the problem. Lydia was obediently making sure the work got done, but she was not grasping the assignment. She was functioning as a technical supervisor, not as a big-picture manager.

"The extent of the missing ingredient struck home when, to demonstrate delegation, she assigned the weekly skill chart updating to a junior administrator. She took an assignment that required qualitative managerial thinking and transformed it into bean counting and ledger keeping. In my mind, this provided the perfect illustration but I couldn't get this across to her either.

"Trying to hold that discussion I further realized that I'd never get much enjoyment from interacting with her. My initial response was to start leaving her out of the loop by going directly to the supervisors reporting to her. They are bright and alert young people who are very responsive to my coaching. I began to think that either would be a great replacement for Lydia.

"But I had to stop circumventing Lydia when I saw that my

actions were depressing her. She's loyal and willing to do whatever she can that's within the range of her capabilities. This brings me to my current situation, for I don't want to hurt her and don't know what to do. I'm committed to helping her, and I'd like to follow through with this commitment. What do you advise?"

As we said when we introduced this story, when it comes to thinking about mind-set, orientational change, people operate with classic misconceptions. Desires for others to change fill people with overly ambitious goals and unrealistic expectations. The genius and the undoing of the American management system is the inability to discriminate between a failed situation that can be salvaged by over-whelming it with time and energy, and one that's impossible to fix. In the case of changing people, ambitions are inflated beyond what's reasonable by lightning bolt accounts of breakthrough orientation changes. But these are generally after-the-fact reconstructions that feature a dramatic moment as if a single insight was the only event required for someone's breaking through. Such misportrayals lead to unrealistic expectations to the point that we have an entire culture that is disoriented. In our experience, a great deal of water erodes the ground prior to the rain that changes the course of a river's flow.

We responded to Erica's lunchtime question with low-key rein-forcement. We told her it sounded as if she had her situation with Lydia sized up fairly accurately. We said that, from her account, it seemed as if there was little chance that the logic and thought pro-cesses* Lydia used would ever match with hers and, without such a change, it sounded as if she would never judge Lydia sufficient for the manager's job. We said it sounded as if her problem was one of how to deal with a situation requiring an action she didn't want to take.

Offering support we remarked, "We understand, it's a very tough situation. Either way you send a signal you don't want to send." Behind our words was the implicit recognition that keeping Lydia in the manager's spot without her orientation changing would eventually be a motivational turnoff to the able young people working in Erica's department; on the other hand, demoting or dismissing a dedicated employee who works sixty- to seventy-hour weeks could

---

*While listening we were thinking of Lawrence Kohlberg's "moral develop-ment" model and how Erica's account featured Lydia as a level 3, "deference to authority" thinker, while Erica was trying to get through to her with level 4 and level 5 logics which Lydia couldn't compute. See S. A. Culbert and D. Lavoie, "Stages of Organization and Development," *Human Relations, 31* (5): 417–438, 1978, for an application of Kohlberg's scheme to communication problems in the workplace.

demoralize Lydia and all the other employees who count on the company's reciprocating the loyal commitment of an individual.

Apparently our words of support constituted sufficient "reinforcement" for Erica to release from the expectation that there was something more she could do to cause Lydia to reason and function differently. Three days later, Erica packaged together a group of discrete, high-level accounting activities that could be performed by someone working independently, gave these activities a functional name, and, with a respectful and face-saving explanation, offered them to Lydia as a part-time job.

Two weeks later Erica called with an update. She said, "I was blown away when Lydia instantly accepted. She told me the job had been getting her down, and that it was time for her to work less and start enjoying the new home she and her husband had recently built. Coincidentally, on the day I announced the change in Lydia's status and the promotion of one of the supervisors, our city experienced a small earthquake. Some of our people joked that it wasn't an earthquake at all. They said it was the people in our building heaving a collective sigh of relief."

Transition categories

This case illustrates two additional advice- and feedback-giving considerations. The first is the level of advice *you provide* in helping the other person to function more effectively. Can that person get by with an instrumental change in his or her behavior or, for that person to function more effectively, is a change in orientation required? The second is what the other person sees as required to operate more effectively, which will determine the level at which this *other person reacts* to advice received, regardless of the level at which that advice was given. Together these considerations take you to one of the four categories of the four-cell matrix depicted in Chapter 11 (see Figure 11.2, p. 211).

If your advice recipient desires instrumental feedback, and you agree that this is the type of help you want to give, then we'd expect the two of you to have an easy time holding Category I (behavioral effectiveness) discussions. If you're trying to give advice aimed at changing an individual's orientation, and you're able to communicate that need convincingly enough for the other person to also desire it, then you can proceed to initiate Category IV (breakthrough learning) interactions with inquiry and discussions that eventually challenge that person's current mind-set.

If you find yourself in Category II (political accommodation), trying to discuss orientation with someone who wants help in dealing with a specific situation or individual, you may decide to first put energy into getting the other person to make the transition to Category IV. To do so you'll have to convince your advice-recipient that it's not just a specific situation that's the problem. You'll need to produce convincing evidence that there is a class of situations in which this individual acts deficiently and that something about the underlying assumptions he or she makes is the cause. Until you get the other person questioning his or her assumptions and perceptions of "reality," you're not going to get far talking about orientation. This is the point where we encountered Erica agonizing about Lydia. It was Erica's repeated inability to get Lydia into a discussion bearing on her orientation that sent her searching out our counsel.

If you and the other person are interacting in Category III (socialization), you probably won't realize it. You'll really have to be on your toes to notice that the other person is trying to draw out generalizable principles and formulas for success from the information and instruction you matter-of-factly provide. If you pick this up, then you need to assess whether the lessons you are giving in the specific situation are those that you actually think the other person should internalize. For example, Barry, the manager in Chapter 8 who used to lose his temper when people failed to carry through on the gun-to-the-head "commitments" he extracted from them, was inadvertently teaching a cadre of young managers to extract commitments and to self-justifiably blame others when those others failed to live up to extracted promises.

On the other hand, if, after appraising the circumstances or expending effort without achieving results, you decide it's unrealistic to expect your target person to move to Category IV, you have the choice of remaining in Category II or III or deciding that it is more realistic to move to Category I. This essentially describes how the CEO at the OceanView Medical Center decided to handle his situation with his marketing manager Laurie. When he realized he was in Category II, he moved to Category I by instructing her to change job descriptions and telling her what to do.

The search for the appropriate advice and influence category certainly applies to Erica's deliberations of what to do about Lydia. Clearly Erica wanted to engage Lydia in a Category IV interaction by getting her to add "a missing ingredient" that would change how she reasoned. In this instance our support, which she interpreted as advice, was aimed at helping Erica face up to the fact that she had a Category II mismatch. This recognition posed a difficult question for

Erica. Would she be willing to release from her need to change Lydia's reasoning and orientation and retreat to a Category I feedback situation where she gives instructions that Lydia dutifully follows? Then Erica could stop upsetting Lydia with feedback and advice that never seemed to sink in. This would allow Erica to concentrate on activities where the company could really benefit from her efforts. Once Erica was clear that accepting Lydia's current orientation was her only option, she decided it was an unacceptable one. Difficult as the decision was, she chose to remove Lydia.

Since assessing the category in which you and your advice recipient are interacting is so key and important, how do you determine an individual's capacity to make the transition from instrumental activities that never seem to be quite enough to orientational, Category IV learning? Certainly you'd hate to mistakenly conclude someone is unable to engage in orientational change when that person is actually able.

We think the way Erica went about making this assessment was, in theory, a very reasonable one. It's the way most of us make our determinations. She tried her best to give advice and feedback at the orientational level and assessed the results. However, Erica also discovered that the process of going the extra mile can be disorienting. She got so caught up trying to get Lydia to change that she began to overlook the dispiriting impact she herself experienced from interacting with Lydia. But when Lydia delegated updating the supervisor charts to an assistant, the problem became sufficiently vivid for Erica to realize that Lydia was dealing with a situation that required resources that she didn't possess.

Milestone conditions provide the telltale

We don't think Erica would have needed our input at all if, at the time of her interactions with Lydia, she had known about and used the four-category and milestone models. With the four-category model, she might have recognized that she and Lydia were interacting in Category II and that she was trying to get to Category IV. Alternatively, because of her own motivation, she might have thought that they were interacting in Category IV but then, with the "milestone model," she would have seen that she had yet to accomplish a single condition required for expecting positive results. If it had been a baseball game, Erica would have realized that if Lydia couldn't be helped to reach first base, she would never have a chance of crossing home plate.

Thus, in assessing the category in which you and another person are interacting and the feasibility of breakthrough learning, we advise you to consider your progress in achieving the three essential milestone conditions—set-breaking, conceptual clarity, and emotional bonding—and your prospects of accomplishing all three. If you can get your feedback-recipient through one or two milestone conditions, in time that person might find a way to score a run. Alternatively, if, after a good deal of effort, you find that the other person's set is not broken, or that he or she is not conceptually clear about what is off and what needs to be set straight in his or her assumptions and reasoning, or if this individual remains emotionally uncommitted to changing something fundamental in his or her view of things, then you need to downgrade your expectations.

Instinctively, Erica went for the set-breaker with Lydia. As accounting manager, "payroll" reported to her. She had ready access to everyone's salary figures. From experience Erica knew that Lydia would instantly calculate percentages and realize exactly what was happening. However, in the absence of understanding precisely what was off, all Lydia could tell was that Erica was not pleased with her and, because she couldn't see any valid grounds, she (mis)construed the message as unfair and abusive treatment.

Erica's next action was to establish some conceptual clarity, which she attempted to do by offering detailed examples when conducting Lydia's performance review. But in the face of Lydia's mind-set objections, Erica watched her concepts turn to "mush." To get her points across she tried holding weekly meetings structured in the way she wanted Lydia to reason. But when Lydia delegated staff assessments to an assistant, Erica once again experienced Lydia striking out.

Intuitively Erica appeared to be following the model. She was trying to break Lydia's set belief that she could be successful reasoning as she did and she had been trying to instill clarity about the type of thinking required. But without a set-breaker and conceptual clarity there was no way to expect Lydia to emotionally commit. That would mean acknowledging that her reasoning was off without knowing how to reason alternatively.

Being a "people person," Erica was again inclined to go longer and stronger in helping Lydia. But she lacked a means of assessing whether or not success would ever be possible outside of blindly committing more time and energy. That's when she approached us for advice and, perhaps, absolution from accumulated guilt. Our model allowed us to track and validate the way she had progressed and to assess the possibilities of her eventually succeeding. If Erica hadn't already gone the proverbial "extra mile," we might have suggested that she try some additional set-breaking and clarification. From her account it sounded to us that her efforts had been very fair-minded and appropriate. Our comments merely provided second-opinion support to confirm her fears of a terminal diagnosis.

We think most lessons that culminate in orientational change are comprehended bit by bit, and in piecemeal fashion, notwithstanding the fact that very occasionally there are lightning-bolt transitions. Furthermore, most people prepare themselves for the moment of change by working their orientation problem in several life domains simultaneously. That is, if they sense that they are being too domineering and overcontrolling in their interactions with people at work, they may experiment with backing off in their interactions with family members and not being so directive and intense with the salespeople they encounter when shopping. For this reason, when it comes to engaging people who are consciously willing to reassess the effectiveness of an orientation, we think about asking questions that pertain to how their lives outside of work are going, and whether they see the issues under discussion appearing elsewhere as well.

But many people are inclined to draw firm boundaries around their work activities and consider all other topics "very personal." And, as we've discussed, getting data from other dimensions of an individual's life will sometimes feel inappropriate. Under such constrained circumstances, which for many people will be most of the time, advice-giving leading to orientational change at work is extraordinarily difficult to achieve. This is not to say that orientational change is ever easily achievable even when your relationship permits utilizing considerations taken from several life domains simultaneously. But when the only usable data for feedback- and advice-giving are work-related observables, we consider the participants extremely fortunate to achieve any type of orientational results.

For example, we never asked Mike, the business affairs executive in Chapter 12 whose boss was pondering whether to promote or demote him, whether there was anything in the feedback he was receiving at home or elsewhere about denial patterns like the ones he was manifesting at work. Reflecting back, there were so many intangibles that made us feel like it was not something that was appropriate to do. Moreover, we never asked him whether he tried applying the lessons he learned at work to becoming more responsive to the realities lived by his wife and children, especially at moments when he knew he was seeing events differently than they were seeing them. If it turns out that his avowed change in orientation is deep-rooted and long-lasting, then we would bet the family homestead that, in both instances, we are correct in our thinking.

That is, prior to Mike learning that there are negative consequences to not engaging the realities lived by associates at work, we believe that comparable resentments existed at home. Likewise, we believe that the breakthrough at work yielded parallel benefits for his family.

Structure for instrumental and orientational learning

We've now laid the groundwork for further sharpening the contrast we've been making between the type of feedback and advice required for instrumental learning and the type of advice required for breakthrough learning, mind-set, orientational change. Different words and actions and different relationships are required depending on how you and the people you seek to advise assess their needs, their problems, and their opportunities. Are an individual's effectiveness problems caused by a need to function more skillfully? If so we're talking advice and feedback aimed at instrumental learning. Are they caused by the individual's operating with a "faulty" mind-set that creates systematic problems? If so, we're talking advice and feedback that begins with inquiry and where specific problems are scrutinized and treated as clues in detecting invalid and self-defeating assumptions that need revising.

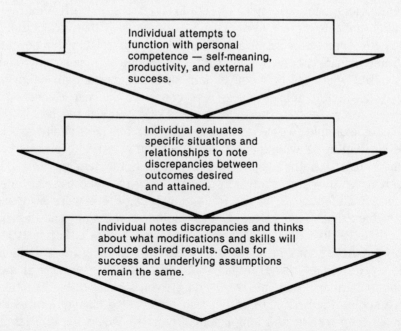

Individual attempts to function with personal competence — self-meaning, productivity, and external success.

Individual evaluates specific situations and relationships to note discrepancies between outcomes desired and attained.

Individual notes discrepancies and thinks about what modifications and skills will produce desired results. Goals for success and underlying assumptions remain the same.

Figure 13.1. Structure for instrumental learning leading to changes in behavior.

The structures for instrumental and orientational learning are parallel. Both begin with the same overarching motivation: the individual's desire to perform competently, taking actions that are personally meaningful and that pay off in terms of productivity for the organization and recognition by others. Both contain the same basic methodology: scanning for discrepancies between goals sought and realized and then seeking remedies aimed at reducing or eliminating the discrepancies. The difference between the two has to do with the level of discrepancies noticed and the type of remedy sought. Instrumentally, the focus is on specific relationships and events and the individual figuring out what changes in behavior are more likely to produce desired outcomes and results (see Figure 13.1). Orientationally, the focus is on classes of relationships and situations and what changes in underlying personal assumptions lead to a more accurate picture of what it takes to perform self-competently, leading to new ideas of what constitutes desired results (see Figure 13.2).

Contrasting these structures reveals dramatic differences about the type of advice and feedback people require from you. When your advice-recipient's goal is instrumental learning, for purposes of changing specific behaviors, that person wants your ideas of what's needed for dealing successfully with people and situations external to him or her. That person wants to know what's required for success

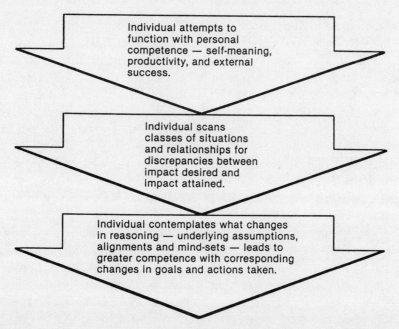

Figure 13.2. Structure for orientational learning leading to changes in reasoning.

in the specific situation, or types of situations, in which he or she is struggling. That person wants to know the requirements of the people he or she is trying to please, which may include you. That person may also want some feedback about him- or herself and the impact of actions taken, but in this context, such needs are more about how to engage externals given personal goals and work objectives already held. Thus when it comes to helping someone instrumentally, feedback- and advice-giving pertains to providing information about what you believe the other person needs to say and do to have the impact he or she desires.

However, when your advice is directed toward assisting people to change their orientations, then your feedback and advice-giving should begin with a focus on internals, not externals. **Instead of giving information, you need to collect it.** You need to learn the personal assumptions that lead another person to behave in ways that you judge counterproductive and to seek outcomes that you read as self-defeating. You need to do this in order to understand exactly what change in thinking will produce changes and adjustments in goals and relationships sought that you are convinced will cause that person to operate with greater organizational competence, personal meaning, and success.

Category IV interactions require teamwork

Thus when you give advice and feedback directed toward Category IV interactions, you should begin by raising questions that get the facts out on the table so that you and the other person can work together to identify key facets of his or her current thinking that best apply to the situation at hand. This contrasts with your getting the facts out for purposes of driving your point home convincingly, such as often is the case when you give instrumental advice. To facilitate Category IV interactions, your primary objective is to expose the underlying assumptions that the other person uses and how they were arrived at, and then, together with that person, to assess the validity of those assumptions when applied to the category of situations represented by the specifics at hand.

The inquiry process we've just described is analogous to how a college guidance counselor might treat a student client. Only after learning about the student's interests, needs, resources, aptitudes, and past performances can that counselor begin to give intelligent direction and advice. Even if the counselor believes he or she already understands the student well enough to give advice, that counselor needs to begin with a recitation of the facts and salient assumptions he or she is making to check for correctness and whether the student is aware of making those assumptions and realizes the career directions that they imply. At some point the counselor will probably challenge the validity of one or more assumptions the student makes and/or attempt to recall past accomplishments for purposes of exposing the student to unexplored possibilities and opportunities or risks that he or she hadn't considered. Thus the student supplies the building block facts and the discussion proceeds interactively with those facts serving as the foundation. All differences in assumptions are explicitly discussed prior to the counselor's taking them as facts.

Likewise, it is important to get the facts that constitute your advice-recipient's reality, and their basis, out on the table prior to challenging and/or questioning assumptions. Of course, we think you can assume that any individual's general motives relate to empowerment: that person's desire to function with self-perceived personal and organizational competence and to be viewed as a producer and contributor. However, please note that we said "self-perceived." This is the sole reality that determines whether your comments will be persuasive. Only when the feedback-recipient perceives you moving confluently with his or her interests, and building upon assumptions that he or she makes, will that person drop his or her guard to actively consider ideas and facts that you see so compelling.

Thus when you think an individual's orientation needs changing, you need to learn about the assumptions that underlie that orientation prior to engaging what you perceive to be the basis for your advice-recipient's disorientation. It's here that many well-intentioned Category IV advice-givers err. Instead of beginning with the assumptions that explain current orientations and behavior, they begin with what they think is "the correct orientation to have." In the process, the advice-recipient misses what the advice-giver believes is too obvious to be missed, and too much of the energy and goodwill expended goes for naught.

Case reflection

We used the just-mentioned line of inquiry in our approach to the Category IV (breakthrough learning) case described at length in Chapter 12. We think it led to the milestone conditions that were essential to John's overcoming Mike's resistance and breaking through with his advice. At first we found ourselves in positions just like the one Mike was in, listening to John's viewpoint and not knowing whether it was correct. We couldn't make a determination until we heard Mike's reasoning and learned that there were no other important variables involved that had failed to meet John's eyes. In attempting to be efficient, our method of inquiry featured us asking Mike to respond to the picture of reality that John had provided us which initially, when we used the term "deficient performer," he tried to deny. Their mind-set stalemate "broke" when Mike realized that the line of reasoning he had been taking was making him appear unresponsive and unproductive, with potential dead-end consequences for his company career.

Establishing the milestone conditions that promote Category IV change

John and Mike's interaction also illustrates the three-plus-one milestone conditions of our feedback model. Accomplishing them required our help, but we think primarily because John didn't have the model. We don't think our role would have been all that important if John had known about it and used it. In fact, we're inclined to think that our role would have been reduced from active catalysts to passive note takers. For your reference, we portray this model in Figure 13.3. It shows that set-breaking and conceptual clarity both need to be accomplished before a Category IV advice recipient can emotionally bond with advice that urges a change in orientation. Anchoring is the after-the-fact activity in which people attempt to stabilize and embed the changes in assumptions that produced a revised or new orientation.

We're now at the point of describing these conditions in sufficient detail for you to use them in taking a psychologically sound approach in providing orientational advice. Using them provides you guidance for assessing the actual category in which you and your advice-recipient are interacting, for calibrating progress, for knowing what you need to work on next, and for comprehending the feasibility of achieving Category IV results. These conditions serve as milestones for navigating in terrain that, by its nature, cannot be accurately predicted or precisely mapped.

Your awareness of these conditions also provides you with a means for knowing when it's time to back off to see what the other person can do on his or her own. It also provides guidance in helping you figure out when you need to release from a clash in viewpoints to work on developing more trust. Of course, as we've seen in several cases, Lydia's included, effecting orientational change may just not be in your control.

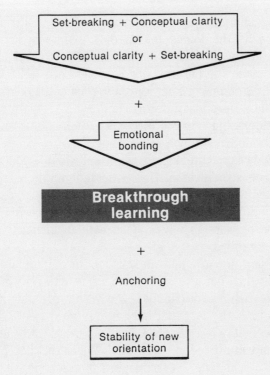

Figure 13.3. Model for milestone conditions that lead to a shift in orientation.

Set-breaking

We first came across the term "set" when we were undergraduates taking psychology courses and studying experimental learning theory. "Set" was the psychologists' terminology for referring to the patterned, predisposed way of thinking and reasoning that an individual is inclined to use when facing categories of situations. For example, if a teacher were to assign a page of twenty-five easy math problems, in word and concept form, to a fifth-grade class, with all but problem 18 entailing addition and 18 requiring subtraction, the psychological "set" established on the first seventeen problems would lead to our expecting a high percentage of the students to mistakenly attempt an addition solution when working on problem 18. But if 18 were preceded with a large sign—CAUTION—we would expect most students to *break their set* and spontaneously adjust their thinking to be on the lookout for some novel consideration or change in approach that's required to solve problem 18 correctly.

In identifying set-breaking as the first milestone condition in Category IV interactions, we are referring to more than breaking a habit or a programmed way of operating. We're referring to habits and programs plus the logics that people invoke in justifying their predisposition for the patterned ways they act and respond. Internalized, "sets" become the natural, unconscious knee jerks that an individual uses when thinking and operating in a class of situations, where "class" is a personally determined mind-set pattern and category. Set-breaking, then, is the disconfirmation and/or invalidation of the mind-set the individual had been using.

Set-breaking is accomplished when sufficient evidence accumulates to convince an individual that a current mode of thinking and operating is insufficient, inappropriate, and defective. The evidence must be sufficiently compelling to make it impossible for the individual to think and operate that way again without instantly recognizing the limitations involved.

Set-breaking doesn't just pertain to orientational change. In fact, if the individual has the skills to operate differently, it will produce immediate behavioral change even without a shift in mind-set. Noteworthy here is the fact that behavioral therapists* conduct their treatment by conditioning people to act differently on the belief that eventually a shift in attitudes will follow. While this line of reasoning has situational merits, we see managers overapplying it. Nevertheless, there are many situations in which it may be the only practical way to proceed.

Short case

For example, a newly appointed executive director of a community service agency called us inquiring what to do about an office manager he described as an "incessant complainer," "a real downer," and "a constant threat to other people's positive morale." He was stymied in trying to create an upbeat office atmosphere as long as Carole was around. He said he had done everything he knew how to do in getting his message across, and that Carole had not shown any visible agreement or sign of change. He said he was down to firing her, but now felt that was impossible since he recently learned she was four months pregnant and about to become a single working mother. He said he knew of no one more dependent on her job, and that in her pregnant state it would be impossible for her to find another job with comparable income and maternity benefits.

To get Carole's attention we suggested the director invite her

---

*Especially those who attempt to help people struggling with eating and substance abuse disorders.

to lunch and hold the following set-breaking conversation that we scripted: "Carole, I invited you to lunch to tell you two things. The first I'd like to tell you right now and the second at the conclusion of lunch. The first is very simple to explain. For me, having an upbeat office is essential. I like to be positive, I like other people feeling good. I want people feeling good about me, about one another, and about working here. I want our people projecting a positive atmosphere to the extent that it rubs off on everyone who comes to our office. Nothing is more important to me. I want this to be the hallmark of my leadership here. And to have it, I need you to change your tone." Then we advised the director to sit back and listen. We told him to expect Carole to take him on a tour of every detail that's off in the office with layered justifications for why she has no alternative but to complain. We counseled him to empathize the best he could, to nod a good deal and model positivism, to take notes on topics he might like to get back to at some other date, and, most important, not to get drawn into a debate or clarification of facts. We said, if Carole asks you about the second item, tell her you want to wait until after lunch.

Then, after lunch, in response to Carole wondering and asking him about his second item, we suggested that he repeat what he had first said, word for word, as closely as he might be able. We told him to say: "Carole, having an upbeat office is essential to me. I like to be positive, I like other people feeling good. I want people feeling good about me, about one another, and about working here. I want people portraying a positive outlook all the time. Nothing is more important to me. I want this to be the hallmark of my leadership here. And to have it, I need you to change your tone." We coached, "Don't compromise your impact by saying one thing more."

Our goal was to help the executive director break Carole's set by communicating that his requirements were not negotiable, no matter what she might say. She was locked in to her job, he was locked in with her, and some key assumptions she made about herself, the other people in the office, and her relationship with him and the others had to change. We counseled, "Perhaps you'll hear more about some glaring problems that also need addressing and, perhaps next week you should get to them. But right now your prime objective is to interrupt Carole's thinking and give the message that your demand is absolute, and that no compromise solution is going to satisfy you."

By no means did we expect that the set-breaking conversation we scripted would, on its own, lead Carole on a path of self-discovery and orientation change. In fact, for us Carole was an abstraction, since everything we knew about her came through the executive director. Our goal was primarily to provide him with a means for breaking through Carole's defenses. Whether that conversation would eventually lead Carole to engage him in Category IV interactions was beyond our ability to foresee. By itself, set-breaking usually leads to instrumental change and is insufficient for producing breakthrough lessons. The individual merely knows that he or she possesses an orientation that does not achieve desired goals.

Set-breaking continued

By definition, breaking someone's set means the other person now realizes the insufficiency of his or her current approach even though he or she continues to use it. That person may reason, "My inability to act differently leaves me with no alternative but to behave in my current suboptimum mode." This person will be in limbo, knowing that his or her performance is nonoptimal, waiting for the clarification or for the skills to perform differently. Even when that person is provided practical alternatives, he or she may not use them due to worrying about the unknowns involved.

Sometimes a mere change in circumstances breaks an individual's set, and sometimes with a corresponding change in orientation. For example, we've seen many instances of people taking the job of someone they had criticized as operating incorrectly, then finding that external forces caused them to reason and act the same basic way as the person they just replaced. This is commonplace among people who switch from a job in the field to a job at headquarters, as they find their mandated agenda switched. Likewise for people taking international assignments who find they need to operate with significantly different business assumptions than the ones they utilized effectively in their home country. The same is true for people who enter a new life category that changes their situation and perspective, such as marriage, the birth of a child, or the sudden onset of a physical or emotional problem in their family. Such changes can shift an individual's priorities and automatically cause former modes of thinking and behaving to become obsolete.

Conceptual clarity

When you are energized, giving feedback and advice with set-breaking impact, you can usually count on your advice recipients being aware that you are convinced they need to change. In fact you can usually count on them having a fairly accurate idea of what you think they should *stop* doing. What you can't count on, however, is their understanding precisely what you think they should *start* doing as a replacement and why you think it is so important for them to do so. When it comes to orientational change, conceptual clarity can be extremely difficult to achieve.

By conceptual clarity we are referring to the sharpness and accuracy with which the orientation substitute and the constituent elements you are advocating register in the mind of the person you are trying to influence and change. Remember we're not just talking about what you send but about the matchup between what you send and what the person on the receiving end feels he or she needs. And we're talking about a difficult matchup to make because the very fact that you're giving feedback implies that your feedback recipient reasons differently from you. Think about it. If you and that other person reasoned similarly, isn't it likely that he or she would long ago have seen the wisdom of what you are advocating and made the appropriate adjustment on his or her own?

Without a precise idea of the orientational change that you are advocating, your advice recipient will be unable to grasp its value. This doesn't mean that this other person won't attempt to change. It means that the most that you'll get for your efforts will be accommodations to you. Instead of being in Category IV, your interactions will be in Category II, "political accommodations." While you are advocating a change in the reasoning and mind-set that precede a change in behavior, your recipient may be attempting to guess what behaviors emanate from the change you are advocating and provide those behaviors as a means of pleasing and placating you.

Once it is clear that an individual needs a replacement orientation, there are two ways to proceed. You, as the advice-giver, can provide it yourself or you can act supportively while the other person searches for it. In choosing your route, keep in mind that ultimately the concept that you frame has to make sense in the mind-set of your feedback recipient.

We know it's meaningless for us to categorically advise you to always be supportive when dealing with an individual who repeatedly doesn't get it when you feel, as Erica did, what's off was clearly communicated in your framing of the problem. That is, if you think the other person is "too thin-skinned," or "too aggressive," or "lacks a certain something," you think you know what the problem is. And when you provide that person ample visible evidence and he or she doesn't agree, your patience is tested.

Finding that the way you have the problem framed does not compute in your advice-recipient's mind should serve as a cue to ask that person, "Do you see a problem in the situation I'm describing?"

Then you ask, "What is the problem?" Then you ask the "why" question, which is some variant of "How do you account for that problem's existence?" If what you receive as a response is too far away from how you see the problem and account for it, then you can ask if that person thinks others see the problem as he or she sees it, and, if so, how that person accounts for the differences. This is the legwork required for getting the "facts" out on the table. Notice that the "facts" are perceptions and feelings generated by experience. Also stay alert for situations in which the other person already comprehends how he or she has the situation framed incorrectly, but doesn't want to say so for fear of your finding that self-acknowledgment too indicting. It's very difficult for someone to say, "I need to be more _____ but don't know how to operate that way." This may have been an important underlying issue in the resistance we encountered in the bus company case, described in Chapter 4 where we instructed management that their job was to support service unit effectiveness.

Of course all actions that you take in discussing "the problem" are actually avenues into the mind-set and thinking that your feedback-recipient is using. They are ways of going to the other person's framework and seeking engagement where that person reasons. Once you have that engagement you can try to build out to your concept and conclusion using the terms, images, and contextual considerations that characterize your recipient's mind-set and reasoning. You're the one who knows where you're headed; if you can't make the bridge, it's highly unlikely that the other person is going to be able to make it, and certainly not by using the terms that more naturally occur to you.

On the other hand, most people who use an orientation that they experience as being criticized are unable to articulate their effectiveness problems independently of the demands they feel others placing on them. They see their performance problems instrumentally as a matter of measuring up to the expectations and needs of people they are trying to please. Moreover, in most instances, they don't even realize that "orientation" is a variable that can be changed. For instance, from Erica's account, it seemed that Lydia was doing her best to satisfy Erica even though she was never clear about Erica's real demands. Apparently Lydia did not see her orientation as a variable that could be changed or adjusted, which would explain why all conversations in which Erica attempted to discuss orientations with Lydia turned to "mush." This is why we thought to ask Erica if she were prepared to live with Lydia's orientation. Erica responded by gerrymandering a job description to include the functions for which she thought Lydia's orientation was appropriate. Afterwards she selected a replacement manager who would be a better match for the way she wanted to work.

In promoting conceptual clarity it is essential that you think twice, and twice again, before yielding to the temptation to hold yourself up as a positive example, for, by definition, this course is steeped in built-in bias. The very fact that you orient differently and, in your own mind, more desirably, is what causes you to spot the other person's problems and to frame what we call the "better" orientation precisely as you do. See if you can pass up this temptation. Instead we recommend you ask the advice-recipient about the people that he or she considers to be more effective, and suggest that he or she talk with those people to learn how and why they reason as they do.

Once that is done, listen to how the advice-recipient frames those differences and give your advice in the form of feedback relative to the new concepts and the modifications that the other person is now inclined to make. In taking this route, you don't need to be particularly compromising. Don't confuse your desire to give support with progress. If you want to reinforce the other person's efforts, try saying something like, "I think you are making progress, but I don't think you've quite got it yet." Figure that you did great getting this far and now you've got to make the most of it.

Emotional bonding

Every manager and every professional in the "change" business understands that advising an individual to change his or her orientation is a hit-and-miss proposition in which serendipity inevitably plays the kingpin role. Most people, most of the time, resist changing orientations, even when provided superior concepts and strong evidence that viewing events in a different way will cause them and their organizations to function more effectively. In such instances, people change the words they use, and they change their behavior. But most people, most of the time, fail to change their orientation. If tangible evidence and rational appeals worked, you wouldn't be reading this book. When it comes to orientational change, it's feelings that ultimately determine the matter. That's why we use the term **emotional bonding.** Engaging people where they really live requires engaging their emotions, not just their heads.

Thus in our experience a surge of emotion is required to catalyze and fuse any advancement in thinking and resulting change in orientation. And not any emotionality, but emotionality that the individual receives as an internal signal that a new way of thinking or acting, that is both personally valid and practically efficient, has locked in. This emotionality bonds the individual to a new way of reasoning and viewing events, and cements this change in his or her consciousness. When this emotional bond is forged, an individual who lacks the skills to implement a new improved orientation will become consumed in acquiring them.

With the exception of unequivocal job or life failure or experience of extreme adversity, we don't know how to specify exactly what will create the emotionality that catalyzes an individual's change in orientation. We do know that abject failure typically embodies each of the three critical milestone conditions. The failure is the *set-breaker*. It stands as clear evidence that the individual's way of reasoning didn't work. The terminology that the individual uses in describing the problem that led to the failure serves as the foundation of the *concept*. The statement of the problem implies the new improved way. And the emotional reaction that leads that person to recognize the failure and to intractably commit to avoiding making such mistakes again, by making an orientation change, provides the *emotional bond*. What remains to be determined is the speed with which the individual develops skill in the new orientation and whether that new orientation is appropriate to use in other life domains. The events that provide the answers to these questions and the requisite skills and reinforcements are the *anchors*. On the other hand, some people erect defenses so quickly that they duck even the lessons of severe setback.

Perhaps it has already occurred to you that emotional bonding is a two-edged sword. While our experience tells us that the vast majority of orientational changes are ones that lead to a greater exercise of personal competence and a greater outflow of organizational effectiveness and productivity, we also have to state that this is not always the case.

Short case

Sometimes people learn the wrong lessons and fuse with the wrong shifts and changes. Failures not followed by the counseling of trusted and reliable advisers can readily lead to perverse behavior and a sour-grapes attitude. For example, we're reminded of an executive whose abrupt and close-minded, overly decisive, critical approach to other people and their business problems was creating a morale mess in the organizations reporting to him. Without referring to any problems we merely asked about his evolution as a manager and his management style. He told us at his level he doesn't get performance reviews, he merely negotiates pay. But at the last review he had, at a different company, in being rejected for president he was told he was insufficiently decisive. Based on what we saw when we walked his new playing field observing the carnage, did this guy overreact! When his new boss asked us what we thought, we told him "counsel him fast." Then we added, "Also try the positive, reinforcing approach. Ask him why he gets so disconnected from the considerate and careful thinking person that down deep you know him to be." The eventual rebalancing was dramatic. But first, for emotional release and bonding, he had to psychologically revisit the moment of trauma and the strength of his feelings about being treated so unfairly at that former time. This was another guy who was out to give a (former) boss precisely the orientation he was calling for.

Quick reflection

Most people dislike the emotions that emanate from feelings of uncertainty and, for many, the anxiety is intolerable. There is even a stock market axiom that goes, "The market knows how to temper its reactions to good news and to bad, but it nosedives with uncertainty." Compare this to people who have to live with a broken set, knowing that some dimension of their current orientation is off but not clear about how to implement the new orientation that promises relief from their previous situation. In such instances it is commonplace for an individual to fuse with a deficient alternative primarily as a means of escaping the anxiety that comes from the uncertainty of not knowing whether the proposed new orientation will really work.

Anchoring

After an individual makes a mind-set–changing orientational shift, that shift needs some rooting for durability. And nothing roots a newly acquired orientation like success and feelings of empowerment. Successful outcomes offer tangible evidence that the individual possesses the skills to carry off the new orientation effectively.

Repeatedly we've made the point that the skills required to carry off a new and enlightened orientation are by no means faits accomplis. In fact, now we can state the opposite. We think that the reason why obvious (to you) and more constructive orientations are so often rejected and circumvented results from an individual feeling that he or she lacks the skills and self-confidence to consistently utilize what is prescribed. This is the old advice-giving saw of leading a thirsty horse to water and then splashing the water in the horse's face in a futile effort to get the horse to drink. When it comes to people trying out new orientations in search of a single, anchoring success, there's a wet crowd milling around the water trough, dying of thirst.

There are times when an individual acquires new skills that create such a surge in self-confidence that they simultaneously serve as set-breaker, clarifier, emotional bond, and anchor. Even reestablishing confidence in former skills, like the aforementioned temporarily overdecisive executive did, can simultaneously accomplish these four milestone conditions. This is often a function role models serve, and one of the reasons why positive role models can be so important. They provide an individual an opportunity to vicariously try out new orientations without having to fear surprise consequences. Little by little an individual can begin thinking that he or she can actually change and then one day dares the experiment. This is a particularly important route for people who are faced with new challenges for which they have no established repertoire, such as women professionals. Recalling their own mothers staying at home to raise children, they carefully observe their contemporaries who have families, trying to anticipate how they might successfully handle the challenges and pressures of taking on the work and family roles simultaneously.

Conclusion

Now that we have deepened your understanding of the milestone conditions that need to be covered in Category IV interactions, we want to take you through two more cases for purposes of further developing your skills in sizing up advice-giving situations and achieving positive results. The next chapter, Chapter 14, begins with some major points to highlight what we hope you've internalized thus far and then presents another breakthrough-learning application. Then we follow with Chapter 15, which contains a short case in which we stop halfway through to see what you would make out of our attempts to hold a Category IV advice-giving interaction.

14

Perspectives to Keep in Mind When Participating in Breakthrough-Learning Interactions

We realize that probably you've been taking with a grain of salt our statements about the low likelihood of your feedback- and advice-giving culminating in breakthrough results. We understand, on this matter we're as split-minded as you. The problem is that we're in too many situations where we feel the importance of the situation creates an imperative to break through.

When someone's personal competence matters to us—perhaps because we care so much for that individual, or because the fallout from that person's problems deeply affects us, or because we have some value-driven, heroic self-image of being able to help people, or because we are so confident that we've got an essential understanding and the data to demonstrate its validity cleanly in hand—then despite the odds we feel compelled to wholeheartedly engage in Category IV interactions. We proceed as if we can actually help that person break through, steaming ahead with full-force commitment, oftentimes on a collision course with disappointment.

On the other hand, we've learned that there are achievements and hidden gains even when we don't succeed and this recognition has added to the number of low-probability attempts we make as well as our responsiveness to cues that tell us it's time to back off. Herein lies the key.

The key to giving advice and feedback aimed at getting your breakthrough insights across, resulting in someone changing his or her thought processes leading to changes in behavior, is your being able to accept that most of the time your well-intentioned efforts are going to fall short of the mark. On the other hand, we don't see your "failed" efforts as meaningless because, performed earnestly, they will probably move the other person ahead.

Thus, when involving ourselves in Category IV interactions, we no longer tell ourselves we absolutely have to break through. We tell ourselves that our engagement and interaction can be assigned some number, maybe number 6, 11, 17, or 34, in the life learning process of another individual who will not experience breakthrough learning and consequent orientational change until at least number 34. If the breakthrough requires thirty-four encounters and, as the fates have it, we turn out to be number 34, then we are the fortunate ones. We get credit for the engagements that thirty-three people before us had without the personal satisfaction of seeing their efforts pay off. When we are particularly attuned to an individual, and through the exercise of sensitivity, skill, emotional involvement, and devotion of time have lessened the total number of encounters required from 34 to 29, then we consider both ourselves and our feedback recipients to be very fortunate, even though our encounter merely served as numbers 17 through 21.

Key points

With this disclaimer, we're got a list of points that we hope will add to your perspective when you venture forward in Category IV interactions giving feedback and advice aimed at achieving breakthrough results. We're listing them under the headings process, outcomes, and relationship to indicate their role in your engagements with someone you are trying to influence and help with a breakthrough insight.

Process

1. There are two essential tasks to be accomplished prior to giving feedback and advice. The first is accurately assessing the level of need. Can the person get by with instrumental learning that changes his or her behavior? Or does the person require something deeper at the level of mind-set change and adjustment in orientation?

The second is assessing how the other person sees his or her need and figuring out that person's motivation. Is his or her goal orientational or instrumental? Answering these questions will tell you about the category in which your feedback is being received, which is essential to your knowing what course of action to pursue.

2. Even when you are convinced that the other person can achieve a breakthrough change in orientations, realize that you'll be doing well merely to establish a dialogue and to make a little progress. Give it your all, but reconcile yourself to being number 6, 11, or 17 in a process that requires thirty-four encounters in finding the right emotional chemistry for the breakthrough insight to sink in.

3. Keep in mind that only two of the essential milestones (set-breaking and conceptual clarity) result directly from your efforts, and even those may not be within your control or your ability to articulately communicate. You may be a party to the third condition (emotional bonding), but this condition is never under your control. In fact it seldom has a linear relationship to any premeditated course of persuasion that you took. Herein lies a most delicate issue. To be a catalyst for emotional bonding, you've got to get involved and in the process you take some level of responsibility. But even when you take a great deal of responsibility, the authority to cause the breakthrough and consequent orientational change will never rest with you. That authority is totally in the mind and DNA makeup of the person you seek to influence.

3. There is no prespecifiable route to positive results. Because you are taking a mind-set–sensitive approach, to your own mind-set and ingrained agenda as well as to the person you are attempting to influence, your influence attempts will begin and end at places where neither you nor the other person has ever been before. The best you can do in charting your progress is to aim toward achieving the milestone conditions: set-breaking, conceptual clarity, emotional bonding, and anchoring.

4. Your chances of making progress are measurably increased when the recipient is able to make cross-linkages between the consequences of an orientation at work and the consequences in some other aspect of his or her life.

Relationship

1. The relationship you establish with your feedback-recipient is essential to keeping the process going. That person needs to see your inquiry as friendly and your motivation as emanating from concerns for his or her well-being, a desire to see him or her succeed, and your knowledge that success means progressing in ways that are both personally meaningful and organizationally productive. To accomplish this you'll have to make sure that your criticizing feedback is performed in a context where your recipient knows that you haven't forgotten his or her strengths. In fact, in your recipient's mind, there are times when the quality you are critiquing is also a strength. Acknowledging the positive while discussing the critical is a key to maintaining your relationship in a form that allows you to make more progress.

2. Achieving positive results requires a "partnership" in which you and the person you are attempting to influence work together and mutually take pride in the results. In other words, your relationship is a vehicle, it may even be the motivation, but it alone is seldom the cause. Having your efforts make an impact on an individual's mind-set and that person deciding to change his or her orientation is always a tremendous accomplishment.

Outcome

1. When you engage in Category IV interactions, keep in mind that the probabilities are strongly against your achieving breakthrough results. Keeping this in mind should help you not to get overly intense when your efforts are frustrated and your experiences direct you to another category.

2. Once a breakthrough is achieved, sustaining it depends on the recipient's acquiring the skills to implement the new orientation. You may have an opportunity to help instrumentally by instructing, coaching, and backstopping the recipient as he or she struggles to operate differently.

Case in point

Now we'd like to tell you a story that illustrates several of the aforementioned points and depicts the open-ended process that you embark on whenever you attempt to push for someone else's orientational learning. It took place in a biotech research company that two years earlier had been bought by an international pharmaceuticals company with headquarters in Europe. We were called by the "Leader" of a group of founders who each had made the transition from lead researcher to full-time manager.

The Leader said, "We need to learn how to manage in a corporate atmosphere where our scientists fear that the parent company's desire to turn a profit will significantly compromise their personal commitments to advancing science. Prior to our firm being acquired, we operated like an independent research laboratory. We would write grant proposals and solicit research contracts aimed at funding basic discovery. But our parent company's profit motive has changed our mandate. Discovery for purposes of scientific advancement is no longer sufficient. Now we are required to consider the product consequences of our research.

"To reflect this change we reorganized and added three new departments. Formerly I was head of research, and every scientist reported directly to me. Now in addition to research there is product development, clinical trials, and government relations. This covers 'the discovery-to-market product cycle.' There was always a finance and administration person, and she continues reporting to me more or less as she always did.

"We also instituted two additional levels of hierarchy to free me up for other activities and to provide some career advancement for accomplished scientists. Of course it also allows them to leverage their contributions.

"The reason I need your help is that many of our scientists are fighting these changes, and it's getting to be a sticky situation. I continue to be pressured by requests to meet with the eighty or so scientists who used to report directly to me. Not only is this an awful drain on my time, but I'm now spending half of the year on the road on corporate-related matters. I want you to talk with some of our scientists and tell us what we can do to get them to make peace with the new mandate and reporting arrangements."

Our discussions produced several recommendations, three of which are germane to our discussion here. First, we recommended that the Leader truly commit himself to delegating and to promoting greater independence. We told him that we heard too many stories of people lower down in the hierarchy putting him in their decision-making loop on issues that they readily ought to be able to figure out for themselves or with their department director. We recommended that he give his directors the decision-making authority that their titles and responsibilities warranted.

Second, we counseled him to adjust his management style from involvement in every substantive decision to involvement in setting goals, establishing benchmarks, and monitoring results. Then, we recommended that systems for project evaluation and performance review be revised and routinized.

Third, we recommended that he clarify, as unambiguously as possible, and repeat whenever an opportunity arose, that the company was now in the research *and* development business and that this was no longer a debatable topic. We advised him to say that, with the exception of some minimal number of speculative basic research investigations, all internal work would be reviewed for its relevance to a product and health need application.

We presented our recommendations in a meeting with the Leader and the directors, who reported to him. The Leader's response was enthusiastic agreement and a total commitment to implement our recommendations. However, there was another reaction we didn't fully understand. While agreeing that we were on-point with their situation, several of the directors were, in our eyes, "underwhelmed" with our recommendations. On the one hand, they thought we covered what they termed were "all of our significant ills." On the other, they felt we had made our points too positively; they said they would have liked to hear more severe criticism and wanted us to do a bit more work to help with implementation. At the time, a request for more severe criticism was a "new one" for us. However, on reflection we figured out what they were really saying. They didn't think that our positive approach would be sufficient to change their Leader's ambivalent behavior.

It took three months of scheduling and rescheduling canceled meetings for us finally to hold our follow-up consultation. Each postponement came with short notice, and after the third we wrote an atypically confrontational letter. In it we intimated that their scheduling problems made us the latest instance of someone with a delegated responsibility being denied the authority to exercise it. The Leader's response was apologetic, and a rescheduled date was set and kept.

Scheduled was a round of three-party conversations with the Leader as one party, us as the second, and, sequentially, each of the five directors as the third. The topic was organizational roles and authority.

Each three-party conversation was preceded by two private ones. In the first conversation we met with the Leader to get his assessment of the director with whom we were scheduled to talk next, and what he thought was required for that person to function "even more effectively" than he or she already functioned. In the second conversation we met with that director to inquire how that person viewed his or her responsibilities and the extent to which he or she felt the authority to exercise them.

Our discussions with the Leader were fascinating. It appeared that he had our previous conversation in focus for he was advocating a need for change. Conceptually he had it clear; he needed to delegate more authority to his directors and thereby reduce everyone's overdependence on him. He told us, "You guys were absolutely correct. Until my directors are seen as having the power to make decisions, their people will have little reason to go to them instead of me." At this point we couldn't tell whether he was making an instrumental adjustment or was actually changing his mind-set and felt he had the skills to implement a change in orientations.

Whatever the Leader was up to, it really didn't make much difference, for in subsequent discussions his behavior consistently belied his stated grasp of this concept. For instance, in describing the finance director, named Phyllis, he said, "I like her just the way she is. I find her conservatism to be a wonderful counterpoint to my clinical trials director, Fred, and his inclination to take too many spending risks." Reciprocally, when discussing Fred, the Leader complimented Fred's imaginative work and described how his presence curbs Phyllis's bent for the parochial. In neither instance did he see a reason to tell Fred or Phyllis that he sees them needing him to moderate the one-sidedness of their mind-sets and to achieve a better balance on their own. And while contending that each required no feedback, he volunteered additional limitations such as, "I don't have any questions about how ably Phyllis handles finance and accounting, but I still need her to run things by me in the areas of personnel policies and benefits, where I consistently find her uptight and stingy." Then he quickly cited two actions she had recently taken, which he reversed after she had announced them publicly.

In every instance we scrutinized to determine whether the director whose style the Leader was reflecting upon actually had the authority to exercise the responsibility that his or her role and job implied and that he or she needed in order to operate independently of the leader. We counseled the Leader, "Of course everyone is working from delegated authority, and ultimately each director has to answer to you. In part, this is the purpose for the discussions we want you to have with them. We want you to hold the front-end discussions about the domain you are delegating, thereby ensuring that your point of view is considered. You can even make your viewpoint an overriding factor in areas of high concern. Your job is to monitor the implementation of classes of activities. If you see things that appear to be departures from conceptual agreements you have with your directors, then you should start asking them about the reasons for those departures, not making their decisions for them. The objective is to take up specifics only when there is a bigger point to be made."

In almost two days of conversation with the Leader, sometimes with a director present, we found reason to make this point repeatedly and each time something was missing in the Leader's response. His set was broken, he had conceptual clarity, but he never seemed to have it internalized. In terms of the milestone conditions, the Leader had not formed an unrelenting emotional bond with the change in orientation he had agreed to make.

Major help came from the product development director, whom the Leader had personally recruited and relied upon as his most trusted confidant. In our three-way meeting he told the Leader that, above everyone else, he saw his colleague Sid, the director of research, experiencing the biggest authority squeeze. Clearly Sid lacked sufficient authority to exercise his "directing" responsibility. In fact, the product development director went so far as to assert that the Leader was reducing Sid to operating as a manager, not a director, since he wasn't giving him any latitude to direct. Then he offered that this is why there's always a line of researchers pestering the Leader's secretary for appointments. He asserted, "The tough thing to figure out is why the rest don't also want to see you. It seems to me that every scientist's career hinges on having their pet projects funded, and who, in their right mind, wants to leave his or her fate solely in the hands of some middleman? On the other hand, if research scientists thought Sid played a decision-making role, they'd instantly see the wisdom of keeping him in the loop."

The Leader was visibly concerned. This director's concern for a colleague's authority was dramatic evidence of the Leader's actions diverging from his stated intentions to delegate. When this director left the room, the Leader turned toward us and asked, "What should I do?" Then he said, "Tomorrow's group meeting may be just the opportunity I need. I've had to preempt your agenda so that we can respond to the latest corporate request for cutbacks. We have to decide which of the new research proposals we're committed to funding will have to be delayed or killed." He asked, "Should I really turn the running of that meeting over to Sid?" We responded by looking dumbfounded.

There was something in the Leader's conversation with the product development director that sparked our intuition. We said, "It occurs to us that some part of your reluctance to delegate may be caused by your need to maintain a solid power base at corporate. While we haven't visited your 'corporate castle,' we've been at several other 'corporates' when 'barons' from the field stopped by. We've seen people at corporate act like power-jealous 'knights' who cunningly interrogate the barons to size up their power to calibrate how much respect to extend. Perhaps you think your power base at the 'corporate castle' depends on maintaining the image that you are pivotal to all the research taking place in this division. You want power, and because your division is a high-tech mystery to them, you are treated as a powerful 'baron' whose contributions they can't do without."

The Leader's face flushed in response to our guess. He had a strong reaction to this metaphor. Quickly he volunteered, "I don't want to be seen as just another message carrier." Then he added, "And I don't know what I would do if I gave away the 'keys' internally. I certainly don't want to wind up in a benign position being referred to as 'Old Uncle Jack.' "

We read his flushed face and the "Old Uncle Jack" and "message carrier" imagery as indications that finally he was emotionally connecting with his ambivalence about changing his orientation. But there wasn't time for us to say much more. The research director was standing outside the door and it was time to discuss his situation.

Sid began slowly, apparently trying to measure his words to not appear self-promoting in pushing for more authority. Listening to his hesitant, slow-paced, and cautious wordings, the Leader interrupted. He said, "Sid, I know I've been involved far too much in your area, and I'm now committed to making the change." Then he described how he thought this manager should get himself more into the "directorship" function and might start immediately by leading the project funding meeting scheduled the next day.

At the meeting, we found the research director very impressive in moving the group through a complicated and difficult agenda and strong-willed in asserting his views, rationales, and preferences. We kept an eye on the Leader, who seemed amazingly comfortable being a participant while not asserting much control. Then, in the midst of a discussion about an apparently speculative project, the Leader took us all by surprise. Stiffening he announced, "I need to call time-out to confer with our consultants." Then he beckoned us to leave the room with him.

Ducking into an empty office and closing the door he said, "God, I don't know what to do now. Up to this point I've agreed with every one of Sid's priorities. But I'm scared stiff of the project he's pushing now, and I don't want to undercut his authority by saying so." We took the Leader's question as acknowledgment that he knew his delegation skills needed bolstering.

We said it was highly appropriate for him to insert his views, but in a "consultative" form. If he had expertise that could save the company money, then the company needed to benefit from his knowledge. We told him, "If there was an expert on top of some mountain in Switzerland who had critical data to share prior to someone making a decision, then you'd want to get that person here as well." But, we advised, "Speak with the consultant's voice, say what you think, but then leave it up to Sid to decide." Within five minutes we were back in the room. As the Leader began to comment, the research director interrupted him, he said "to clarify." Apparently the Leader had his "facts" incorrect and it became clear that this director was easily up to making the decision that needed to be made. The tension visibly left the Leader's body as it seemed both his and the research director's new roles clicked in. He began to give and take just as anyone might in a consultative conversation. The research director made the decisions.

The rest of the meeting went very smoothly with the Leader taking the lead only on matters that pertained to integrating what the company, now a corporate division, was doing and the plans he heard at headquarters. Afterwards, he took us to lunch. He wanted to talk about the meeting. He was exhilarated, delighted with the new role he had taken, and intrigued with the nuances. Together we reviewed his roles of coordinator of planning, oversight of operations, and monitoring of results, technical consultant, resource procurement, and linchpin to corporate. Now that the Leader had greater role clarity, pejorative and saccharine images of "Old Uncle Jack" and "message carrier" never entered the conversation.

Milestones achieved

Changing a mind-set and an orientation is never easy. It entails tremendous complexity, and one can never prespecify the events that enable an individual to actually bond with a more productive orientation. Was it the castle analogy that produced his emotional bonding and the Leader's ultimate resolve to change his orientation? Was it the product development director's confrontation about the treatment of his research director peer? Was it the relationship the Leader developed with us? Was it a connection between what was happening in his office and something he thought of that happens at home? Was it the insight that leaving the driving to someone else didn't deprive him of a role in calling attention to points of scenic interest? Was it something else we have yet to identify? Perhaps it was all these things; the point is that we will never know. In our experience, the situations that carry sufficient emotional impact to create bonding are impossible to predict and are often the result of happenstance.

Nevertheless, for illustrative purposes here, the Leader apparently experienced each of the three critical milestone conditions. We think our initial consultation **broke his set.** Our letter and the three-party role discussions with his directors no doubt contributed to **clarifying** the vicissitudes of the overdependence problem and the need for him to grant authority to go along with the delegation of managerial responsibilities. And, as described, somewhere between the three-party conversation with the product development director and the simile of the corporate castle, the Leader had an **emotional bonding** experience that allowed him to commit to a change in orientation. We think **anchoring** took place when Sid performed as ably as he did and in the instructional skill-development conversations we had with him in our caucus and at lunch.

This Leader's experience demonstrates another instance of how people who get involved in Category IV interactions and who possess the capacity for breakthrough learning have to struggle along and grope their way through the process. It illustrates our conclusion that breakthroughs entail the changing of one or more underlying assumptions, and this requires the simultaneous presence of all three milestone conditions. The theory says that absent any one of the conditions, the changes the advice-recipient makes are far more likely to be instrumental than orientational. He or she merely takes specific actions that upgrade a basic course of behavior. Present any one or two conditions, without the other(s), and the person will not quite change his or her thinking. Whatever progress follows will be the result of discipline and raised consciousness but not internalized thinking and changed perceptions.

Now that we've made our points and reinforced them with several case examples, we're ready to move on to everyday applications of Artifact of Mind, new mentality thinking. That's the purpose of Part IV. If you like, you can skip directly to that section. However, in Chapter 15 we present a brief "anchoring" case for you to use in applying your insights about the conditions and parameters of breakthrough learning.

15

Breakthrough Learning:
Case Study and Exam

By reading this far you've taken the intensive course and you are ready to pass the exam. The exam comes in the form of a case and some questions we'd like you to answer—first when we stop in the middle to raise them and later at the end. The case concerns Geof, the president of a well-respected advertising agency, who called with a request for "project management" help after hearing about our efforts at Dewey, Cheatem, & Howe, the advertising firm mentioned in Chapter 5. The first questions are quite basic: (1) What did Geof learn? and (2) Were these the lessons he needed to learn?

On the phone Geof said, "We heard about the team-building help you gave the executives at Dewey and we need some of the same. In particular, we need help developing more flexibility in our staffing and servicing of client accounts." In person he told us the details.

He said, "Four years ago I took over the presidency of our firm's Los Angeles and San Diego offices. In three years I took sales from 150 to 250 million. Last year the recession peaked and our sales were back to 200 million. Our clients were in trouble and were feeling forced to cut back. Looking at their situations, I could readily see we weren't working the way we should."

Geof went on, "Our clients' needs dictate that we change. Instead of selling media and print campaigns with intangible and hard-to-measure results, we need to get closer to their problems and give them whatever is needed to make their business results show a gain. For instance, today the direct mail firms can come in and show our clients exactly how much a dollar spent will pay off with increased sales. We too need to think about direct mail, product displays, and every other avenue that promises to help our clients show a profit. This means developing greater client empathy and more flexibility in the types of services we offer. When direct mail is warranted, we need to be the ones proposing it. Then we need to line up the direct mail experts and broker their effort. And we need to get the costs of our services down, which can be easily accomplished through flexibility in how we organize and cross-project sharing of resources."

Continuing, he said, "We've got to break from an industry tradition of segmenting roles and relegating staff to a single client and not sharing them with other project teams. And we shouldn't be sitting back listening to clients talk with the sole intent of selling artistic advertising and high-profile TV campaigns. Our account executives need to reach deeper into programs; our program people need to think more broadly than scanning for opportunities to push their artistic specialty; our creative people need to brainstorm all clients without concern for whose autograph is on the finished product; and we need a flexible staffing program to avoid costly periods of underutilized professionals sitting around unloaned to another account or project. Our clients can't afford our spending their money on program slaves who hang out waiting for the next module of work."

In response, we raised the obvious question about courses of action taken and results to date. Geof answered: "So far I've been unsuccessful. I've preached to them individually and in groups. I've seen them nod enthusiastically and then watched them leave my office to carry on as usual. Even my partner Stan, the head of creative, gives strong vocal agreement while hoarding resources and, with his leading glamour account, sticking closely to his accustomed routine. I even have difficulties getting him to critique other people's accounts, and he is supposed to oversee all creative input. And I get the same schizophrenic reaction from my boss, the worldwide president. In one breath he claims that everything I say makes good sense and then, in the next, he calls me a 'heretic.' "

We asked, "In your business, isn't it a plus to be considered a heretic?" This caused him to laugh, exclaiming, "That's a hell of a question!" Then he told us, "I'm not exactly sure what my boss thinks. He made his mark developing the media and advertising system, and I think he believes it is working successfully in most of the company's other offices." He went on, "As long as my boss talks as traditionally as he does, there are limits to how hard I can push."

Reflecting for a moment he mused sarcastically, "Not that pushing harder would overcome the inertia in our office."

The topic switched to organization structure and the staffing hierarchy. Geof took us through "the chart." Examining it we noticed that Stan held the title Chairman and Head of Creative, which positioned him slightly above Geof. Taking note of this, we asked, "Do you think we ought to meet with Stan to bring him into the loop of what we will propose doing?" Geof acknowledged that this would be an excellent move although, he assured us, "Talking with Stan will be a mere formality."

A breakfast meeting was proposed. It went along just as Geof predicted it would—an affable encounter with but perfunctory discussion of our thoughts for proceeding. The only interesting addition was Stan's asking for a list of references. Geof knew all about our work at Dewey and we just assumed that he would have told Stan.

We sent Stan a list of references and made a date to begin on the second Friday morning. In the meantime we formulated a plan for counteracting staff resistances to change. It featured switching the responsibility for proposing changes in the agency's approach to the people whose careers depended on working more effectively. We wanted to put Geof and Stan in the role of reacting to staff suggestions in contrast to being the advocates and pressuring people to adopt their ideas. We were extremely interested in Geof's reactions to our proposal for changing the momentum.

That Friday we were met in the reception area by Geof's assistant, J.T., who quickly took us aside to tell us that Geof was working at home today and that we would have to call him to arrange another meeting. When we asked to use the phone she hesitated, saying that she didn't think this would be a good time to contact him. When we asked what might be a good time, she rescinded her earlier statement, saying, "On second thought this is as good a time as any, in fact he might really want to talk to you now." In response to this odd chain of conversation, we asked, "What happened, was Geof fired?" She broke down. Nodding her head and sobbing she replied, "Yes, but you've got to keep it a secret. It just happened yesterday and won't be announced until next week. I left word on the answering machine at your office to cancel. When I checked with your secretary this morning she said you hadn't called in and she didn't know how to reach you."

When J.T. regained her composure we asked whether we might talk with Stan. She explained that, knowing we were coming in and unable to head us off in time, she had broached this with Stan, who told her he was too busy. While she was telling us this, who but Stan should happen by in the hallway, stopping to give us a major greeting and inviting us to come down and see him when we finished with J.T.

We told Stan we knew. In response, he quickly indicated that he had a great deal of reorganization to accomplish and that he wanted to continue our project and that he would get back to us next week, which he never did. Then, as if to explain what had happened, Stan reflected on what he was contending was Geof's fatal flaw: "Geof was unable to bond solidly enough with the agency's clients. Now I've got to drop everything for a while to concentrate on building back relationships with clients to make up for years of what Geof failed to do."

Geof wasn't answering his phone that day and his machine wasn't picking up, so we couldn't leave a message. However, we did reach him Saturday morning to invite him to a Monday lunch. He sounded grateful for the chance to talk and accepted appreciatively.

At lunch Geof recounted that plans for his departure had been revealed to him in a meeting with the agency's worldwide president. He said it appears that his dismissal had actually been staged four months earlier and that notification had been delayed pending the outcome of negotiations with a $20 million-a-year client that had, two weeks earlier, announced it would be switching to another agency. He said it was an account on which Stan had refused to share resources, contending that the client was a lost cause. Because of this their proposal went forward without the agency's best creative talents being involved. Geof said, "What really hurt was watching Stan consume himself in the nonessential details of his pet account while my guys were working day and night."

Geof said, "The coup to unseat me was led by Stan, who lobbied headquarters with an ultimatum. I was told that Stan had declared that either I be dismissed or he would quit on the spot. My boss said the creative guys felt Stan was indispensable and that all the brass were concerned that Stan's leaving could result in the departure of our agency's largest and most prestigious long-standing client. And all this was despite the fact that I was the fast-tracker who had been tabbed to be the junior-most member of the corporation's elite seven-person Futures Group. Talk about sandbagging. Here I was struggling to install the very model that the company is betting on for its future, and I get knocked off because the model encounters local resistance."

We commiserated with Geof about his feelings of being sandbagged and unsupported. Then we inquired about his relationship with Stan and what might have provoked Stan to take such extreme action. Geof replied, "For years I've been after Stan to discuss our

philosophical differences. He's a very insecure person who has difficulties being forthright. Several times I took the initiative, saying,
'Stan, I know we see things differently, let me tell you my views and
then I want to hear how you see it and discuss what we see differently.' But when I'd ask Stan for his views, I could never get him to
say very much."

When we took up Stan's complaint about Geof's neglecting client relationships, Geof took the offensive. He said, "Stan's criticisms
are entirely unfounded. He and the account people would criticize me
for not spending time with low-level client representatives and miss
that I was in the room next door with their guy's boss." He went
on, "Stan would express annoyance whenever he heard about one of
some client's junior guys running uninformed. Frankly, I never saw
that as wholly our problem since I always made sure that things were
covered at the top. Nevertheless, lately we've been doing a much
better job of making sure everybody at a client's operation gets the
message and the word."

Geof finished his account by saying, "Don't you agree that it
was Stan's insecurity that caused him to fear me and want me out?"
He was seeking validation for his reasoning and conclusions. This
adversity was teaching him some important experience-based
lessons.

Midpoint exam

Now, for your first two test questions:

1. What did Geof learn?
2. Were these lessons he needed to learn?

Take some time to think about your answers before reading on.

Stopping the story at this point can readily lead to your thinking
that **the lessons Geof learned were mainly negative, political, and instrumental.** In his mind, he had been treated to some
of the roughness of high-level organizational politics. At a minimum
he learned to be more alert for backstabbing, coalition building, and
perhaps the need to give better facework (i.e., to present a better
image) to people with whom he was expected to team. He was probably thinking that self-survival comes before getting overly involved
in changing the system, even if changing it actually improves things.

We responded to Geof's request that we declare that his problem
was caused by Stan's insecurity by telling him we thought differently.

We answered, "Frankly, it seems like more than his insecurity was involved." Geof asked what we meant.

We answered, "It sounds like you didn't really need him and, as the situation evolved, his actions clearly show that he felt he was better off without you. Everybody communicates differently and, if you had really needed Stan's intellect and judgment, you might have put more energy into figuring out how to get it. Knowing of your success, we'd guess that there are many situations where you go out of your way to learn about a client and what you must do, specifically and sensitively, to get into dialogue with his or her viewpoints. Your premise is that Stan is more insecure than the average person and, in our judgment, he probably is. But if you actually needed Stan, then it would follow that you would have been more solicitous of his views and more active in creating the circumstances for an "insecure" guy like him to open up."

Geof was visibly emotional and broke the tension by leaving the table to get more coffee. When he returned, still shaking with emotion, he said, "I know I failed to get him involved. There was a lot about Stan that I did need but I can see how he never felt I was really listening." He mentioned a couple of instances to illustrate and then gradually switched topics to reflect on his prospects for future employment. "I think the advertising business as we've known it is bankrupt," he said. "I need a situation that treats advertising as an integrated service tying media and print in with merchandising and retail. I've got several ideas about how to accomplish this and am open to all opportunities in a range of situations that I have just begun to explore."

We asked, "What are your plans for networking and getting another job?" He replied, "I know many important and well-situated people, it's just that I've got a problem in that I'm not sure exactly how to approach them."

To us this was a deeply revealing statement that seemed to tie in directly to Geof's problems with Stan. We responded, "It's interesting to hear you express that difficulty since, to us, what needs to be said is basic and quite straightforward. Geof looked blank-eyed, as if he couldn't imagine what to say. We responded, "You merely tell the person you are between jobs and need his or her *help*." Geof responded, "That's the difficult part, I have a lot of trouble asking people for help."

We saw this as an opportunity to lend support. We said, "Geof, people like to be needed. Why do you think we're here? It's more than our liking for you or that yours is an interesting case. It's validating for us to feel needed by someone for whom we hold so much respect and who is as talented and accomplished as you are. No doubt the people you would like to contact will each have their own personal agendas. But, most likely, included in their agendas will be an altruistic desire to help someone whom they see as talented and able as you." We added, "Almost everyone feels this way; probably Stan does too."

The last statement was formulated for impact, and it struck home. It extended our previous comments about Stan's not feeling needed by Geof. In response, Geof self-critically reflected, "That was also a big problem for my ex-wife, and it was my last girlfriend's major grievance as well. Both complained that I didn't need them enough, but in actuality I did. It's just that needing someone creates emotions that are very difficult for me to express out loud. Telling someone that I need them is almost impossible for me to do. In fact, I think that my typical response to needing someone is to feel too dependent and to begin pushing that person away." For a few emotionally charged moments, no one talked. The silence seemed to embed the point.

Final exam

Now, for your final exam, can you answer these questions? This time we're not going to answer them for you because they are actually more prompts for your self-reflection than they are important questions that deserve your objective response. Take your answers as evidence of what you've learned so far and perhaps as a diagnostic of what you need to ponder further. Here are the questions:

3. What lesson(s) did Geof learn as a result of our continuing the conversation? (Hint: Use the words "mind-set," "orientation," and "responsibility" in your answer to this question.)
4. Are these lessons different in character from the lessons he was learning when reflecting on what his mind-set was teaching him prior to our intervening?
5. If your answer to number 4 is "yes," how would you characterize the differences? (Hint: Don't forget the two levels of change we've been emphasizing.)
6. What is required for people to get the deeper lessons that their experience might reveal without being distracted by what they readily conclude at the surface? (Hint: The terms "trusting relationships" and "the need to know" might come in handy.)

7. Why could we see the errors in Geof's reasoning? Would you have seen them? How do you account for why you could see Geof's orientation problem while he did not? Would he have seen yours? (Hint: Don't forget the power of being an outsider whose viewpoints are not biased by being a stakeholder with a self-sealing and self-protective mind-set.)

8. Why, as outsiders, do we "always" see what we believe are "critically" important issues that the "other" person fails to see? (Hint: Don't forget that we think that the Artifact of Mind is the only insight that can make the new management theories work.)

Concluding point

There is one concluding point we'd like to underscore in this case. It's food for thinking about the Geofs in your life. Had we not voiced our opinion, not given our feedback with the advice it implied, Geof might have settled for the instrumental political lessons, thereby missing the opportunity to upgrade his orientation and improve his next situation.

Being an "outsider" affords all of us daily opportunities to see others doing what we all do daily—actively disregarding feedback and advice and mistakenly rationalizing their experiences to find ego-satisfying ways to bolster themselves when facing a sensitive moment or setback. In this case, there was a happy ending. Geof learned a key orientational lesson that enabled him to network successfully in finding his next job. The lesson may have made it possible for him to succeed at it, as well as to allow the people who respect and admire him to give him more advice.

We're now ready to leave the focus on categories and breakthrough learning interactions and strike out in another direction of pay-dirt applications. In fact, getting the real "dirt" on pay is precisely where we're heading next.

IV

Applications and
Conclusions

16

Performance Evaluation: The Capstone Event in Giving Feedback and Advice

It's always struck us as a strange and amazing fact that a high percentage of managers and professionals receive direct and substantive feedback only once a year. That time, of course, is the company-mandated annual performance appraisal and pay review. Paradoxically, it's the precise time people are most likely to resist learning. In their minds they've come to negotiate next year's pay and want to hear neither what they are doing wrong nor how they might profit from doing something differently. So there they are, trying to put their best foot forward while the person conducting the pay and performance review is trying to extract a confession that there are critical functions to be performed more effectively and essential lessons to be learned. When we see such a situation we always question the group-think that can get otherwise intelligent people to go along with such "a program." After all, every reviewer is also a pay-review–recipient and has firsthand reason for knowing better.

It's a question we've been pondering for years. How can any rationally thinking manager expect a subordinate to openly admit that there are essential lessons to learn at the precise moment that subordinate is most focused on getting positive marks, moving ahead, and maximizing pay? Why don't reviewers catch on? Why do they go up to a year at a time, storing their choicest and most challenging feedback, and then delivering it at the precise moment the person they are purporting to help is least likely to accept it?

The pay review is the moment when people come prepared to explain, argue, and debate the seriousness of any slurs to their records. Their interest is mainly in knowing that their sacrifice, hard work, and imaginative contributions have been seen and valued, and that the system is going to pay off. It's time to optimize payments and rewards. In short, for feedback-recipients, it's time to get what they deserve, and their motives sometimes extend to getting as much as they can get.

Nonetheless, this is the time that performance reviewers have chosen for feedback-recipients to self-candidly reflect. They also want recipients to take stock of their strengths and weaknesses and to know the next steps required in making progress. They want them to know the skills and experiences required. All of this is presented on a continuum ranging from significant deficiencies to be remedied to next steps in one's growth and evolution. The reviewers have conscientiously taken hours, stretching into days, to review the facts, to conclude, and to negotiate with their bosses how much of an increment will be paid. In many instances they have reasoned their way back from numbers that someone else determined to a feedback script primarily aimed at justifying those numbers. Now they need to convince the recipients.

Of course the annual performance review also serves as an internal control mechanism against cowardly managers who are reluctant to confront those errant performers whose daily actions are a drain and burden to the effectiveness of the system. It forces managers to face up to their responsibilities to efficiently staff and this means only with performers whose value justifies what they cost, both in dollars and in opportunities. It forces managers to put people who aren't sufficiently contributing on notice that their performance is—please note this semantic correction—*perceived* to be inadequate.

Politics are involved

Secondary, political considerations are involved as well. It's seldom that a reviewer steps forward into one of these sessions without receiving "consultation" from higher-level management. Once that takes place the reviewer becomes a "spear carrier," and his or her credibility and image get tied to carrying out these instructions and agreements. No one wants to be seen by higher-level management as a "wimp" who, while "administering" a performance review, got talked into believing that the recipient has been misunderstood, undervalued, and, most indicting of all, underpaid! Consequently, we seldom find much give on the reviewer's end. There's lots of head-nodding, empathetic expressions, and sincere-sounding statements like "I can really, I mean really, see where you are coming from." But it's rare to find openness that leads to a reversal of the conclusions the reviewer held prior to discussing them with the recipient. The situation is structured for something else. It's structured to convince the recipient he or she has been treated fairly and to use that person's desire for progression in pay as the motivator for orientational change.

Secondary political considerations extend to the recipient's side as well. Often that person finds him- or herself in a "catch-22," in which he or she wants to argue that a piece of critical feedback was invalid but fears that the act of arguing will be interpreted as defensiveness and supporting evidence that he or she doesn't deserve more pay. Thus it's commonplace for someone on the receiving end of what that person perceives is an unfair criticism to bite his or her tongue and docilely accept the bum rap. The recipient nods and smiles in an attempt to project an image of "openness," while, inside that person, stomach acid drips at an ever-quickening rate.

"Scientific" methods are involved

To circumvent the frustration and the angry feelings that can erupt when performance reviews are disputed, many pseudo-scientific systems have been implemented. There's the Hayes plan, in which job functions are broken down into operations and are rated "objectively" with points assigned for degrees of difficulty and responsibility. More points, more pay. There are industry surveys that provide averages for what people performing similar categories of jobs are paid. These are used to tell people how their pay stacks up, but usually only when it exceeds the industry average. There are schemes in which all the people in a managerial or technical category are rank ordered, from 1 to (we've actually seen) as many as 120! Then pay is distributed by rank with modifications possible for retention needs and other factors not included in the performance ranking. There are plans in which performance goals are set at the beginning of a pay period with predesignated performance benchmarks and bonuses for exceeding modest standards of accomplishment. There are schemes in which self-ratings are solicited with the reviewer and the recipient sitting down together to compare and discuss the marks they awarded to performance and production in various categories. We've even heard of salary pools assigned to an entire work unit, with the peers within the unit being asked to meet and divvy up the dollars in a way that they perceive to be fair. The latter is based on a logic of "who knows the value of one's relative contributions better than one's teammates?"

Over the years we've heard just about every wrinkle on how to conduct a performance review but nowhere have we heard stories of more diligence exercised than in our own backyard at the university. If we took the time to detail the review process that we professors go through in evaluating one another for promotions and pay increases, you'd find it hard to imagine a more elaborate system or one in which incremental benefits achieved for time and energy expended are more costly. We'll spare you the details other than to say that academics often take a year or more to conduct a review with, from our vantage point, primary emphasis placed in multiple committees defending their "independent" and "objective" assessments. And the "de-spiriting" is substantial. Only a small percentage of professors reviewed escape with good feelings about the system or themselves.

The eye of the beholder

Now to the point of this chapter. What if the goal of the annual performance review were to conduct the feedback- and advice-giving candidly and open-mindedly with the focus on the recipient's learning? How might that process go and how might you proceed given what you now know about advice-giving?

In answering this question we begin with the insight that "organization is an artifact of the mind that views it" and the premise that, when it comes to sizing up organizational events and evaluating an individual's contributions and value, what you see depends on where you stand. It leads to our seeing that until you, as the feedback- and advice-giver, realize your own motives and perceptual inclinations, it's going to be very difficult to make your statements sufficiently engaging for the other person to trust what you have to say. It also leads to our seeing that before you can successfully give advice, you need to be able to be an open-minded listener and to be perceived that way. To us the bottom line is that the structure of the annual review has to change. In the current structure, when you are in the performance and pay reviewers' roles, there is no way you can be open-minded.

The Artifact of Mind insight assumes that everybody sees the same events differently, and whereas the bias is systematic, it is not contrived. It is a dual result of the variables in one's own performance effectiveness equation and the agenda one assumes on behalf of the organization. The "Artifact" insight underscores the point that just as performers are working off self-interested, personal-competency agendas, all evaluators are too. All of their own personal-competency issues are involved in how they assess someone else's results. Thus when a performance is judged flawed, two viewpoints need to be processed simultaneously. In the context of the Artifact of Mind insight, calling one opinion objective is merely an assertion in which the person with the power, not necessarily the person who is more accurate, gets to decide what is deemed "objective" and "correct."

This is not to say that performances and the orientations that underlie them should not be systematically discussed and evaluated. It is to say that all assessments are relative to the personal-competency motives of the evaluators and to a corporate point of view. The value of all "indisputable" output standards—sales made, new products delivered to market, increased profits, reductions in costs, awards received, and so on—can become issues for debate. In short, no judgments rendered should be disconnected from the short- and long-term personal agendas of the person making the assessment.

The goal of feedback is supposed to be "learning"

When it is performance and pay review time, and your objective is to set the stage for your feedback-recipient's learning, then one action, above all others, dramatically improves your chances that the interaction will be a success. That action is separating performance from pay discussions, with the performance review following the pay discussion by a long enough period of time, be it one day or six weeks, to punctuate the fact that pay is no longer the topic. The separation needs to be a sufficient time for pay recipients to release from their disappointments and to finish verbalizing frustrations that, to the reviewer, might seem self-indulgent or self-inflated.

We think that what we are proposing is entirely reasonable given the behind-the-scenes events that usually precede a review. We've been alluding to the fact that most discussions in which pay determinations are made take place with the recipient out of the room, with conclusions that are seldom open for renegotiation. When this happens, the pay reviewer bends the truth whenever he or she intimates there is anything to negotiate. The most honest way to "administer" the pay review, then, is to write down the dollar figure, stick it in an envelope, and hand it to the recipient. This modality communicates that the pay decision is not readily influenced. After the recipient has opened the envelope, then you can explain the reasoning that went into the dollar determination.

Without the benefit of the Artifact insight, most pay reviewers are inclined to focus on what they see as the strengths and weaknesses of the recipient's performance with platitudes and innocuous statements that don't provide any substantive critique. When they are really desperate, they focus on work habits such as dress and punctuality, instead of the true reasoning behind their evaluations. In the guise of searching for more insight into the recipient's activities, they argue that you can't get acceptable output with the existing work habits, which only causes the conversation to deteriorate. When this is the focus, the bottom line becomes a recitation of the recipient's imperfections and inadequacies.

Separating pay review from performance preview puts the focus where it ought to be. The focus of the pay discussion should be on explaining what the system appreciates, not in general, but for pay. This is important information for a pay recipient to hear. It clarifies what pay follows from what action in stark enough terms for the pay receiver to reflect on the meaning of the message being conveyed. This is "hardball" time in which pay recipients learn what they actually need to do if pay is their primary consideration, and then to evaluate the personal trade-offs. It's also an opportunity for them to establish what they want, or are "purchasing," in the way of personal orientation, experience, learning, and stability of employment in place of the pay increment they wanted but did not receive.

Proceeding this way avoids relationship-confusing terms like "I deserved" or "You get credit." Inside the company it's a market economy. People don't get paid what they think they deserve and they get lots of credit that never falls to the bottom line. It's not a matter of getting "screwed," it's a matter of getting what the game will pay.

Hearing an explanation of one's evaluator's thinking can lead to self-reflection and learning. When this happens, you can expect the learning to be instrumental. The pay recipient thinks about what actions and behavioral adjustments will best allow him or her to maximize the outcomes of a particular alignment and mind-set orientation. In your holding such a discussion, we think it's a good idea to tell recipients *not* to just grin and bear it. Remind them that the number in the envelope is probably a "done deal" and that for purposes of preparing for the next meeting you are interested in hearing straight-out what they think. Keep in mind that some of the words and feelings you are listening to are cathartic expressions necessary for paving the way to subsequent open-mindedness.

Previewing performance, not reviewing it, is how the company and the individual profit most

The next conversation is the feedback- and advice-giving discussion. In contrast to what was formerly called a performance review, this conversation might be a performance ***preview.*** The objective should not be to evaluate the recipient; it should be to arrange the stage for subsequent success. As performance ***previewer,*** your focus should not be on telling the other person what you think, but rather on finding out what he or she thinks, and interacting with that. You want to learn about the person's self-competency objectives and to find a role in helping him or her to realize them. It's in this context that you can cover candidly what you think the other person didn't bring up.

In other words, **your job is to actually "team up" with that individual,** which entails identifying what you can do to help that person achieve his or her brand of competence and discussing the impact of the expression of that brand of competence on the corporation's effectiveness. Throughout this book we've been talking about how every attempt at giving advice is an opportunity for the advice-giver's learning. When the issue is reframed from "evaluation" to "teaming up," the only way to conduct the conversation is to conduct it interactively with the goal of two-party learning. This is not only fair; it's the critical precondition for the pay recipient's learning.

Thus when the annual performance review is feedback for purposes of reinforcing strengths, self-correction, performance improvement, and learning, the discussion needs to be held under optimum conditions, which means that there are at least four different opportunities for learning. Two opportunities are addressed by each party learning about the conditions the other is working to establish for performing self-competently. Two are addressed by each party having the opportunity to learn how his or her needs for personal competency affect the competing pursuits of the other person. Each party thinks about the accommodations and adjustments that he or she might make in facilitating the actions of the other.

Case in point

After listening to us carry on about the problems inherent in conventional pay and performance review practices, a division manager named Pete was convinced to try it differently. Afterwards he talked about his experience.

Pete said, "When I stopped to think about it, I figured I had nothing to lose. If I told you how much time I used to waste each fall preparing for and conducting the reviews, you wouldn't just think I was nuts, you'd know I was. Under no circumstances were the results ever worth the effort. I would spend hours and hours following the company format for calibrating performances and formulating pay increases, only to see the figures I proposed subjected to an inconsistent application of standards by self-indulgent upper-level managers. The result was that it always fell back on me to sell my people on rationales I never really held for why they failed to get what they were expecting and, in many instances, I thought they deserved. I realized that the same personal attribute could be seen as a plus or a minus depending on the viewer's motive of the moment.

"Long ago I realized that the boxes I was supposed to check and the numbers associated with them were systematically upsetting to my people. About five years ago we had thirty 7-point boxes, now that's been simplified to nine. But when we had thirty I had this strange experience. I had given a star performer twenty-six 7s and four 6s. When I gave him the sheet I watched incredulously as he turned red in the face and got mad as hell. And when he refused to talk about his feelings, that really set me thinking. About a week later I realized he was right and I went to apologize. I said, 'Chuck, you are absolutely right, all I was trying to do was to establish a little credibility for myself with the guys I report to. The entire review was angled at getting you to be more diligent in keeping me in the decision loop so that I could answer my boss's questions. I never doubted that you were doing things right. I can see how you might have viewed those four 6s as an underhanded way for me to win an argument that we've been having for years.'

"The next year when the review form was down to nine items I decided to conduct an experiment. I gave each person a form to fill out as preparation, to see firsthand how they saw themselves. The results were horrible. With Art, whom I've known for years and who trusts me implicitly, I said, 'Art, you know damn well that you're not a 7 on "Communicates well with subordinates." And you certainly know you are much more than a 4 on "Effort expended" and "Diligence." How come you gave yourself such peculiar ratings?' He answered, 'Truthfully, because I was sure you would raise the 4s and I thought my 7 might get you up to a 5 or a 6.' I laughed and said, 'Now I've got to give you a 7 on psyching out the system.'

"So here's how I did it last month, and it really made a difference. I'm sure next year it'll go even better since the reorganization that took place just before reviews threw a monkey wrench into the process. This was the first time I reviewed five of my nine guys; three had been reporting to me for only two months.

"Following your suggestion, I began by scheduling two meetings with each person, roughly two weeks apart. I scheduled the first meeting for an hour and held it in my office. The second meeting was scheduled in the other person's office and set for an entire morning or afternoon. That really got their attention, since many have had to wait days to get just fifteen minutes of face-to-face time with me.

"In my office I told them, 'I'm going to give you the figure that management, myself included, has worked out for your next year's pay. I'm not going to get into the equity of the increase but I will answer any questions you have about the thinking that went into it.' I then said, 'I'll do my best to answer questions pertaining to your pay and how we reasoned, what I value about your strengths and what the company is willing to pay you for. Next week, I want us to focus on how we're going to work together next year. I will tell you what management is expecting of you, and then I want to discuss what I can do to help you produce results. I also want to know what others might do to better support your operations. If it turns out that a half day is not enough, then we'll schedule another appointment.'

"Two weeks later I went to their offices and said, 'I'm here to learn how you see things and I want to tell you how I see them too. In thinking about how you conduct your operations I came up with some areas where frankly I don't think I understand what you're up to very well and where the reasoning behind your actions isn't evident to me. Probably you think something similar about me and how my management efforts affect you. I'll try my best to be open so the conversation should really go two ways.'

"A majority, but not all, were able to embrace the spirit and get into it with me. In those instances I probably learned as much about myself as I did about the people in my group, except I got evaluated seven times. Hearing all those people tell how the way I reason and act affects them challenged my stamina. Thank God it wasn't an entire group purging themselves all at one time. One of the managers asked to have a buddy sit in on the discussion, who turned out to be another newcomer to our group. Suspiciously I agreed. However, when the meeting was over, I felt it had been very successful and that the buddy would be an invaluable resource in translating and coaching the guy who asked him in. Next year I'm inclined to invite others to do the same.

"What I learned about others during the review meetings was

critical. But what I learned about my impact on them was even more profound. Acting on my premise, that I'm supposed to do everything in my power to help the people reporting to me succeed, and your premise, that I don't really know what constitutes success for others until I understand specifically what the other person is trying to achieve and how he feels he needs to go about it, the conversation goes quite differently. And keeping it focused on tomorrow rather than worrying about the past seems to make a big difference. There was not a single instance of the bickering and arguing about facts and events that drove me nuts in previous years. At least two guys didn't understand what I was doing, but they seemed to appreciate my making the effort. I still faced the old 'if–then' questions. Several asked, 'Pete, if I accomplish "X," then can I expect "Y" in pay?' In every instance my sincere answer was, 'I don't know.' And frankly, I don't. In this company, the real power always seems to come from two levels above me.

"The downside is that now they are judging my effectiveness on what's happening to them. I'm worried that I set expectations for helping that I may not be able to keep. My people are counting on my being around more and I've got a boss who likes to send me out of town. That makes me nervous because I fear that keeping up on their affairs is going to be a significant drain on my time. I asked them to keep me posted, less on events and more on their thinking, and once again here I don't think most understood what I really need.

"My plan is to hold a series of management team meetings. I'm going to announce the topic and the questions I have in advance and ask people to say what they think and advise. I want them to see that they can learn from one another's thinking. My plan is to act as a facilitator, not the leader, and not state my conclusions until near the end. I may have to ask you for some help, because when I tried something like this in the past, it produced a lot of upmanship and image posturing. But I realize that we've got to do more of what you're calling 'mind-set management.' "

Case reflection

We felt that Pete's actions and thinking were dead-on with the Artifact of Mind insight and our thinking about the need to separate pay from performance and the need to conduct performance *previews* instead of pay and performance reviews. The one drawback seems to be the time it took for him to conduct all these discussions, not to mention what he anticipates in the way of follow-up. Having nine people report to you is time-consuming. Most experts would say a maximum of six is more desirable. The initial half-hour meetings consumed four and a half hours; the nine four-hour preview discussions brought Pete's "review" time to more than forty hours—a full work week. Beyond that, there was preparation time and meetings with bosses, and that probably took half a week. That is a lot of time to dedicate for pay review, but not excessive when you consider that the bulk was spent on relationship building, learning, and mind-set management.

The jujitsu principle

Several aspects of Pete's realization and experience applying our constructs deserve summary conceptualization. But before doing so we'd like to tell you one more story to further illustrate what we think you should be after. It's an application in a conventional setting that we made many years ago. At the time it was our most ambitious undertaking and, in the process, we learned a performance evaluation principle that, to that point, had only been subliminally in our sights.

We call it the jujitsu* principle of performance evaluation, and we think it applies 100 percent of the time. The jujitsu principle can be stated very simply: **When a *valid* evaluation takes place, the evaluators learn as much, or more, about their performances as the evaluatees learn about theirs.** We believe the obverse is true as well. When evaluators don't learn as much about themselves as they do about the people they evaluate, the deficit provides an important signal. And when they don't learn anything at all substantial about themselves, this fact should be taken as a 100 percent signal that a dominating, bogus, invalid performance review and evaluation has taken place.

Case in point

The site of our application was a government organization in which civilian employees were intermixed with military, and where rank and hierarchy will always count. Because of the unique nature of the organization we've found it a difficult one to disguise. So in this one instance we're not going to try. It was the 600-person technical organization charged with fixing all the "broke ships" in the Pacific. These are the technical engineers and experts who fly in the dead of night to where the malfunctioning equipment is located, often shinnying

---

*Jujitsu is a martial art in which you attempt to gain a competitive advantage by going with your opponents' momentum and utilizing it on your behalf.

down a helicopter rope onto a rocking ship that's steaming to a classi-
fied military position, to earn an admiral's commendation for fixing
the ultra-high-tech "whatyoucallit" that the on-board ship's company
couldn't spell, let alone repair.

Our clients were not these daredevils and the steel-nerved Red
Adairs. Ours were the people who managed the operation, who en-
sured that the technical know-how and Department of Defense funding were always there, and who interfaced with fleet commanders
fielding emergency calls and scheduling functional check-outs for
technical exotica. When we asked these people if they would mind
being identified, they answered, "Hell no—not as long as you spell
our names correctly."

Our connection was made through the captain heading the command, whom we met in a leadership seminar held at the university.
He invited us to his San Diego headquarters to meet the about-to-
retire civilian technical director (TD) who had overseen this operation for more than sixteen years. TD had a reputation of never meeting an officer, from admiral to ensign, that he couldn't insult or intimidate, yet he had an ability to recruit and train the "weird-brain"
technical experts that the Navy couldn't do without. The captain and
the successor TD wanted to change the culture to make it less fear-
laden, more people-sensitive, and more personally developmental.
They were looking to institute a performance review system that
provided managers more feedback and insight into how they were
performing, with identified areas for personal and organizational improvement.

The captain would be off to his next assignment in a year and
was looking to leave a legacy. Typically a command was for two or
three years, and then rotation to bluer waters. The new technical
director was bright and alert and had the "required" unpolished and
tough, craggy exterior. He had been in "monarchy" training for several years under the retiring TD, being groomed without knowing it
to follow in his predecessor's footsteps. But inside he had the value
system and sensitivities of a holy man; he just needed some reassurance that people wouldn't lose their confidence in him if he exhibited
overt sensitivity. If we had told him this at the time, he would have
had us for lunch.

This is a situation that we could go on and on about because
the vignettes make for extremely entertaining storytelling. But our
purpose here is to summarize efficiently by giving you the structure
of how a systemwide scheme for performance evaluation can be
transformed into advice-giving management development. For Navy
purposes we didn't call it either. We called it "leadership training"

because, at the time, that's the budget category in which they could fund it. Incidentally, today, five captains later, this command with the same TD is operating an incredibly sophisticated total quality leadership program that is a government knockoff of TQM. Just in case it wasn't apparent, "leadership" is a high-currency term in the military. They don't hire managers, they breed leaders.

Here's the structure of the program we proposed and carried out over a six-month period in dealing with the top three and sometimes four levels of hierarchy. Even though the civilians reported to the military, the organization chart was fairly typical, and standard hierarchy. For ease of following along, consult Figure 16.1.

First we met with the captain and the new TD to discuss the management of the command. We needed to hear their management philosophy and their ideas about what needed improving. We wanted to get their self-assessment and evaluation of their military-civilian teamwork. We also wanted to hear them characterize their individual

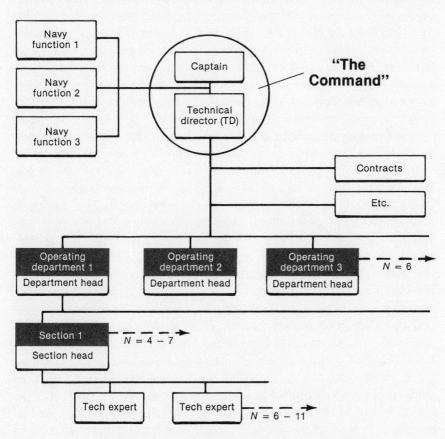

Figure 16.1. Organization of the command.

management styles and what they saw as the pluses and minuses of their command and their individual styles and the impact of these on people. We felt they gave us the full window-dressing picture, but that didn't bother us at the time. The process we were embarking on was going to get the "goods" for them like no one else involved. The missing level of candor didn't matter, they were about to get ten or more reviews.

Next we turned our focus to the management of Department 1. We wanted to learn that department's mission, and we wanted to hear their assessment of that department's management and productivity and what they saw the top two levels of department management needing to improve. Eventually we were after a picture of how they saw the effectiveness and developmental needs of each department head and the section heads who reported to him or her. Yes, one of the department heads was a her, and she turned out to be as good and as mentally tough "a guy" as any of the "hims."

Then in came department head 1. The captain and the TD briefly introduced us and went over the ground rules for our helping the head take stock of his department's management and the basis and effectiveness of his management style. Before leaving, the captain and TD made a date with department head 1 to return for a give-and-take conversation. It would take place after we held performance-effectiveness conversations with that head and then between him and the section heads who oversaw the technical experts.

Then we went with department head 1 for a discussion that paralleled the one with the captain and the TD except with him, instead of covering only section head 1, we discussed all five people reporting directly to him. We asked him to discuss them one at a time, beginning with the section's responsibilities and the styles of each manager we were about to meet. We wanted to know pluses and minuses and what he saw as the next steps in each section head's development. We told him the same thing that we told everyone else with whom we spoke, that we would keep his confidence and never reveal his reflections up or down. Our goal was to facilitate management, oops, "leadership development," through self-review and an exchange of performance-effectiveness perceptions.

Each of our individual meetings was preceded by a questionnaire sent out with cover letters explaining the "leadership development" activities, one jointly from the captain and TD and another from us. People were told that the questionnaires were intended as a mechanism for collecting their thoughts in preparation for two discussions, first with us and later with their supervising manager. It was for "their eyes only," not to be shown to anyone else. The entire process was explained, including a culminating off-site meeting to discuss the corporate implications of what those who participated learned.

Included on the questionnaire were questions about what that individual did especially well and what he or she thought was sometimes problematic, as well as similar questions of pluses and minuses about the help and direction received from the person who was their line boss and "superior." Also included were questions inquiring how that person evaluated the functioning of the command and what he or she thought was needed for it to function even more effectively. Although we did not collect these questionnaires, we would often begin our interviews by asking "How did you answer Question 1?"

Then we set dates with that department head for three-party conversations with each of the section heads working under him. Those sessions were preceded by individual conversations with the section heads in which we discussed their style and self-evaluation, what they saw as the next steps in developing as a manager, and a review of the quality and character of the department management being received as well as an assessment of the overall functioning of the command.

By now you probably have spotted how we were utilizing the jujitsu principle of performance evaluation. Each evaluator would be receiving an evaluation by each of the people reporting to him or her while each evaluatee received only one evaluation and then by a boss who was charged with helping him or her to perform more effectively.

Our focus was on consciousness-raising and self-assessment— identification of competencies, areas for development, and, generally, preparing our discussant for a performance discussion with his or her boss. We were functioning with the assumption that in-depth and candid self-reflection is the essential first step for performance discussion and progress. The format provided us with two levels of briefing on any individual whose performance was to be judged and previewed. While we were not about to reveal specifics, we were equipped to ask, "How do you think your hierarchy views what you just described?" and to comment, "We may have gotten it incorrect, but we think there are some areas in which they see you differently. You may want to inquire about this later on when we meet with your boss." Then, at other times when discussing strengths or the help or lack of help that an individual received from the hierarchy, we would counsel, "You may want to bring this up for discussion when, later on, we meet with your boss." This made sense since the next step was to bring the two together for a performance planning **and** developmental steps discussion.

We played a low-key role in the discussions with the boss. Mainly we wanted to keep the focus on people growing and improving, helping the boss find better ways to deploy, facilitate, and coach. Having gone through self-reflection with us as a sounding board, most section heads scored high in our category of candidly engaging issues. Some did not at that time, but may have later on; there's no way for us to tell. There were a couple with suspected alcohol problems who kept the conversation bland and played things close to their tattoos. But those who were candid paved the way for the department head to be candid in return, and in most instances we were left with the feeling that important issues were being addressed. We felt optimistic that this was merely the jump-starting of a discussion that would extend out over time. Candor was assisted by the fact that most were Navy veterans and engineering types who are often inclined to be quite stark when discussing what they consider "facts." What's more, most were in job classifications that provided civil-service protection.

During these discussions we took two types of notes. One was on what we thought the boss should be learning and the other on implications for the structure and organization of the command. After meeting with all the section heads reporting to department head 1, we met alone with him for an intensive discussion. We asked what he learned about himself and command management and structure from his discussions with the five section heads. We wanted him to identify both specifics and themes. Since we had taken part in these discussions, we had a basis for interacting with his reflections and were free to contribute our thinking. After this review and discussion, the department head was ready to keep his date with TD and the captain.

The structure for this meeting was relatively free-form. The only thing we requested was that it begin with the department head telling the other two what he had learned from his part in the exercise—about the department's operation and management; about himself and his management style, effectiveness, and needs for development; and about the command and how it might operate more productively.

After the meeting with department head 1 we remained with the captain and the TD to review what they learned and might do to support what had been discussed and to begin the next round with department head 2. The format was the same. What changed was the quality of the briefing that we received. Now that they had seen tangible evidence of what was possible, their guards were coming down.

We repeated the process with six departments and three small military groups and with a couple of professionals with administrative specialties, such as the person whose unit was in charge of contracting for exotic technologies and the person managing the computer facility.

The culmination meeting was an in-depth discussion with the captain and TD about the conclusions they were coming to in assessing the command's management, as well as what they had personally learned. We were especially interested in their thoughts about cultural change and the strategic human resource planning they were trying to implement, aka "the new management mentality."

The captain received numerous comments that he was aloof and image-conscious to a fault. Many situations had been brought up about how his lack of engagement had created problems for people, with implications for the fleet. The TD received feedback about being intimidating and perceptions that he had been explosive and overly directive in areas he had delegated, attributes that seemed to mirror complaints made about his predecessor. In response, the two set out to buddy-up in coaching one another and, from our limited vantage point, their progress was swift. As we intimated earlier, the ultimate benefactors of any review process should be the guys at the top.

At the end, as if to role-play the new mentality and the culture change these leaders were after, the captain and the TD hosted a department heads' meeting. Paralleling what the department heads did when meeting with them, they began with a report on what they learned both personally and organizationally and then gave an overview of what they planned in the way of culture change for the command. After an hour of give-and-take feedback and discussion, the TD went to the board to write down suggestions for the culminating off-site event involving each of the people who partook in the "leadership" activities just concluded.

Principles of performance evaluation

In the context of this book, the programs described and the results obtained probably strike you as feasible and practical. But we'd like to return to the introduction, in which we alleged that the vast majority of people conduct the performance evaluation quite differently, and most are so anesthetized by habit and training in the established "program" that they fail to recognize the bogus elements, even when they are on the receiving end. Using the former mentality, the need to accumulate power and to manage one's image make the former way of proceeding totally logical to the point that most people lack the ability to even conceive a plausible alternative.

The two cases described illustrate several Artifact of Mind– inspired practices about how to conduct performance review.

First, and foremost, contrary to conventional logic, **it's preferable not to confuse yourself or anyone else by intimating that amount of pay is a valid indicator of quality of performances rendered.** Certainly there are times when pay bears a linear relationship to performance, but there are too many times when it does not to get into a practice of citing yesterday's faults, seen through the alignment filters of a hierarchical superior, as the justification for not awarding more pay. Our advice is to decouple the two and not to risk the possibility of jeopardizing good relationships by getting into a mind-set debate that won't accomplish anything practical. We recommend the pay reviewer going quickly to the bottom line and explaining its basis as candidly as the recipient cares to hear it. If the recipient doesn't want clarifications or the rationale, and you're sure of that, we'd say, "Forget it," although if it were us, we wouldn't forget it until we knew why.

The second important practical point is to **get pay issues out of the way and out of consciousness before holding performance discussions** because, on this topic, the principal objectives should be reciprocal learning and your giving support. This requires relationship cultivation and protection.

Third, **whenever possible hold performance *previews*, not reviews.** A fractured quote, probably misattributed to Yogi Berra, applies here: "History may be prologue, but tomorrow is another day." When control issues are not central and the spirit of teamwork is engaged, then *previews* are discussions in which the reviewer is asking "How can I assist you?" empowerment questions, in contrast to "Here's what I require" control statements. You can require till you are blue in the face, but requiring doesn't necessarily make for positive results. Involvement and assisting does.

Fourth, **avoid giving others reason to see a performance preview or review discussion as an instrument of domination.** This requires sensitivity and careful monitoring because people are conditioned to see it that way even when it's not your intent. The jujitsu principle should serve as the telltale: When evaluation takes place validly, the evaluators learn as much, or more, about their performances as evaluatees learn about theirs.

There are many other practical applications of the artifact of mind insight; the next two chapters take up some more. But one that we find especially interesting, that we don't take up in this book, is "truth telling" and what constitutes and promotes the telling of the truth at work. It's one that we've written about,[1] and we think you would conclude as we did when you internalize the Artifact of Mind insight: Truths are relative to the mind-set of the viewer; people can relate to telling you what you want to know only by knowing your mind-set and agendas; asking for truths that put someone's interests at risk is a practical matter as well as a moral one; there are many ways for people to not tell you those elements of the truth that you most want to know about without lying; and as a truth-seeker, you need to factor in the motives and agendas of the person that you are asking when interpreting the meaning of what you have just heard. And there's more.

Note

1. See S. A. Culbert and J. J. McDonough, "Trusting Relationships, Empowerment, and the Conditions That Produce Truth Telling," in F. Massarik (ed.), *Advances in Organization Development* (Norwood, N.J.: Ablex Publishing, 1993), Vol. 2, pp. 154–170.

17

Breaking Out of the Program

When we began this book, we characterized the progressive new management models as conceptually correct and on course toward producing teamwork and effective corporate results. We staked our turf as promoting the mentality that enables people to implement those models effectively. We defined that mentality as one that relates to people as subjects, not objects; as distinct individuals pursuing overlapping but different personal-competency agendas in contrast to role-determined, interchangeable component elements of the corporate "program" and system. We contended that making this transition was the prerequisite mind-set "organizational" change for putting the new models into practice.

In this chapter we examine what it takes to break through an individual's indoctrination in the former mentality using a "problem-posing" methodology. "Problem-posing" is a method for challenging the reasoning that embeds dysfunctional orientations, especially when those orientations result from an individual's adherence to an external "program." It's a method that has applications in many settings, from advice-giving at work to the teaching of mind-set "organizational" lessons in the management classroom.

The structure of this methodology is amazingly simple; in fact, you may have already noticed it in our case accounts. It's a method that has the advice-giver or educator working both sides of the street. First, the advice-giver raises the recipient's consciousness of the "program" by posing problems that the program creates that can't be adequately addressed and reconciled within the logic and format of that program. Then, with the problem posed and the resulting limitations and dysfunctional consequences of the program grasped, the advice-giver runs across to other side of the street "to support," not direct, the recipient's contemplation of the problem and that individual's options for dealing with the dilemmas created by it. Of course any person's options are constrained by that person's skills, and thus support often means coaching on the skills required for exercising certain options.

Now we want to illustrate what it takes for people to make the transition from their indoctrination in the "program" of the former mentality to see that their perceptions and reasoning are essential contributors to the organizational life they lead and, in many instances, to determine the course of organizational events. We see this as the ultimate realization that the new mentality brings. Using the former mentality, people are inclined to see hierarchy, people in power, and prevailing assumptions about the marketplace as constraining factors that force them to override their own experience and sensibilities to view events in the programmed way. But the new mentality, with its "organization is an artifact of the mind that views it" underpinnings, invites people to take more active roles in construing the organizational scenarios they live and in framing the problems that need solving at work. When people realize this and change their mentality, they brave levels of responsibility that challenge even the lion-hearted.

For example, consider the challenge and squeeze a courageous manager found herself in when, in a problem-posing encounter, she learned that "her organization" was a derivative of her mentality and, to an extent far larger than she had ever dreamed, hers to determine. Using the former mentality, she could see herself as a "good guy" member of the management team working hard to identify and solve service problems by fixing problem personnel. However, after a conversation in which she comprehended the distorted view of people and their personal competencies that underlay her corporately programmed mentality, for at least a few moments she faced up to her role in perpetuating her company's effectiveness problems and began considering the alternative actions she might take.

Case in point

This conversation took place as we were returning from New York City to Los Angeles on a five-and-one-half-hour flight. We were flying United, and the skies seemed friendlier than ever. To begin with, the plane wasn't particularly crowded, there was none of the customary bumping and squeezing in the aisles, and there was plenty of over-head space for carry-ons. Then, before leaving the gate, a United Airlines ambassador wearing a name tag with a mid-level manage-ment title came over to welcome us personally, shake our hands, and "on behalf of all of us at United Airlines" to personally wish us a wonderful flight. Her warmth seemed genuine. Turning around, we noticed she was going down the aisle giving the same big greeting to everyone, regardless of class of service.

Still at the gate, a flight attendant announced that United wanted to hear from us, and that we would be receiving "forms" to use in rating the flight. The forms arrived immediately. We put them aside, amused about the number of rate-busters who were already busily filling them out. We reasoned, "What's to hear from us, our plane hasn't left the ground."

At the time we were in an intensive work mode and were far more interested in being left alone than receiving good service. But this was a "survey" flight, and we were going to be very well taken care of, regardless of what we wanted. We didn't want booze, we didn't want movies, we didn't want seconds on the dessert cart, we didn't want inquiries about what else we wanted. In our opinion, it should have been visually clear: All we really wanted were our writing tablets and to be left in peace. Repeatedly we learned this is the one service that's not available on a flight where service is being evaluated.

As a contrast to this "survey" flight, we thought about another United flight when the guy next to us had repeatedly rung the atten-dant call button while two attendants socialized up the aisle from him. Apparently deciding he could wait, they continued their conversation and then walked off in the opposite direction. Easily ten minutes later, perhaps more, when one of the conversing attendants arrived, she started with a wisecrack, saying, "I'm glad to see that you aren't sick, I was afraid from the way you were ringing the call button that you had an emergency." Then we rocked with laughter when this quick-witted guy shot back, "When I have an emergency, I'll book it on a different airline."

An hour out of Los Angeles there was an announcement that an attendant would be by momentarily to pick up the completed forms. Impulsively we pushed the call button and, in a wink of an eye, an attendant materialized. Attempting to be humorous, although in ret-rospect we could see how we were a bit obscure, we asked if we could speak with the "top cop." Nevertheless, the attendant didn't hesitate for a moment. We were amused that he seemed to know precisely what we meant. Off he went and almost immediately we got Vera.

Talk about impressive people; Vera is a public relations find.

We found her professional, intelligent, socially appropriate, and, best of all, interested in hearing out our viewpoints when, making sure we smiled warmly so as not to offend her, we said, "This form is idiotic."

Taking the seat next to us, Vera responded by giving us all the responsibility for our slur and criticism. Pleasantly and tactfully she inquired, "What do *you* find wrong with it?" If there was ever a doubt in our mind, we knew then that Vera was "management."

Turning the tables back on Vera, we said, "Is there anything about it that you don't like?" Nondefensively she was willing to take the test. Her expression was thoughtful and she strained to find something, perhaps the color of the paper, to criticize. Obviously she was partial yet, at the same time, was trying to be open-minded. But she couldn't find anything and because of this appeared a bit embarrassed that she couldn't. Her curiosity was aroused. We had posed the problem and she seemed very interested in hearing what we had to say.

We started with the obvious and then we tried to state what was more fundamental. We said, "Vera, who is this questionnaire evaluating?" She said, "All of us, the entire airline. We want our customers to have good experiences from the time they pick up the phone to make a reservation to the moment they leave the airport with their baggage." "But Vera," we said, "Look at these questions! Don't you think they really emphasize the flight attendants and the services they provide?" She agreed. Continuing, "Vera, there's no question about it, we can't recall ever having better service, and we didn't even want it! If United really wanted a fair test of the service, wouldn't you make your survey a surprise to your attendants, by handing the forms out shortly before landing?" Apologetically she agreed.

Then we went for the managerial "jugular." We said, "Vera, we see this as an exercise in which you guys in management blame the victims." From the look on her face she didn't have the foggiest idea about what we were talking about. Explaining, we said, "You guys already know what's wrong with your flight attendants. It's implied by the existence of these forms and the survey itself. What's bothersome is that you are asking us, as passengers, to do your dirty work. So we feel a little manipulated that you ask us for an 'objective' listing of your flight attendants' sins so that you can beat them over the heads with our critical comments. And let's say that you beat them into submission and, for the sake of argument, that they are totally responsive and mend their ways. Don't you think the problem is something deeper and that next month you will be able to compile a new list of different sins?"

We could see by the way Vera settled back in her seat that she was intrigued with the viewpoint we were expressing, so we kept on going. We said, "Vera, why don't you ask attendants what they are doing wrong and why they fail to do their jobs the way you in management want them to? How about focus groups or some other mechanism to really get out what's on their minds?" She said, "I agree, we really ought to do that next." We said, "Actually, you don't need to. You already know 'the problem.' We certainly do. We've known it for years." She looked perplexed. We said, "We're United regulars, in fact the reason we're sitting up here is because United has rewarded us for being regulars." Now that our loyalty was not in question, her attention was riveted. We said, "When teachers act like your attendants typically behave, we call it 'burnout.' " Now she was excited. She said, "Our management calls it 'complacency,' that's the problem with the attendants on most of our flights." This was a funny moment for us—all of a sudden Vera wasn't "management." To engage in straight talk, Vera had to abandon the team.

Having dropped the charade, we joined her definition of the problem. We responded, "Remember earlier we called it an exercise of *you* in management blaming the victims? When teachers are burnt out it's often because they are in a 'program' that requires them to repeat the same routines without sufficient latitude to deviate and to interject enough of themselves to make their work personally meaningful."

Then reflecting on our years of experiences with United flight attendants we said, "In California we used to have a regional airline called PSA where the front of the planes were painted with happy smiles and the attendants were encouraged to be themselves while doing their jobs. We passengers never doubted that our service and safety needs would be taken care of, but in addition we received human treatment by human beings and, because of that, we all enjoyed their latitudes. When they spilled water on us, they called us clumsy and we laughed. And they didn't have to give us a twenty-five-dollar dry-cleaning coupon to make up with us. In fact, we remember one announcement in which a flight attendant going through her preliminaries deadpanned, 'If for some unforeseen reason we experience a sudden drop in altitude, an oxygen mask will drop down. Then, *after you're done screaming,* take the mask and. . . .' Those attendants had a good time with us, and their energies communicated to the point that passengers joined the joking and were friendly to one another."

Taking our image literally, Vera responded, "Oh, our executives are much too conservative to allow something like that." Excited, we responded, "Vera! You've got it now!"

We said, "Go back and tell the executive members of *your* management team that it's time to stop wasting the company's money on entrapment surveys and public relations shams. Tell them the problem is that passengers feel like objects who are passed through the program, whether or not that program fits their individual needs. For example, our desire to work today was a bad matchup for the services that your attendants were unflaggingly going to give us in order to score high on the survey. Tell them the symptom is, *your* terminology, 'complacent' attendants who are in a program that limits their personal expression. Tell them the problem is, *your* terminology again, *our* 'conservative' management that forces attendants to make the 'correct' response irrespective of who is standing in front of them or how they, as distinct and unique individuals, are personally reasoning. Then tell them that the problem-solving methodology is bogus—it features addressing the problem of straitjacketed attendants by further taking in the seams."

We thought we got to Vera when she said with apparent wholehearted sincerity, "You are absolutely correct. In fact, and I probably shouldn't tell you this, we're getting beaten up badly on our Pacific routes for exactly this reason. I wish I could take you back to tell our executives what you just told me."

We responded, "Vera, that's your job! This is your company; in fact, didn't you just go ESOP? You go back and tell those guys on *your* team, who also work for you and the other employees, to lighten up and reexamine the consequences of their conservativism." Spontaneously she blurted, "Oh I couldn't do that." Quickly we said, "Vera, think about what you are saying! You are admitting that you are part of senseless activity that blames well-intentioned employees, employees who have been numbed into complacency by a program that won't allow them to put enough of their real selves into their work, that's about to solve this problem by constraining them further, and you aren't willing to tell the guys on *your* team, who create the policies that cause these problems, what you perceive they are unwilling to hear. Is this a conspiracy or what?! Exactly what do you propose to do when they stretch out their hands to receive the results of the survey so that they can once again convince themselves that they have done their jobs of ensuring that improvement is taking place?"

At this point we interpreted Vera's eyes as pleading for mercy; she had no immediate answer for the problem we had posed. After an uncomfortably long silence we did something we seldom do when we are formally consulting. We backed off. Breaking the silence we complimented Vera for giving us the kind of attentive hearing that we always dream of getting from our students.

On the way out of the plane, Vera made a big point of running up to us to vigorously shake our hands and thank us for "opening my eyes and helping me see the light." She gave us her card and was so cordial and made us feel so good that we were instantly willing to absolve the airline for the too many minutes we had just spent idle after landing, waiting on the tarmac for an open gate, long after the surveys had been collected.

Case reflection

We wish social protocol permitted our calling Vera to find out what she eventually did. Steeped in the theory of the new mentality, sometimes after a problem-posing "hit," we just "run." We never expected to go this far in our conversation; in fact at the time Vera engaged us in conversation, all we had intended to do was to decompress from our work mode with some light, entertaining conversation. But her sincerity and straightforwardness caused the discussion to build.

There's no question but that we got carried away, for we never intended to put Vera in such a tight squeeze. Asking an individual to take responsibility for effectiveness issues that those above in the hierarchy aren't facing can make that individual feel overwhelmed and burdened. As we see it, our discussion led Vera to view an organization knot that she experienced tied too tightly to disentangle. Each of us faces knots like this that we work around. But outsiders, who see them differently, often give a tug on a loose end, and, to our surprise, frequently the knot unravels. In the situation with Vera, we think all we did was call attention to what, subliminally, she already knew but didn't want to face out of lack of capacity to fix.

Developing the skills to see and challenge the program

Throughout this book we've tried to convince you not to expect people to see the light and to instantaneously transform themselves to become that which the new models require of them, no matter how conceptually vivid and progressive the specifications for new conduct might be. In fact, herein lies a potentially fatal problem. Few of the new models specify the conditions and processes required for people to open themselves to being influenced, or for developing a mentality that relates to individual mind-sets as distinct from corporate-desired ones. Yet without openness to influence, and a willingness of work associates to take an active interest in the quality and focus of one another's thought processes and modes of functioning, the new models become just another set of performance stipulations and top-management–instigated obstacles to personal effectiveness.

The keys are personal consciousness and organizational mutability. But consciousness in a system that people perceive can't be changed will drive people crazy as they uncover a cascade of flawed practices and anachronisms that inhibit personal and organizational productivity. The Artifact of Mind insight leads to our believing that no system should be upheld too rigidly, no matter how much energy and effort went into conceiving and conceptualizing it. Just as people need to be open to self-scrutiny and learning from feedback and influence, so does any management system whose executives are sincere about people finding individualistic ways to function with empowerment. Herein lies a fine line. Any system that is perceived as closed to influence is readily experienced as a "constraint." On the other hand, there is little doubt that a system that is "too mutable" runs the risk of units deviating too far from corporate competence and the market strategy, breeding confusion, dysfunctional politics, and leadership chaos.

Where will people get the training they need to internalize an Artifact of Mind mentality to view people as subjects and to view corporate programs as artifacts of mind and open to change? Until they are open to change we can only talk about new motivational and intimidation approaches aimed at getting people to perform as the "system" requires. Once the system is seen as open to change, we can talk about empowerment and the modifications required to make the system more user-friendly and marketworthy.

Required is a problem-posing process that introduces people to the fact that, ultimately, each individual determines the reality he or she lives and that the "organization" is merely a set of agreements intended to provide people sufficient structure to efficiently address joint business concerns. Ideally this type of education should take place early in life before the dogma of objectivity gets so embedded in one's reasoning that it becomes too rigidified to overcome. Successfully employing progressive new management models requires that people see the program open to their influence.

Course in point

At UCLA's Anderson Graduate School of Management we've made several systematic attempts to provide this education, and it's illustrative to now share what we think was our most adventurous and successful undertaking. It was an effort initiated over twenty years ago in a course called "Individual Problem Solving and Complex Systems." We always thought that this was a title that told students the goals of the course but very little about what they were going to experience. We were on the quarter system, so the course ran ten weeks.

The faculty made it a requirement for all entering MBA candidates. Classes met twice a week for an hour and a half with the stated expectation that an equal amount of time was required for out-of-class, small group projects and activities, with additional time for reading. Because the topic was at the core of what our faculty felt management students needed to learn, the faculty's pet name for it was "The Nucleus." The students picked up on this term and at moments when they felt their struggles with the material were particularly perplexing, they good-humoredly claimed they were being "nuked."

The students were divided up into sections of twenty-five to thirty, each section having a different professor and a different curriculum corresponding to that instructor's disciplinary specialty, but each with the same learning objective. Although the terminology "organization is an artifact of the mind that views it" wasn't in existence at that time, in fact its coining derives partially from our experiences with this course; in one form or another, our teaching objective was to explore its real-time manifestations.

In our sections, we arranged the structure to pose problems that would cause students to make the subject matter personal to themselves. Until they had the Artifact of Mind insight internalized, they would perceive the class as "structureless," which, for many, proved to be extremely frustrating. We would refute their use of the structureless label, contending there was plenty of structure and that their problems resulted from the fact that it was a different structure than the one they were accustomed to and preferred. We asserted that some structure was provided by the assignments they had to accomplish, but most was provided by students themselves and the mind-sets they individually used when construing events, including what they were, at that moment, misperceiving as the absence of structure. We would tell them, "If you want to see your structure, try discussing what is missing and see how what you require is slightly different from what others believe is missing. When there were no instant takers, we would explain, "This is a class in which thirty people are taking thirty different courses, and we won't know what you are studying until you tell us your individual topic. Likewise, we won't know why it's important for you to study that topic until you've given us some insight into the meaning it holds for you and why this is the particular time you've chosen to study it."

On the first day of class we also talked about our roles. We told students, "In this class we're breaking from convention to operate less as course teachers and more as problem-posers, facilitators, and process consultants." Then, using Paulo Freire's[1] terminology, we introduced the terms *conscientizaçâo** and *problem-posing.*† We gave students an instruction sheet that described the assignments, the organizational forums for accomplishing them, and the system for grading their performance.

The first assignment was for students to get themselves into four-person "support" groups, which, by the third week of the term, would be meeting a minimum of two hours a week. The only constraint we put on the groupings was that all matchups were tentative until everyone in the class felt satisfied. We stated our responsibility for optimizing the productivity of the whole, which generated a concern that everyone needed a viable group to which they could wholeheartedly commit.

The instruction sheet explained that 40 percent of each student's final grade would come from the average grades received by the three other students in that person's group on those students' end-of-the-course papers. In other words, we told the class, "Almost half of your grade will rest on your ability to influence and advise three other people in their writing of 'A' papers, while their grades will be based on their abilities to influence and advise you and the others that you are coaching."

The remaining 60 percent of each student's course grade was to come from that individual's performance on learning criteria that the class as a whole thought were valid and would recommend. We told the class that the grading criteria needed to promote and measure intellectually valid production for an MBA degree and discriminate between performances.

Also assigned was a weekly paper that students were asked to hand in at the beginning of Monday's class and which we would return with written comments at the beginning of class on Wednesday. The idea was to provide fast enough turnaround for students to benefit from our comments before writing their next paper as well as feedback they might find useful in gauging their participation in

---

*The uncovering of the social and cultural program.

† The intrapersonal dialectic that derives from facing effectiveness issues that cannot be reconciled using the logic and format of the extant social program.

Wednesday's class. The topic of each paper was "What I learned that was *personally meaningful* to me during last week's work on the course, which included classes and support group meetings, and specifically what accounts for the personally meaningful label I attach to that learning." When some students wrote, "Nothing was personally meaningful," we would respond by asking what would have to happen to make something personally meaningful and to explain what that said about them.

We asked that final papers be on the topic of "What I learned about myself from reviewing the eight 'personal meaning' papers I wrote as a collection." While the weekly papers were not graded, the fact that the final papers would be graded provided students a reason to take writing the papers and our comments seriously.

While the format for each of the nine papers was relatively unstructured, we did ask students to be sure to document each assertion of meaning and learning with descriptions of the events in which the signaling feelings and cognitions occurred. We also requested that they specify the background reasons that explained why one classroom event or another was especially meaningful. These requirements were our structured way of insisting on self-reflection. The final paper focused students on process. It required them to review their previous weekly papers and to chart the events that cued their learning and the progression of personally meaningful insights developed.

The students quickly caught on that helping their teammates write a top-notch final paper required that they track one another's classroom experiences and weekly statements of learning. This made reading what their teammates were writing, contrasting their experiences, and learning the basis of their different reactions to the same classroom events a prerequisite to their offering feedback and counsel. We were making our contributions by commenting and raising questions on the weekly papers and clearly stating when we were unable to see what was personally meaningful in what a student was describing. Because these weekly papers were not graded, and because our comments were personal reactions, we had a great deal of latitude in making them problem-posing and provocative, which, we hoped, would serve as constructive prompts for self-inquiry. We would write comments like, "I don't see what's personally meaningful here; tell me what I need to know to understand why you felt this way given that I don't think everyone else would have felt the same experiencing the events you cited." We would even include comments like, "To me it appeared that you were emotional when Greg challenged your logic in class on Wednesday. Were you? If so, does this relate to what you are discussing here?"

For students, the class oscillated between extreme frustration and excitement. Several aspects were particularly frustrating, especially the initial ambiguity about what was expected of them and their uncertainty about what work-group participation and personal output would be instrumental to getting a high grade. The term "personally meaningful" was almost always perplexing, especially for young adults who had spent most of their life going to school and, more recently, had been in the lower echelons of organizations. By and large they had always been in positions where the system stipulated the criteria for getting ahead, what they were expected to produce, and the standards used to judge the quality and quantity of their production. In other words, they had always been focused on the external "program." In contrast, we were asking what constituted valid production on internal criteria. This was a question that many had never before had to engage and justify out loud. In using the term "personally meaningful," we were asking them to invent their own programs.

When receiving comments that we failed to see what was personally meaningful about what they wrote in their papers, students would get angry. In class they would aggressively ask, "Who are you to decide whether this is personally meaningful to me?" Typically we would respond by referring students back to their "support" group for a second opinion. Could anyone else see what was meaningful and understand why they concluded as they did based on what they had written? For some it took as many as three or four unsuccessful attempts before they began writing about their experiences in clear enough terms that the personal meaning might be visible to interested outsiders. Of course everyone received direct help from support group members who had gotten to know them well enough to raise relevant and important self-searching questions that they could superimpose on classroom events. It was here that we fell in love with "open-ended questions" that led people to self-scrutinize their experiences of classroom events for data that could be useful in addressing personally meaningful issues related to functioning with enhanced self-competency.

Eventually students discovered that their abilities to bring important questions about themselves, about how others think, and about how the system works, are what make any activity or class like ours a personally meaningful experience. Identifying significant "open-ended" questions became a source of excitement and eventually exhilaration. As students developed a capacity to create learning opportunities for themselves, they stopped blaming us for not doing our job and failing to "lead" the class as we were "supposed to." **They discovered that scanning for self-meaning lessened their dependency on us as "the system."** Identifying meaningful self-questions gave students what they needed to know to direct class discussion in ways that were particularly relevant to their interests, and they became increasingly conscious of doing so. They learned that discussing organization process was actually a methodology for redirecting events. They learned how to superimpose meaningful personal agendas on almost any organizational activity. And they learned the importance of being able to make their personal agendas visible, for doing so set the stage for others to provide on-point feedback in areas that they had designated for self-improvement and upgraded work effectiveness.

Inevitably, classes would go through a period of attempting to erect criteria for evaluation prior to deciding what would constitute intellectually valid production and how they might optimally accomplish it. When someone would point out this dynamic, many were confronted with their tendencies to let concern for external success supersede their needs for personal meaning. Pointing out this dynamic typically provoked self-reflection as these students recognized their tendencies to endow meaningless activities with value based primarily on their beliefs that they could score highly on them.

We always thought we gave students major direction to solving the large class production question by assigning "personal meaning" as the topic for weekly papers. We intended the "lack of structure" to give students the opportunity to learn about the roots and arbitrariness of "organization" as well as the importance of building an organization that was determined more by function than form. The latter was an easy lesson to illustrate as classes inevitably would make the mistake of deciding on organization before they decided what they wanted to study and the optimal processes for doing so.

Always we found blatant parallels between what we witnessed in class and prototypical organizational behavior. At various points we found it impossible to resist the impulse to discuss them. We saw instances of groupthink, conflict avoidance, disregard of others, overdependency on the "program," counterdependence, domination by a single dissenter, form over function, norms that reflected gender and racial status; the list was open-ended. We felt that explicating these dynamics and exploring their underlying assumptions helped students to rethink their socialization and view the anxiety-reduction kneejerks that prevented them from taking a more self-directed and organizationally productive direction.

Whenever possible we tried to lead by asking questions aimed at keeping students focused on Artifact of Mind subject matter. For instance, with respect to their initial assignment of identifying members for their small group, we would ask, "What do you need to learn about the twenty-nine other individuals here to make a valid decision about the people who might be the best resources to have in your small group?" and "What do you think others might need to know about you to identify where the natural chemistry exists?" Typically some students would try to deny the validity of such questions and propose that support groups be composed based on numbers drawn from a hat. Then our job was to challenge them to examine the underlying reasons for their resistance. With an intonation of irony we might say, "Oh, that's interesting. You are assuming that personal chemistry isn't important for teamwork, more or less like people in a business setting might assume when they assert that anyone they work with is more or less the same to them." Ultimately this was an opportunity to help students state the determining, unspoken issue about how they feel anxious whenever selection or rejection takes place.

The fallback position for students not being able to agree on what constitutes valid intellectual production, and the criteria and means for measuring it, was an exam based on two books, "assigned" as background reading, which most students had no immediate motivation to read. We told them that the class was sponsored by an institutional system that requires production in exchange for course credit *earnings* and that we discriminate for contribution by awarding a range of grades as performance "pay." We explained that faculty and students in other sections would readily understand, and that the *system* was easily satisfied by our following the "program" and giving an exam—even if the books and the exam were completely extraneous to the educational effort under way. We asked them how they would feel if they were in another section and thought there was a grade giveaway program taking place in our section. Any group suggestion had to pass muster by being justifiable on terms the system could appreciate. But form has a way of taking on a life of its own and, at various points of discussion, students could hear themselves falling back on the position that an exam on objective material was the only fair way to measure learning gain. On the other hand, also without thinking about the actual course content, some students quickly picked up on the idea that, by playing their cards correctly, they could save a lot of time by avoiding an exam, for there would be no need to open even one of the fat books.

Over six or seven years of teaching this course, we never had two classes work out exactly the same scheme for solving the large class assignment. Some students got personally explicit in the large class and some kept personal disclosures for support group discussions, primarily using the large class as a laboratory for their observing their teammates' leadership and task-group participation styles. And each time we taught this course, the class devised a somewhat different classroom structure to use for promoting relevant learning and measuring accomplishment. In twelve or so sections, we never gave an exam.

There's no need to take up the specific solutions worked out by specific sections. Experiencing and discussing the process was where they learned about the Artifact of Mind insight and internalized their education. Firsthand they learned that people with different mind-sets see the same situations differently; that people with different needs naturally invent and prefer different organizational structures, which they propose with a rational logic of what is objectively best for the classroom *organization* that does not disclose their self-interests; and that the only efficient way to decide on the classroom's organization structure was to learn about the intrinsic needs and preferences of the students in it, and to design a system that could address those *consumer needs*.

Another source of problem-posing–provoked learning was provided by students in other sections being given entirely different assignments and different instructional support. This created an institution-wide dialogue on precisely the educational issues you'd like to think MBA students talk about outside of class. They discussed what constitutes valid MBA education and what experiences and technologies are relevant to operating as a manager. Students were interested in how the faculty could possibly contend that the same course existed in so many different formats and forums. They compared notes and envied those who were involved in experiences that sounded less perplexing and seemed to be a better fit for their needs, talents, and interests in earning a good grade. The result was the evolution of a management school culture in which students exchanged and contrasted their experiences and challenged their *top management* to explain its rationales.

During the first few weeks of the quarter, when the students were truly baffled, it was not unusual to hear expressions of upset and disparagement of the class. By the end of the term, it was commonplace to hear the same students making positive statements about the class, with about 85 to 90 percent ranking it as an extremely valuable educational input. Many became ardent enthusiasts, giving encouraging messages to incoming first-year students. But the strongest endorsements came from alumni surveys, when graduates registered their appreciation for this course as highest among the most valuable aspects of their MBA education.

Course reflection

There's no doubt about it, each time we teach an experiential course we are provided additional Artifact of Mind insights. Even today, more than twenty-five years after encountering the theory, writing about it often and thinking we know it so well, we continue to tease out new Artifact of Mind propositions. What's more, just as the students bonded with the people who were in their small groups and sections and formed lasting relationships, so have we. We've bonded with the faculty who taught parallel sections, and we've developed several enduring collegial relationships with students who are now alums.

The Artifact of Mind educational experience and the legacy of "The Nuke" are apparent in the orientation sessions we give MBA students entering our program and the two-quarter group field study projects they are assigned at the end. They are explicit in several human systems and organization behavior courses where students are encouraged to treat case material personally and to contrast their reactions to course content with the reactions of their student associates, examining the reasons behind basic differences. They are present in leadership and professional development courses in which students are asked to describe their own leadership styles and to analyze the formative experiences and models that cause them to lead and participate the way they describe. They are present in marketing courses in which students are asked to interview a variety of people and to partition diverse consumer needs with specific match-ups in appeal. They are present in business-economics courses that highlight issues relating organization form to transaction-cost economics. They are present in residential kickoffs for executive curriculums. Notwithstanding all of this, at least some of us yearn for the opportunity to once again take up these lessons at the systemwide level and to go at it full blast vis-à-vis the new management models and the new mentality requirements.

The program

In this chapter we've used the term "program" to refer to any standard, fixed method of thinking and acting used to meet an organizational requirement or to pursue an organizational objective, regardless of the interests, needs, values, abilities, and circumstance of the people who are required to use that methodology. While "programs" are not negatives per se, they often contain elements that are deleterious to the well-being of the people who are expected to comply with their tenets. Insisting that people knuckle under to a corporate-level program without exception for personal qualities, self-interests, and local circumstances is possible only using the former mentality.

The Artifact of Mind insight helps us understand that, at their roots, programs are the products of social agreements and basic assumptions about the functioning and motivations of man. There's nothing wrong with programs when people have the choice to buy in. In fact, we often hear people utter statements like, "I buy the program." Problems arise when buying the program is forced on them, or when they lack sufficient information, either about the program or themselves, to make the "buy" decision on personally valid grounds.

We fear unexamined programs for their capacity to do human harm by thwarting an individual's basic nature. We applaud examined ones when they serve the needs of people along with the needs of a system that serves people. In fact, by definition, all the progressive management models are "programs." They take agreed-upon company goals and establish a set methodology for achieving them. Whether they are "good" or "bad" rests with the mentalities of the people perpetuating and enforcing them. The new programs quickly regress to be no more than a repackaging of the old when they are applied using the former mentality. This mentality treats people as objects to be reshaped.

The new mentality offers you a means for humanizing programs and advises staying open-minded about changing the program when it doesn't match up with the specific individuals whose effectiveness is supposed to be enhanced by its existence. Using the former mentality, a person either conforms to or leaves the program. But, using the new mentality, you quickly see that the system or the individual or both can change. And the methodology is different from that of the former mentality. Instead of enforcement and control, the new mentality methodology is "problem-posing." You begin with the problem and give all parties an opportunity to voice their personal-effectiveness agendas and concerns. The resolution requires politics;

however, with problem-posing the politics include the possibilities of renegotiated agreements and cards-on-the-table fair play. Even when the end results are the same, the feelings and relationships will be entirely different.

The next chapter presents a book-summarizing case of a situation created when a newcomer entered an organization, sensed the presence of a nonconstructive program, and instead of "loving it or leaving it," decided to take a crack at changing it. In the process this newcomer engaged a range of new mentality issues, so that including it here provides a very nice summary of the themes in this book.

Note

1. See P. Freire, *The Pedagogy of the Oppressed* (New York: Continuum, 1992).

18

How the Artifact of Mind Insight Instructs Us to Act

Throughout this book we've been describing cases that demonstrate there's something different and unconventional, perhaps a bit counterintuitive, that goes into our thinking about organizations and the circumstances in which people find themselves while trying to perform competently at work. We have been attributing our perspective to the directions we receive from our knowledge of the Artifact of Mind insight. Now we'd like to state precisely the prominent managerial lessons that we hoped would come to your mind as you read the case stories applying this insight along with us. To accomplish this, we need to tell you one more story.

Case in point

A friend of ours, Stu Richter, had an assignment consulting to the president of a major league, professional sports team. Impressed with his performance, the president asked Stu to come to work full time, creating a new position called "Vice President of Operations." The salary sounded good, the perks were terrific, and the career opportunity sounded great. But when Stu Richter hedged his enthusiasm by telling us "I'm *inclined* to say yes," we asked, "What's causing your reluctance?"

He responded, "I see two problems. First, I see a great deal of incompetency and inefficiency. There aren't many professionals in the front office. Most of the employees are old-timers, sycophants, and former players whom management doesn't want to replace. Second, one of the key people who would report to me is marginally competent and, based on my experiences, is unquestionably an assassin-caliber backstabber." When he asked what we thought, we knew just what to advise.

We answered with a question, "What's the chance of getting the president to fire that guy before you come in?" Stu responded, "That's precisely what I was thinking." To reinforce his point we said, "Tell him there is nothing to be gained by your coming in and developing a dangerous reputation when, in fact, that guy's presence represents someone else's dirty laundry." Of course, our major concern was that one morning we'd sit, coffee cup in hand, reading the morning paper and find Stu Richter's name in the organizational obituaries with cause of death listed as "stab wound in the back."

Stu Richter responded by saying that's just what he expected us to say, and that the president had told him he would do whatever it took to support him, so that one guy out the door before he took over ought to be a piece of cake.

Stu decided to raise the topic of cleaning house without mentioning anyone's name. The president implored him to take it easy and see how the people shook out. He told us the president reassured him that, after he came on full-time, if he still thought "personnel shifts" were necessary, he would have the president's 100 percent support. And Stu thought he would, and that the president's response was reasonable.

After Stu had spent three months on the job, we asked him, "How goes it?" Stu answered, "Dynamite." He was clearly enjoying himself and felt he was performing well. When we asked about the "backstabber," Stu Richter told us, "That guy is still at it." Then he added, "But my guy isn't doing anything that the majority of the others in the front office aren't also doing." Stu told us, "They're a bunch of amateurs who enjoy sitting around telling incompetence stories that feature the screwups of the last guy who left the room. That's part of their inefficiency. Everyone is so afraid of the gossiping that no one wants to leave the room to go to his own office and do some work." He added, "Once, to signal them to stop, I abruptly stood up and walked out of the room backwards. I told them, 'If someone is going to stab me I want to see his face.' " Joining our laughter, he said, "But not to worry, I've now got 'the goods' to take this guy out."

We responded, "If there's an epidemic of backstabbing, then allow us one hypothesis about the cause. That president of yours must be pretty tight with the praise. The dynamic you're talking about comes from people who can't get positive strokes. It's their lame attempt to compensate for having to work without affirmation. They attempt to build themselves up by putting another guy down." Again, Stu said, "Dynamite," adding, "I've got to find a way to take that one up with my boss." Coming from an individual of Stu's caliber, that "dynamite" was flattering.

Then we asked, "What 'goods' do you have on this guy?" Stu said, "Before I took over, the president had asked my guy what could be done about the pattern in which seats are sold. We have a bad situation created by the sequence in which our computer sells seats after the season ticket orders are filled. We get some strange patterns in which the arrangement of empty seats make the stadium look less filled than it is, particularly when viewed from popular TV camera angles. My guy's answer was that the cost of redoing the computer system would be prohibitive, in excess of half a million dollars. Then I met the marketing director of a ticket merchandising company at a league meeting in New York. He thought his company could easily solve our problems so, inconspicuously, I had one of his specialists in to size up our situation. I'm now convinced they have a ready solution, which I verified by calling the ticket people of three other teams. The cost would be $30,000 annually, including software maintenance and yearly upgrades."

Now it was our turn to say "Dynamite," but we followed with a longer answer, one that Stu had not expected. We asked, "Can we make a suggestion?" Stu Richter nodded, "Of course you can, why do you think I'm telling you this?" We then advised, "Take the president into your confidence and tell him that you want his cooperation in trying a confidential experiment. The $30,000 versus the half-million-plus should clearly document your point. But tell him that you want to use your study to win your guy's loyalty. Tell him that you plan to low-key it by giving your guy the ownership of your software study and asking him to run with it, implying that he can have all the credit. Tell him if there's further backstabbing and a failure to win your guy's loyalty, then you want the authority to boot him out, no if's, and's, or but's. Knowing that you've done more than just go the extra mile to make this guy a success should win your president's cooperation." In response Stu said, "Dynamite, dynamite." We were pleased because we knew, from past experience, that a double "dynamite" was a 7.2 on Stu Richter's scale.

Managerial lessons

Now we'd like to state the lessons. We've got nine listed here. You may have more.

First, and foremost, the Artifact of Mind insight leads to our seeing that **management is a mind-set technology.** Since the organization in which a person works resides in that person's mind, engaging an individual requires that you visit the location at which that person conducts his or her organizational business. As much as possible, this is where we try to spend our time. We try to puzzle out how the individual thinks and what needs to change for that person to conduct business more effectively. What we see as off in that person's behavior, then, often serves merely as a clue to engaging that person's mind-set.

In the preceding example, Stu had to engage the president's mind-set and he had to engage the mind-set of his errant performer. The exercise we proposed was aimed at engaging both, providing the president with a chance to see Stu taking the extraordinary positive team-building step and his errant performer a chance to see what team play could do for him and to decide whether that warranted his loyalty.

Second, the Artifact of Mind insight leads us to assume that **management entails psychology, lots of it, and there's no getting around this fact.** But many managers are extremely reluctant to acknowledge this. For years we've been treated to comments like, "Analysis is paralysis," "Watch out, here comes the Doc," and "Lie down everybody, we're going to be psychoanalyzed." In our minds this is all camouflage. These managers know full well they use psychology all the time but are reluctant to acknowledge this for fear of having their competitively framed motivations exposed or being told they need to become better "psychologists" if they hope to accomplish what needs to be done.

There's a corollary problem that needs mentioning here. A wide gap exists between the formal frameworks that the fields of psychology put forth and the type of packaging required to make psychology easily accessible and readily available for managerial consumption. The psychology we use and practice with managers is mid-level and practical. It derives neither from "psychoanalyzing" people nor from "psyching them out." It derives from sensitively applying principles that emanate from the Artifact of Mind insight. This is the level at which managers can readily apply the psychological training that they have received from their lifelong experiences with others, as well as their personal knowledge and sensitivity. While this level does not require formal psychology training, it nevertheless requires sensitive and empathetic applications.

In the example, we thought it was important to get Stu Richter thinking about the circumstances that could lead a group of diverse individuals to play out a mutually destructive dynamic. Our hypothesis about the president not giving positive strokes was generated by our thinking, "How could well-intentioned people, who desire to perform with personal competence, wind up in a routine of constantly putting one another down? Certainly this was as much self-destructive as it was other-destructive." Once we thought this, the hypothesis we offered Stu quickly sprang to mind.

Third, the Artifact insight instructs us exactly how to talk to people when we want to help, manage, or advise. **The absolute best way to talk with people is to *listen*.** Please don't get the impression that we're saying "listen quietly" or "listen passively." That couldn't be further from what we do. We don't just listen, we concentrate and try to ask darn good questions. Then we listen. What makes our questions so darn good? They are focused and pointed at learning how the other person thinks. Thinks about what? About him- or herself, the other people, and the organization in which he or she works and lives. We're listening to sensitize ourselves to the critical variables in an individual's personal competency equation.

For example, we knew Stu Richter's mind-set well enough to know he's one of the capable, well-intentioned, team-oriented guys that every company benefits from having around. He's aware that he's got a backstabbing fifth columnist in his ranks, and he's open-minded about having that person rehabilitated, particularly if he can get some important teamwork loyalty and competency lessons across. Among other things Stu's guy needs to learn is how to go about finding solutions to problems he doesn't personally know how to solve. In the scenario we proposed, behavior was to speak louder than words. Stu would raise a behavioral question and then he would listen to his guy's actions. Stu will need to determine whether his ticket guy will act and talk any differently in response to the obvious help Stu provides him.

Fourth, the Artifact insight leads us to see that **imperfect people are often good enough performers once they get their orientations adjusted to fit their alignments, and their alignments adjusted to fit both personal and organizational effectiveness needs.** Some will find this an overly rose-colored view of the world, for certainly technical competency is also very important. Nevertheless, we contend that orientations and alignments are the critical variables that need to be engaged if for no other reason than to figure out what another person is good enough to be trusted to competently do.

When people have the right orientation, they have ways to succeed. Then they are aligned with their competencies and can afford to defer to others for help, which compensates for their limitations. People who are aligned shouldn't have to confuse organization matters by pretending that they can competently do what they cannot. Their credibility is established and, hypothetically, they can afford to reach out to their teammates to solicit appropriate help and support.

In this example, we interpret the president's actions in recruiting Stu Richter to be a step of resolve toward professionalizing his front-office team. And when Stu raised the topic of cleaning house prior to joining that team, the time when one can be coldheartedly "objective," the president essentially said, "poco a poco." Stu read into the president's communication "We'd like to go forward fortifying and rehabilitating our existing team as much as that is possible." This meant that he accepted that they had limited performers who might be "good enough" with the proper orientation. In response to the president's direction, Stu got on board with helping to change the company culture and people's orientations, taking a stand by explicitly calling the group on their destructive backstabbing dynamics. If the hypothesis we ventured is correct, we'd say the next step is giving people some positive feedback and the opportunity to experience success.

Fifth, the Artifact insight directs us to see that **organizational life is inherently and inescapably political.** To turn your back on this dimension because it conflicts with the way you think organizations ought to operate is more than just a little naive. It is downright self-destructive and dangerous. Holding a vigil for organizational politics is unsavory to all of us; it's an affront to everyone's sensibilities. But the Artifact insight clearly instructs that everyone has a constant motive to influence how others think about the situations in which we are functioning. This is the basis of organization politics. To be effective we've got to interact with people who naturally see each situation differently. Only by explicitly facing up to this political dimension do we have the opportunity to play the politics out on the high ground, without getting dragged down too far into the muck and mire.

In our example, that's exactly what Stu had to do. He needed to avoid slipping into the muck with Meyer—that was his guy's name. Our suggestion offered him a possible way to turn his situation around. If Meyer was capable of being loyal, he was going to have a chance with Stu. Stu could use that loyalty to give Meyer advice, suggestions, and instructions to compensate for limitations in Meyer's thinking and technical training. Without that loyalty, Stu would have to constantly fear that each pointer would be interpreted as a security-threatening criticism. This would create the conditions for a backstabbing response. The situation was structured for Meyer to receive some valuable affirmation.

Sixth, the Artifact insight instructs us that **the way to play the politics out constructively is to problem-pose instead of subliminally and covertly manipulating solutions to problems that the other person probably has framed differently.** This is a theme that's been more embedded in our viewpoints and discussion than we've explicitly communicated. Problem-posing is an attempt to evenhandedly state the issues that are in apparent opposition by stating the dilemmas for all parties—self, other, and organization—thereby inviting the other party to clarify and to help with the solution. It leads to treating the people whose actions you would like to influence as subjects who are party not just to the problem solving, but to the problem framing. The alternative is to treat people like objects who can be manipulated, covertly influenced, and involuntarily moved around to produce the solution you envision for them.

Stu engaged in problem-posing when he cut the president in on his dilemma. He did this before he took the job when he exposed his law-of-the-jungle thinking. He wanted Meyer out and he posed the problem for the president's input. It was a good thing that he did; a less collaborative approach could have placed him at early odds with the attachments of the president who was about to be his sole boss. Then he posed the problem again when he brought the president in on his scheme for capturing Meyer's loyalty.

Seventh, the Artifact insight leads to our accepting that **self-interests and opportunistic thinking are ever-present in an individual's motives, and to fight this is absurd. Instead of searching for ways to control them, it's far more practical and productive to search for constructive ways they can be served.** As much as anything, it's the actions that management takes to support people seeing the linkage between their own self-interests and the needs of others and the company that constitutes the fundamental managerial act for promoting teamwork.

This was the inspiration for the advice we offered Stu that evoked his "double dynamite" reaction. His offering Meyer ownership of the software study was an attempt to show him that his very survival, let alone his prosperity, was dependent on having others support him, with clear implications for the teamwork quid pro quos that Stu expected from Meyer.

Eighth, the Artifact of Mind insight leads us to see that **trust and trusting relationships are the bedrock components of managerial effectiveness.** Without trusting relationships, what you learn about the organizational world in which the other person lives is going to be minimal and distorted. You won't see a whole "real person." By and large what you'll see is the real person acting defensively. Others will cover up and make your accurate understanding of them difficult to impossible. You'll have surface knowledge of one or two key variables. In the absence of deeper knowledge and other variables, you'll be inclined to distort the significance of the few variables that you know. This will lead you to incorrectly interpret their actions as, for example, "extremely aggressive" or "technically naive" or "assassin-caliber backstabbing," because you lack balance and more complete and deeper knowledge. And it will be difficult to correct your exaggerated interpretations because, in your mind, you are thinking that you caught them red-handed. Perhaps you did, but it's a lopsided view of that individual. This is what leads to bum raps and stereotypes that exaggerate the human deficiencies of imperfect people to the point that you view these deficiencies as core disqualifiers.

The fact that we instructed Stu to take out insurance by confiding his scheme to the president reflects our sensitivity to the tides of organizational politics and the essential issue of not going out undefended in a world that has yet to demonstrate it can be negotiated safely. Moreover, it was an opportunity for Stu to establish both that he is a trustworthy team player and to give context to the harshness of the actions he might need to take if he failed to create a bond of trust and loyalty with Meyer.

Ninth, the Artifact of Mind insight tells us what real teamwork is about. **Real teamwork is a mind-set that clearly depicts the organization's vision together with a commitment to increasing the effectiveness of each and every person who plays a critical organizational role.** Teamwork includes knowing what others, who you assume are good enough because they are the resources you've got, require to realize their potential and, in an effort to help move your organization ahead, doing your utmost to provide them the context for functioning effectively. It entails cutting people enough slack to do what they know is right and enough knowledge of you and the organization to figure out what is right for the unit as a whole.

Recall our alignment-centered definition of empowerment in which we stated there are three components—self-effectiveness, organizational effectiveness, and recognition for one's value-added contribution. The Artifact insight instructs that there will be no spirit of cooperation when people feel they have to fight and compete to establish a base-level security or just the opportunity to have a little success. Teamwork, then, requires managerial actions that make it easier for individuals to realize their obligations to the company and to themselves simultaneously and to have their contributions recognized. To do so your actions and their actions must be more than self-empowering: they must be empowering to one another as well. Actions taken to ensure reciprocal empowerment constitute the core contribution that an effective manager makes.

In the preceding example, Stu attempted to be a team player by *not* going along with the status quo. He called the group on their destructive dynamic, grasped the importance of giving Meyer a face-saving opportunity to succeed, and was looking for an opportunity to coach his boss on the team benefits of giving affirmation and being more explicit about what teamwork requires and how to help others succeed.

In conclusion

We want to conclude with a message that we hoped would leap out of the pages of this book for you. While the insight that "organization is an artifact of the mind that views it" is tremendously powerful, it's an insight that goes against the grain of what people are used to and have been taught. Thus we find that it takes a lot of hard work to really get it. You work at it and get it again and again, and then, little by little, it gets you. It gets you by delivering small but essential insights that you never dreamed could be so practically important to learn.

The Artifact of Mind insight invites you to extend the same sensitivity and empathy to others that you self-interestedly extend to yourself. Others need success too, and they will try their darnedest to achieve it, one way or another. And part of what determines the path they take lies in how you engage them, particularly when you see pockets of ineffectiveness that can be readily changed by a shift in orientation.

Above all else, valid feedback-sending and advice-giving requires fair-minded analysis of other people's personal competency needs and understanding that people bring their entire lives to their work. To be a resource to another person you must seriously and empathetically consider what the whole person needs. If you say "I don't have the time," our retort is "You don't have the time not to." From the standpoint of organizational effectiveness, it's clearly the most efficient action you can take. Acting otherwise immediately leads to organizational dynamics that ultimately are as burdensome and destructive to yourself as they are to others. Teamwork, then, is the artful practice of promoting self, others, and the organization and actively using your awareness of other people to assist them to evolve increasingly effective orientations. As we see it, at its core, teamwork entails learning enough about people and their personal competency needs to actually make yourself useful to them. This is the *new mentality*.

EPILOGUE

You've just read a book about what you need to consider psychologically prior to influencing others and attempting to give them **great** advice. No doubt you also encountered several points where thinking about taking a psychological approach with others led directly to thinking likewise about yourself. You may have thought, *"I'm not just studying their psychology, I'm studying my own,"* and *"I'm not merely interested in helping others evolve their mind-sets to function more effectively, I'm interested in my own mind-set progression and effective personal functioning as well."* These possibilities occurred to us from the beginning. In this respect we've been shadowing you.

Actually, our first attempts to write this book addressed issues of orientation and breakthrough learning from exactly this perspective. We focused on the self-psychology required to get the deeper level meaning of the feedback you receive—especially when, because of Artifact of Mind biases, the substance of the feedback you receive is always going to be at least a little off. But after months of flawed progress, we discovered that, for us, this was going to be a "flat earth" effort. Each head of steam dropped us off the edge. Only after we switched our approach were we able to achieve valid results.

Assuming, for the moment, that we had persisted in addressing the topic of what you need to know to engage in breakthrough learning on your own, what do you suppose would be missing? When we put it this way, you probably understand immediately. To get the substance of the feedback you receive in the ballpark of what you might find usable, especially given your natural skepticisms and resis-

tance to letting others box you into a category, the conditions would
need to be far more optimal than any reasonable person could ever
expect. Feedback- and advice-givers would need to know a good deal
more about your life and how you think and reason than they do;
they would need to be able to discriminate between levels of learning
in providing you with feedback that's appropriate to the lessons they
think you need to learn; they would need to put what's best for you
ahead of what's best for them and count on you to trust that they
had, in fact, done so; and they would need to perfect their techniques
of making problem-posing statements and taking a mind-set sensitive
approach, not to mention their capacity to accurately size up the circumstances you face. **Unlikely!**

When it comes to helping you engage in orientational and breakthrough learning, we think there is only one person who knows you
well enough and that you trust enough to make specific prescriptions.
Of course that person is you. Not only do you know yourself best,
but—talk about responsibility—you're the one who has to live with
the results. Given all this, you might then reason, *"What's with all
these other people, why get them so involved?"*

The reason for getting others involved is precisely the reason
they need you to be involved. No matter how developed your self-
reflective capacities, there are significant limits to what, at any moment, you can actually learn about yourself. These limits begin with
the Artifact of Mind biases that systematically focus and distort everything you know, learn, seek, and see. They include the difficulty
of dealing with feelings and how, at one moment, you are capable of
responding to the shock of a strong feeling by completely ignoring its
presence and, at the next moment, can become so consumed by it
that you lose sight of all else. Then there are the limits of living in
an unpredictable world where circumstances over which you feel little control require a brand of practical coping that quickly overrides
your intended course. There are many other limits, both capricious
and serious, and you better not overlook the spiritual, which, when
you're in touch with it, can be all-consuming.

There's no doubt about it, when self-development and mind-set
progress are the issues, you need others just as much as others
need you. Their feedback and reactions serve as heads-up alerts and
direction finders, and your relationships serve as benchmarks for assessing progress. And just as others need you to learn about them
prior to your exerting influence, you need them to learn enough
about you in order to get the substance of their feedback "accurate
enough." This entails your being personally present, spontaneous,
open, and candid with the people you're inclined to trust.

While you need other people to be involved, you don't want them controlling you. You want to invent yourself. You never want to think that you are the result of designs created by someone else. You want to look in the mirror and feel good about the person you are evolving into, while the people who provided valuable reactions, feedback, influence, and advice remain in the background. We think this is totally appropriate. If you absorbed the advice you received without making appropriate adjustments, you'd be walking around looking like a Picasso construction. However slight the adjustment, you must give the feedback and advice you receive just the right twist to bring it into proper focus.

When others are up-front and aboveboard with you, and possess some reasonable level of consciousness about their motives and agendas, we don't think you have much to worry about in the way of misdirection. Under these circumstances, equipped with Artifact of Mind insightfulness, we have 100 percent confidence in your abilities to self-reflect and to make the most of their recommendations. Don't put too much heat on yourself: you shouldn't expect superhuman one-trial learning. And if you find evidence that you are making repeated errors, then find people whose alignments you understand well enough to trust their motives to honestly tell you what they think. In all likelihood, they are close to the right issue even while citing the wrong specifics. It's up to you to sort through the "hay" to find the proverbial pony.

But other people aren't always as we just described. Even when they are, their competence and congruence can be difficult to spot in a sea of people whose misdirection is caused by operating in the former mentality, giving feedback and advice that prominently reflects their intent to control you. Herein lies a big complication. Just as it would be a lot easier for other people to take your advice if they could take your concern and interest in their well-being for granted, so would life be easier for you if you could think their advice-giving motives were primarily to help you. But they can't make that assumption, and neither can you.

This line of reasoning takes us back to the situation you faced prior to reading this book, but with two additional perspectives, for now you are familiar with the Artifact of Mind insight and the psychological tenets that derive from it. You now understand precisely what you need to learn in gauging and correcting for their biases; likewise now you are more conscious of your own mind-set inclinations and difficulties in open-mindedly hearing others out. What remains to be determined is whether this added understanding and consciousness will allow you to learn sufficiently from your interactions with others.

We hope that reading this book has provided you with the means for decoding other people's words in search of a message that's relevant to the self-questions your experiences raise, and that you are no longer quite as put off by other people's lack of objectivity, defensive routines, and confounding surface behavior. We hope you are able to see what's to be gained by tuning into the music that accompanies the feedback and advice you receive, even when the words seem way off the mark and even incomprehensible.

Opportunities for making yourself more wonderful rest within the fabric of almost every corporate event. It's up to you to reflect on those experiences, and to tune in to what people are telling you, at times even incoherently, to better learn from your experiences with them in adding to your personal competence and feelings of empowerment.

GLOSSARY

Advice Suggestions about how an individual can achieve greater effectiveness by changing some activity or thought process. Whether "effectiveness" pertains to what's in the best interests of the person being advised, the advice-giver, and/or the organization is always a matter of perception and often the subject of debate.

Agenda-biased outsiders People perceived by a potential advice-recipient to possess self-interested motives and/or partisan work agendas that systematically detract from the "objectivity" of advice they might offer. Often such people are referred to as "stakeholders."

Alignment The personal strategy that underlies how an individual is inclined to structure situations and see events in promoting what is personally important and empowering. It provides the logic that person uses for pursuing self-effectiveness interests and personal and organizational goals and commitments simultaneously. An alignment accounts for what an individual sees as an opportunity to demonstrate competence and what that person sees as a threat. It accounts for what an individual sees as important when evaluating someone else's efforts. And it accounts for what an individual sees as his or her unit's mission and the actions that will lead to that mission being achieved.

Anchoring   Actions taken to reinforce a new way of reasoning and perceiving organizational events that cement changes in orientation and behavior.

Artifact   Any object, concept, or structure mentally manufactured by an individual with an eye toward subsequent uses.

Artifact of Mind   A shorthand way of expressing the psychological tenet, "organization is an artifact of the mind that views it."

Blaming the victim   A widely used management practice whereby the people with hierarchical power avoid taking responsibility for organizational problems, and/or having their limitations publicly viewed, by framing problems to emphasize the deficient performances of people who are most negatively affected by the existence of the problem and who lack the power to convincingly assert differently. This is a situation where a manager blames the problem on a misperforming subordinate, and not on his or her own inability to coach an otherwise able person to play a more effective and productive role.

Breakthrough learning   An experience in which an individual undergoes a basic change in reasoning that produces a change in orientation. We reserve this terminology for changes in the assumptions an individual makes about him- or herself, others, and ensuing organizational events, which are seen as having the potential to produce win-win-win organizational approaches and results.

Conceptual clarification   A clear, concisely stated concept that simultaneously communicates the reasoning and resulting behavior that will more consistently enable an individual to achieve his or her and the organization's goals and what about that individual's reasoning has, up to this point, been ineffective.

Directives   Demands, requirements, and stipulations for operating that an individual feels entitled to make regarding another person's organizational objectives, methodologies, and modes of operating.

Emotional bonding   The act of an individual emotionally fusing with a new orientation to such an extent that it becomes ingrained in one's consciousness, influencing future thoughts and behavior, almost regardless of the situation or constraint.

Empowerment   The feeling an individual receives from believing that he or she is (1) performing competently in a self-meaningful way while attending to all important personal and professional concerns and life situations; (2) producing output that, as the individual views it, the company needs to receive from someone occupying his or her role and position; and (3) knowing that key evaluators and associates recognize and appreciate the essential value added by his or her presence and efforts.

Ends–means analysis   A form of situational analysis, often used in casework problem solving, characterized by people beginning with what they assume is the desired outcome and reasoning backward to figure out what characteristics, contributions, interactions, and processes will cause that outcome.

Feedback   Reactions from an individual that, directly or indirectly, communicate how he or she is affected by someone's thinking and/or behavior. These reactions are communicated by means of words, tone, innuendo, and behavior, expressed or withheld. Generally they are assumed to be reactions of the person providing the feedback, but they may be expressed as those of other people, known or hypothesized, or of a named category of people.

Former mentality   *See* Mentality; Objectivity.

Influence   Conscious attempts to get another person to believe, reason, and/or act as the initiating individual deems advisable. Frequently the appeals that accompany an attempt to influence are steeped in the win-win logic of what's in the target person's best interests and the interests of the organization.

Insiders   People who are thought to perceive and experience a situation similarly because of shared culture, personality traits, self-interests, work responsibilities, or personal and work-unit stakes.

Instruction   Information an individual conveys as the appropriate and skillful way to conduct a particular activity. However, whether information is taken as instruction, or as feedback, advice, or directive, is determined in the mind of the recipient.

Instrumental   Specific actions, styles of behavior, and interactions that are primarily the result of an ends–means analysis directed at getting successful results given existing assumptions and thought processes. These are actions taken to carry out an existing and often fallible orientation, not those taken to develop a new one.

Jujitsu principle of evaluation A principle alleging that a valid evaluation, in contrast to a "blaming the victim" one, results in the evaluator learning as much or more about him- or herself and the effectiveness of actions taken as the people being evaluated learn about themselves and their actions.

Management The function of staging the conditions for others to perform effectively.

Mentality The personal assumptions that underlie an individual's self-concept, view of specific others and categories of others, and beliefs about the nature of the organizational system and the interaction processes required for teaming up with people at work

The *former mentality* allowed people to assume that stipulated organizational requirements were fixed, that others could be treated as categories of objects to be directed and manipulated, and that self-interests are partitionable in performances at work. It featured a control-oriented formulation in which cooperation was often merely a tactic in a strategy of domination.

In contrast, the *new, Artifact of Mind, mentality* views organizational requirements as mutable, people as but discoverable subjects, self-interests as omnipresent, dominance as a tactic, cooperation as the desirable strategy, and needs for control and influence to be met through deep knowledge of how other people perceive and create organizational reality.

Mind-sets The distinctive viewpoints, needs, and agendas that determine how an individual views and engages categories of events at work.

New Mentality *See* Mentality; Objectivity.

Objectivity The belief that there is a standardized view of people, situations, or organizational moments that yields a perception and judgment that all fair-minded people would hold. "Objectivity" is a positive, sought-after condition in the former mentality, but a non sequitur in the new.

Objects *See* People as objects.

Organizational politics The interpersonal dynamics initiated when people (with different personal motives and ways of performing competently, with different organizational agendas, and who naturally perceive all events opportunistically) attempt to persuade others to go along with their self-interested ways of perceiving, staging, and structuring events in an effort to ensure their competent performance in them.

"Organization is an artifact of mind that views it" The psychological tenet that holds that everything pertaining to life and productivity in an organization is a matter of individual perception, inextricably influenced by the personal-effectiveness needs, self-interested motives and work agendas of the perceiver.

Orientation A mind-set that distinctively characterizes and stylizes an individual's behavior and determines how the individual postures him- or herself in relation to some category of activities, relationships, or circumstances. Orientations are the attitudinal and behavioral consequences of the personal assumptions an individual makes about him- or herself, others, and the system.

Outsider An observer who is not seen as a primary stakeholder or as personally affected by what is taking place in a situation; one who is presumed to live a life that is sufficiently independent of what is taking place to render a neutral and unbiased judgment.

People as objects A way of considering people as interchangeable components defined by some personal characteristic, job title, expectation, or category of deployment, and/or by certain "objective" standards for performing that are alleged to be embraced by almost everyone in the system.

People as subjects A way of seeing people as unique and distinct individuals whose needs, resources, ambitions, and perceptions of competence cannot be known prior to inquiring into them.

Personal competénce The core ulterior motive for the self-interested perceptions people have at work. It refers to three key dimensions of self-interested perceptions simultaneously. First, people want to perform competently with respect to themselves. That is, to the extent that it's possible, they want each and every action they take at work to mesh with and serve all of their personal needs and life agendas. Second, people want to perform competently in exercising the responsibilities that go with their jobs. They want to see themselves competently producing what they think the organization should be receiving from someone in their role and position. And third, people want key others to view them as performing competently.

They want others to see them working in an effective manner, turning out value-added product that's essential to the corporate effort. *Also see* Empowerment.

Personal equation   The juxtaposition of personal variables emanating from a desire to perform with personal competence in all life situations simultaneously that bears on every situation and challenge an individual experiences at work.

Political action   Any action individuals take, individually or collectively, in the service of getting others to value them and their production.

Political dynamics   The result of people with different self-interests transacting with one another to get events construed, framed, and contextualized in ways that facilitate both their production and their personal and organizational well-being.

Problem-posing   A methodology for raising consciousness and performing a collaborative type of advice-giving. The advice-giver poses what he or she perceives to be the dilemmas the other person faces, inquires whether this is a plausible framing of them, and asks the other person to respond. After the advice-recipient responds, the advice-giver modifies his or her framing of the "problem" to include the recipient's views, frames the modified view for the recipient's "approval," and when the modified view is judged mutually compatible, enters into a problem-solving discussion.

Program   Any standard, fixed method of thinking and acting used to meet an organizational requirement or to pursue an organizational objective, regardless of the interests, needs, values, abilities, and circumstances of the people required to use that methodology.

Self-interests   Personal concerns that affect motivation and behavior and are influenced by one's assumptions, agendas, stakeholdings, and goals.

Set   The patterned, predisposed way of thinking and reasoning that an individual uses when facing a category of problems, people, and/or situations.

Set-breaker   The events that finally, and incontestably, signal to someone that his or her reasoning and orientation are insufficient, inappropriate, inaccurate, or defective and require changing.

Socialization The social processes by which rules, meanings, mores, and standards are culturally transmitted to an individual, often without knowledge of the transmission, and are reinforced and enforced by group sanctions.

Subjects *See* People as subjects.

Teamwork An active commitment to learning enough about people—their personal competencies, needs, and mind-sets—to be able to work collaboratively and complementarily with them.

Win-win A situation or problem that an individual frames in the structure of doing what's best for the company which, by "coincidence," also is best, or good enough, for him- or herself. By and large, win-win thinking leads to tactical outcomes in which one succeeds in the moment. Occasionally, the win-win is between two individuals, with the interests of the company being left out. The latter is called either collusion or corruption, depending on the consciousness of the omission. Very occasionally an individual frames the win-win leaving him- or herself out of the formulation. This type of formulation is called sacrifice, loyalty, or stupidity, depending on the vantage point of the evaluator.

Win-win-win A situation or problem that an individual frames from the vantage point of the best interests of three parties: self, other(s), and organization. When that individual's assessments are fairly accurate, especially about what others see as being in their and the company's interests, win-win-win thinking builds positive relationships and loyalties that constitute a strategic resource for each of the three parties.

INDEX